SHARE

Chris Yates
Linda Jingfang Cai

SHARE

How Organizations Can Thrive in an Age of **Networked Knowledge, Power** and **Relationships**

B L O O M S B U R Y   B U S I N E S S
LONDON • OXFORD • NEW YORK • NEW DELHI • SYDNEY

BLOOMSBURY BUSINESS
Bloomsbury Publishing Plc
50 Bedford Square, London, WC1B 3DP, UK

BLOOMSBURY, BLOOMSBURY BUSINESS and the Diana logo are
trademarks of Bloomsbury Publishing Plc

First published in Great Britain 2020

A catalogue record for this book is available from the British Library

Library of Congress Cataloguing-in-Publication data has been applied for

ISBN: 978-1-4729-4267-8; eBook: 978-1-4729-4268-5

2 4 6 8 10 9 7 5 3 1

Typeset by Deanta Global Publishing Services, Chennai, India
Printed and bound in Great Britain by CPI Group (UK) Ltd, Croydon CR0 4YY

To find out more about our authors and books visit www.bloomsbury.com
and sign up for our newsletters

This book is dedicated to our children:
Anais
Eden
Solomon
Youjia (蔡优嘉)

They will inherit the decisions that we make today.

CONTENTS

PREFACE

We need to introduce ourselves before you read on so that you may understand a little about who we are and why we wrote the book. Though from time to time we alternate perspectives, in these pages we speak as one voice. In many cases, it will be obvious who is speaking, but in others it will not be. This is partly because sometimes we wish to protect an organisation or an individual, and partly to allow you to focus on the story. For all of our stories, the point is in the *experience* we describe.

We lean on experiences, some theory and some science. We hope that the blend will enable what we want to say to be heard. We are not professional writers, but hope that sharing some thoughts may help in the world. We chose the title *Share* for the simplicity of the word. Power – its centrality and our love and fear of it – is minimised when we share. In the transformation of our organisations and our society, we think this simple idea of sharing may be the key to future success.

CHRIS
As I talked about writing this book, I got a range of reactions. Some said, 'Yes! Something needs to be said.' Others said, 'Wow...good luck.' And then there were those who said, 'You are part of the corporate world; you won't publish the truth, and you won't be brave enough to discuss what needs to be done.'

Some were really angry. Most of my friends do not work in the corporate world. They told me that we should tax and hurt the corporations, burn the whole lot down. They reacted with anger but with no plan, at least not one that looked back to learn from failed policies of the past. Most just smiled politely and quickly changed the subject. What brought such mixed reactions to this book about our faceless corporate world?

Corporate individuals

This corporate world is so powerful and yet we seldom see our world corporate leaders in public or in the media. They have spokespeople and consciously design and brand the image they need us to see.

Most of us who work in this world are not individual sinners. No one comes to work every day pledging to destroy the planet for future generations. We work in corporations, like a mixing pot. Many have humble backgrounds, with interesting and diverse life stories. Some come one or two generations from very humble backgrounds. Some attended good private schools. I rarely come across bad people. No one seems to get up each morning and say, 'I plan to screw the world today'. Most are not chasing the next shiny bonus with no regard to morals or the impact their decisions make on the planet. They live within, or just above, their means and comfort so that they can afford to live separate from most. They have less crime in their lives, as they can afford to live in ex-patriot or middle-class areas; they gentrify older areas of the city dramatically, disrupting and creating communities. They focus on their children's education. This is the corporate dream.

Global impact

It seems everyone, everywhere is talking about climate change, and yet we are not living as if our lives depended on big, urgent action. Across the world, we see forest fires and hurricanes and more refugees and people in slavery than at any point in history by sheer numbers. We become numb to the tragedy brought daily to our lives. Refugees drowning seldom makes front-page news any more.

People link the planet's woes to the greed of corporations and their endless pursuit of growth and profit. I have read that the seas outside Seattle are polluted with opioids and those around the UK polluted with antidepressants. Both are damaging wildlife along the shoreline. I feel sorry for the animals and the people. It seems we don't stop to talk about these things. We are facing the largest refugee crisis in human history – today, for millions of our global citizens – yet we don't talk about it enough.

I've met some of the world's most talented and gifted people at work. Some now have a survivalist backup plan. People are prepping, all over the world. They talk of the next world war, some imminent disaster for nature or mankind, or all three...In order to progress, does humankind really need culling every so often? Do we have to fight through horror and overcome adversity to create the next phase, the next big push? To adapt to the next thing? Wars help us do that. We know from neuroscience that we naturally become super-motivated when under threat.

I don't believe we need to suffer such drastic events to grow and adapt. So, I decided to write some things down. I talked to my friend Linda and she offered to help. We thought our difference in perspective might be interesting. She has a Chinese and communist upbringing. I have a Guyanese–English–American upbringing. I am an Atlantic child. Really different, of course, yet both corporate warriors, thrown together.

A unique perspective

There is joy in being a minority in the corporate world. You get the best of both worlds. I get to do the corporate stuff and sometimes get to step into the world of relative privilege, which allows me to walk in the shoes of the so-called Anglo-Saxon, to which the vast majority of the planet, including almost all Anglo-Saxons, have no entry. Then I get to be from the Caribbean. And a football fan of my beloved, tribal QPR (Queens Park Rangers), which provides sanity in the mosaic of my life. The beauty of my friends who are fans of the football club is that they represent such a mix of society: shopfitters, graphic designers, hospital porters, DJs, senior civil servants, plumbers, train drivers, real estate agents, lawyers, promoters, small business owners, accountants, artists, local government officers, programmers, prison officers, and whatever it is that Dave gets paid for.

For all my corporate background and seeming privilege, I always feel different. Some things *are* different: taxis don't always pick me up; sometimes I don't get served in bars and restaurants; I get asked for ID more often than my colleagues; I feel nervous in front of the police for no reason (well, I do know the reason). But...I get to mix and assimilate with a wide group of people; I look like I am a local everywhere I go, except in some parts of Asia. I think that the ancestors who got me here had things harder and so smile to myself, nod to them, I stand as the product of their legacy and sacrifice, they faced sharper pains on their shoulders and so I carry on.

Russians, Irish and black people, as examples, have unique stories in this Western world. Many were the downtrodden peasant/slave at one point, and some of us came up, at least in terms of income. Often, we are attracted by the baubles of fame, designer clothes, branded alcohol, anything shiny, really. (Old money does not behave like that. It is invisible.) Most were just attracted to the power and freedom that money brings, and power is selfish.

Money does not buy you love. Money buys you privacy. It always has. We have an assault on privacy ahead of us; it is one of the giant frontiers of our data-enabled world. The poor always had this issue. It was only as our data became the living expression of our lives that privacy concerns became so crucial for the powerful. The poor have no privacy; they are exposed to the public eye, on the street and in documentaries, but we only see this on days with low-impact news stories.

As I visit the offices and attend the conferences of the corporate world and look at everything that happens around me, I increasingly believe that the way change management is done is horrible. Change management is how we enable humans to adjust to change by understanding their position and then crafting solutions to resolve the risks and fears through creating *shared* understanding. So many of the world's problems exist because no attention is paid to things like belief and purpose, no empathy or care taken to evidence change management as a concept. I see it in how in life we transition from one thing to the other. At each stage of significant human transition, opportunities are presented to us to shape and rewire how we think about things; we are at a unique stage in human history right now, and, I think, at one of those points where a new philosophy or idea can be seeded. That is why I decided to write some things down.

I'm writing this book partly because of what I feel is a unique perspective on the world. I wrote the book *Rewire* because I felt that the work on diversity was so poor in organisations and needed some fresh thinking. *Share* is really a book about change and empathy again, one written in hope.

I was born in the UK, which gave me an entrance to the world as a British citizen. That stroke of luck creates a certain confidence in the modern context. I grew up for a while in Guyana, in South America, in a so-called developing country, gaining a view of what it was like to live in an extremely different environment. I then got a high school and college education in the UK in the 1980s, making it through university without debt, from a relatively humble background as an immigrant child from a single-parent family in a 'new' country.

Somehow I have soaked up many experiences. In New York I witnessed 9/11 with my very own eyes. I've walked away from car accidents in which I should have died. I've been in subway stations, on mail trains and in desolate roadside cafés where I was faced with a clear and present danger and the possibility of death, and yet am still alive. I do feel blessed.

Purpose
I've visited dozens of different countries across the planet; I am one of those privileged to travel the world. And then I am part of an even smaller group who sometimes choose to go off the beaten track.

I worked in the corporate world feeling as if I were alone, not one of *them*, not one of those people chasing the dollar – as if it were all really an apprenticeship for something else.

As human beings, we all want to share our unique perspectives. I had the opportunity to work for one of the world's finest service brands, building understanding of how people think about change in a focused, competitive way. They (we) built a shared sense of belonging, a shared purpose, to drive a high-end service culture. I learned there that, to deliver exceptional service externally, the *internal* culture has to be a reflection, or the core, of what you are trying to build. If the inside is hollow and just a set of phrases and productivity measures, then you cannot achieve a customer service reputation for solving problems or creating solutions for the client with agility and care.

I worked for one of the world's largest banks in the middle of the 2008 financial crisis. In banking, the core element is integrity. For a bank to build trust in how it operates, at its core even the smallest actions should be done ethically when dealing with money, whether it be from corporations, governments or citizens. If you are not treated with integrity and in an ethical way within the company, why should you conduct your external business in the same way?

We helped to drive such a culture, to unify the bank across national and international borders and embed a global ethical mindset – and practices – through values.

I then joined one of the largest American manufacturing companies – working on how to build a culture that centred much more on the individual – to bring nobility back to the workplace in manufacturing. Given the history of union antagonism in the US in recent decades, how could we rebuild trust at the factory and community level? Why should factory workers trust management and adopt new practices when it might mean cutting back on the workforce, and why should individual workers care about the product and quality? Well, we learned that we want to feel as if we are all in this together – that we have a shared purpose.

'I remember seeing a film about one of the great French vineyards. The chateau employed people to pick the grapes every autumn and at the end of each day laid on a sumptuous dinner, the idea being that treating the workers with respect and care would have a positive impact on their work, and that would influence the quality of the grapes.'

So, a belief is formed that for a thing to be practised, to be entirely truthful to itself it must be built from its core. If you want to be authentic, you have to be true in the way you behave when no one is looking. It's not a new idea, but it is something we need to learn again and again.

Perspective

One thing that I've seen increasingly in my travels is that conscious change-management practices – or lack thereof – determine how we run our societies and the planet (i.e. planned or just carelessly). As humans, driven by fear, ignorance or power, we often take a short-term view and are distracted by the next shiny thing. Not just the big stuff like trade, politics and religion – but how we feel about ourselves. When we pay too little attention to the future, we mess with people's values, and too quickly we are led into war or other serious conflict.

I keep coming back to the fact that maybe there's some reason why I'm still alive today and have been given this seemingly unique life and perspective. We must all find some meaning for our lives. The reason for my life might just be to share my unique perspective with other people and hope that it doesn't get lost before I die.

I believe that the world is built around empathy. From empathy comes trade and sharing, and thus society at its core.

In a society historically run by men, we tend to fight and compete to solve things. At our core, we are just aggressive. I have enjoyed physically fighting other males. For part of my life, a good weekend night out consisted of drinking large quantities of alcohol, dancing, eating curry and having a fight. A top night out in my late teens and early twenties in the tribal (Viking-influenced) UK.

In our 'advanced' society, we have developed sports, games from the time of the ancient Greek, to channel this feeling, to allow a time to fight in a ritualised way. Sport allows us to gather in packs and replicate hunting and fighting. I feel it – I've done it. I have participated in large groups at demonstrations, football matches and other events where I felt part of something. The neurochemical rush is incredible – a natural high.

Today, there is much evidence of this rush along with too much corporate power. Power must be better distributed for society to change. Locally and globally, corporations have control over our world, over natural resources, over other humans on a vast scale, and even over the weather. If our distant tribal ancestors could see us now we would appear to have the power of gods.

Anyone who has read George Orwell's *1984* will be familiar with the idea that a period of permanent competition leads only to permanent death, permanent friction and permanent grind of competition within a context of limited resources. For one system of government – or one team – to win, there has to be huge loss. I was fascinated by the story of the first emperor of China. From a lifetime of endless war, he sought to create a kingdom to bring to an end the endless grind of destruction of human life played out in one country over centuries. I am interested in this approach, one of sharing versus permanent grind and loss.

My favourite games are the board game *Risk* and the digital game *Civilization*. Both are strategy games, and there are basically three ways to play:

1 *Grind* away at each other in a slow, pointless and permanent fight until players drop out. (If players are equally equipped, games can last for days, until a fatal error is committed – usually a rash, all-or-nothing attack on another player.)

2 *Fight* until only one person is the victor and then they can drive new concepts and ideas and be ruler of all. (This takes a long time and includes mass destruction.)

3 *Share* science and trade with each other and evolve, adopt new practices from each other as a core philosophy, and live life in harmony. (The game becomes a little bit boring, but there is less death.)

In his dystopian classic, Orwell also writes about the dangers of forgetting (or revising) the past. We forget sacrifice. Now we see only the movies about the wars and they clash with the overload of our days and they fade. It is hard to keep perspective and to save a space for history as we lurch from one drama to another in the daily news. Is any one atrocity 'worse' than the other? I heard a story in the news recently about a little girl in a war zone who watched her father melt as her family sat together at dinner. A missile had struck their home. This year. Now. As we write this book.

I heard a poem by a father who watched the son he had raised alone, fleeing war and the horrors of a refugee camp, drown on a cold Mediterranean night in his arms in the water.

We have fought wars in order to prevent this horror that now is constantly in our news and that no longer shocks us. We openly express our desires and expect a reaction. We are now an 'I' society. The prefix 'I' is even there, right up front in the name of a popular personal device. In the non-collective when we are dulled, evil rises. We forget the sacrifice that brought us to where we are and thus miss that, in doing so, we call down the heavy price of sacrifice upon our children that comes with our indulgence of 'I' and the numbing of who *we* really are and can be. We are all born with the potential to shine. To choose our destiny. We can decide how we react and not be passive.

What to do?
How can we take learning and apply it to our future, so that we have a choice?

Back to my personal perspective. There's something interesting about being black in a mostly white corporate world that makes you feel a little bit on the outside all the time. One of the many privileges of my position and background is that it allows me to slide across invisible societal borders and visit a multitude of social perspectives.

I have conversations in boardrooms as well as in a local pub in west London. I have conversations with the white parents and the ethnic parents in the private school PTA, bridging both worlds. And I spend my holidays with family in what would be called an 'ethnic minority' culture, feeling the superstition and belief systems of that culture and experiencing that range of world views.

In that context, I have the privilege of listening to people expressing their feelings. I have travelled with a curiosity that makes me talk to taxi drivers, bartenders, cleaners and waiters. In my corporate life, other than the office cleaners I am often the only black face. They smile at me in the corridor; I get special favours as they sometimes give me the look that says, 'I see you there, "brother"'. A smile, a nod of acknowledgement, an extra mint on my pillow or discreet advice to tuck my shirt in.

Sometimes I seek guidance from strangers (and give it) in airports, at bus stops and in cafeterias over the world. I have learned that we have more things in common than the differences that keep us apart – a cliché, I know – but mostly, we don't really know this about each other, because few of us get to travel and to test this, to have perspective. We are kept from building our own discovery of perspective by our media, our social condition and the opportunity that luck, class or wealth bestows. For some, even when travel is an option, it is done in a sanitised way: they stay within their social class and experience the golf club and global service standards of the same hotels. It is possible to travel the world and stay in your own world. Like the old royalty of Rome, the cities today are increasingly built around an idea of a standard global service offering and thus 'local', for many travellers, is never really understood.

This perspective of living in and seeing different places gives Linda and myself a unique angle from which to speak through this book. Maybe you, our readers, will create a little different path for your society, your corporation or your personal life, no matter what your background. Our hope is that something in the book may resonate with you. And, with perspective, bring about change.

Our main question is: do we believe that our corporations should hold the most power in the world today? To regulate their power for the long term is difficult; they compete by shaping the legislation, by buying the national and international politics they need. It is the nature of competition. To drive a new world, there must be *intent* – from the internal working of each leader, and each manager – to imagine a new way of sharing, with empathy from the core of the organisation, and demonstrate by their daily choices that such organisations are more empathic to our planet.

Could we influence the corporate collectives around the world to make a choice to share? For that richest 1 per cent to share and truly enrich, or save, many lives? To try something different?

LINDA

When Chris first pitched the idea to me about writing a book together, I thought it was crazy. I loved writing and storytelling as a kid and young adult – I even participated in competitions and performed onstage – but writing a book in a second language for a primarily Western audience sounded...mad. Then I realised that most of my hesitation resulted from my internal struggle to navigate different cultures, value systems and perspectives: one I was born and raised in, and the other that I spent the last 20 years trying to understand and master. With struggle and pain comes experience and insight, and I convinced myself to share what I've learned, for it might be useful to other people.

When I was writing, I often thought of Chinese students pursuing careers in the West, Asian Americans straddling their cultural heritage and adopted culture, who search for their identity and belonging. I also considered non-Asians who want to understand Eastern values, scholars who increasingly turn to traditional Chinese teaching, including Buddhism, Confucianism and Taoism, to complement Western philosophies for work and life; and I even included global companies that have to manage diverse teams and build an inclusive culture.

China

It is hard to describe the China I grew up in – so different from the powerful China that now has formidable influence on the world economy and geopolitical landscape. The China I grew up in had recently experienced a 30-year-long internal chaos of world wars, civil wars, the Great Leap Forward, mass famine and the Cultural Revolution. It had very few allies outside its borders and had four billion poorly educated and hungry citizens to feed. Living standards were so low that everything from sugar to oil was provided with monthly coupons calculated by household heads; this I remember vividly. There was no market economy, and hardly anything to buy in the shops, even if one was lucky enough to have extra money. There was little perspective of what was going on in the outside world.

Ironically, people were less stressed or unhappy compared with how they feel today. To start with, everyone was paid the same, roughly six dollars per month, whether you were a doctor or factory worker; income inequality was nil. I grew up convinced that hard work – not being born into the right family, neighbourhood or social class – was the only thing that would get me ahead. Then there was a strong sense of community. Competition was frowned upon, because we had to stick together to fight the common enemy, which was the 'Evil Capitalist West'. Lastly, the honour and purpose: whether, rightly or wrongly, people embraced the ideology of Socialist New China. Soldiers gave up their lives, scientists rejected comfortable lifestyles in the West to come back and work on research projects, workers dedicated nights and weekends to complete construction projects. There was a reason to make those sacrifices, and it was honourable. No one talked about money much, because there was none.

After I moved away, every time I went back to Shanghai (which now has two of the top ten tallest skyscrapers in the world – China has five in total, including one in Hong Kong), I heard my people talking only about money: the stock market, property prices, second citizenship to avoid taxes (which is illegal), job hopping for more pay, etc. I saw them stressed, envious about what others got and anxious about what they might have missed themselves. I talked with my peers, who vaguely remembered the world we grew up in; they would occasionally lament the meritocracy and 'pureness' of the mindset back then. I read scholars, authors and social media bloggers criticising this new way of life, saying, 'We lost our soul'. China has succeeded at, or even exceeded, what it set out to accomplish when Deng Xiaoping launched the economic reform and 'Opening Up' initiatives in 1978. We are undoubtedly the best student of the Western market economy and biggest beneficiary of globalisation. But at what cost?

Change

The last two decades saw me working and living in seven different countries on three continents. I have advised international companies and led global functions through digitalisation, workforce transformation and other large change initiatives. What I have seen and experienced prompts me to reflect on what worked and what didn't in change management and to dig deeper to interpret tactics and processes:

- why are organisations today often characterised as being inefficient, slow and unable to change?
- why are leaders of our modern institutions often deemed by the public to be untrustworthy, or even corrupt?

- how do we convince our children that corporations are worth all their talent and aspirations if they want to make the world a better place?

It took over four years to complete this book project. During this period, I had a significant experience which, in hindsight, served as an inflection point for my personal leadership, my relationship with family and my professional pursuits. In a nutshell, I was offered the role of leading an organisational effectiveness initiative for one of the largest fast-moving consumer goods (FMCG) companies, answerable to the board. I had reached the pinnacle; I had huge power over the markets' organisational blueprint and headcount numbers. After five months, the company achieved the target it had set itself in terms of financial savings, but I left the company depleted, deeply disappointed and confused. I felt I had failed.

I spent the next few months soul-searching and speaking to trusted mentors and other professionals in order to try to make sense of my experience. I realised that what had happened was a clash of my people-oriented personal beliefs and the company culture that is aggressive and competitive; it was an ill match between my democratic, long-term-focused leadership style and the cost-cutting, short-term-focused context the company was in.

Immediately after I left that company, I was headhunted by a couple of others which were embarking on similar initiatives. Funnily enough, even after I openly shared my reflections, my style and my concerns, these companies were keen to hire me to 'get the job done'.

Purpose
What I learned was that modern corporations are hardwired to deliver shareholder returns and meet Wall Street expectations to such an extent that human capital is just another resource to be maximised. They all advocate workforce engagement, but, when

push comes to shove, they prioritise cost efficiency and profit margins and end up leaving employees to their own devices.

There is an acknowledged, substantial gap between education and employment. Millennials struggle to get on the career ladder and start their lives. The current employed workforce needs to be re-skilled and up-skilled to suit jobs in the age of post-artificial intelligence and robotics. Governments, educational institutions and corporations all wish someone else would do more to bridge the gap. What those who sing to the tune of *Make America Great Again* don't understand is that globalisation has caused the ship to sail well past the point of no return. America might be able to take the jobs back, but there will be fewer jobs, and everyone will end up paying much more for goods and services. The golden days when a middle-class family in suburban America could comfortably enjoy holidays, health care, college education for the kids, and retirement with pension are long gone and will never come back. We need radically to rethink the purposes for which corporations are to make a profit if we want to avoid a full-blown class war.

What I also learned is that human behaviour is conditioned by incentives. In the short-lived executive job I had, I was offered a generous performance bonus in addition to basic pay and another multiple times as a long-term incentive. This is not even outrageous for an executive comp. When there is so much vested interest, it becomes easier to say, 'Business is business', or 'We have to move on without you'.

But it's never just business.

We tend to forget that organisations are comprised of people. Corporations are actually a relatively new structure made hundreds of years after tribes, guilds, associations and mom and pop stores.

A few years ago, when I was engaged on a workforce migration initiative for a financial services company, I travelled to offices that were due to be closed in small and medium-size towns across America to tell people their jobs were going to mega-hubs that the company thought would deliver higher cost efficiency and economy of scale. One manager told me, 'I used to have an open-door policy and two chairs in my office. Anyone could come in to talk about their work, families and personal problems. Now, all my team is either gone, or in a different city. I don't know why I need the two chairs any more.'

His story stuck in my mind. I wanted to do more for those who want to embrace change but struggle because of a lack of new skills and mindsets.

Leadership
In my current position as head of learning for a big corporation, I spend my time articulating and developing the next generation of leaders, particularly in driving change, delivering results through collaboration and building an inclusive work environment in the context of digitalisation and working as *one*.

It was a conscious career change, because, at least from my point of view, simply relying on the help of a limited number of experts, through consultants or other change agents hired from outside (I was one of them), is not going to be enough. An internal change or organisational development function is not what's needed to be truly revolutionary. In my case, I battled with an existing, old leadership paradigm, yet I needed the recognition and support from the very same groups I am supposed to challenge and provoke. Leaders at all levels must change themselves to act as role models for people to own the change. It starts with a complete rewrite of the leadership definition and focus.

Family
I graduated from an elite business school in the UK and married a Midwestern American boy from my class. We now have a beautiful seven-year-old daughter who ticks all the boxes of the typical overachieving Asian American.

The birth of my own child brought me closer to my parents, who for years have felt an invisible wall between us because I live in the

West, I speak English most of the time at work and at home, and they feel that my values have been influenced by Western corporate values – analytical, task-oriented and ambitious. I find myself wondering how I can teach my daughter the best of both worlds.

Having been raised as a Chinese person, it strikes me that the Eastern way of teaching and learning is so different from that of Western practices. No Chinese parent will say, 'She doesn't have a talent in maths'. If you don't get a good grade, that's because you didn't work hard enough. But it stops the minute school finishes. Once entering the workforce, the teaching is: 'Keep your head down' (The wind breaks the tallest tree), or 'Do not voice your true opinions' (Think three times before you speak; if you don't have anything good to say, don't say it).

Asian Americans are by far the most neglected minority group when it comes to promotion.[1] As I occupy more senior roles in corporations, I often notice I'm the only Asian person at my level. At the time of writing, Goldman Sachs reported that 27 per cent of its US professional workforce was Asian American, while less than 10 per cent was in management.[2] It's probably the same as women and employees of colour in terms of systemic bias; however, the difference is that Asian Americans complain less and seem content with the situation, perhaps due to the teachings and traditional wisdom I have cited, or because we are pragmatic – life is not ideal but at least it is comfortably paid.

The reason for writing this book is not to be angry, but through reviewing what happened with HR, corporate culture and leadership in the past hundred years, to endeavour to forge a way forward in a volatile, uncertain, complex and ambiguous (VUCA) world.

We believe that the old capitalism is not sustainable, or at least not sustainable enough, while over-consumption is destroying the planet, and subsequently the human race. Social mobility is only a dream, with the top 1 per cent of the population in developed countries controlling 90 per cent of wealth today. And income equality today – in the US, a CEO earns 312 times more than the average worker, compared with 20 times post-Second World War[3] – is pushing societies to the verge of collapse.

I wish for a better world for my daughter than I experienced growing up. I believe that especially for those of us who are well educated, who have earned certain positions or influence in our respective institutions, we need to have the foresight and commitment to improve the current situation. If we don't, no one will.

NOTES

1   Kuo, I. 'The "whitening" of Asian-Americans', *The Atlantic*, 31 August 2018.https://www.theatlantic.com/education/archive/2018/08/the-whitening-of-asian-americans/563336. Accessed 17 December 2018.
2   Ibid.
3   Mishel, L., and J. Schieder. 'CEO compensation surged in 2017', Economic Policy Institute, 16 August 2018. https://www.epi.org/publication/ceo-compensation-surged-in-2017. Accessed 17 December 2018.

HOW THIS BOOK IS STRUCTURED

The book is divided into four sections:

SECTION 1
We discuss the wider context, the macro view. The point is to engage the reader in linking the role of the organisation in the context of history. We discuss some of the important things happening in the world today. We talk about the fear we see and try to make sense of why we might be here. We introduce the concept that the role of the organisation, the individual and society are connected, and we also discuss the big idea of the book: *the share-based organisation*.

SECTION 2
We focus on the organisational context, a micro view. We zoom in on tenets of current people practices and organisational practices, and provide evidence of why HR is lagging behind the fast evolution of societal, economic and business models. In the context of what is called the *fourth industrial revolution*, we highlight why we think many current practices are ineffective.

SECTION 3
We introduce some new ideas and reflect on theories that we think will help shape the way forward. We describe what the desired future state for agile organisations might look like.

SECTION 4

We outline a tactical, 4-Step-change approach to make things happen. We also provide further examples, observations and reflections to invite you, the reader, to be part of the change.

SECTION ONE

CONTEXT

I

CONWAY'S LAW

'Any organization that designs a system (defined broadly) will produce a design whose structure is a copy of the organization's communication structure'

— Melvin Conway

In this chapter:
- an examination of the role of the organisation to drive change;
- the link between society, the individual and the workplace.

HOW DO COMMITTEES INVENT?

This was the central question of Melvin Conway's 1968 paper on his observations of software creation within a nascent Silicon Valley. His point was simple: organisations need to intentionally design complex systems (projects, products, technology, advertising campaigns, etc.) to deliver a desired outcome. That is their purpose. Therefore, any system that is created is necessarily the sum of the inputs introduced into the design, and how those inputs are communicated and translated into decisions is crucial in predicting its effectiveness. If we wish power to be distributed in an organisation, it must be intentionally designed for people to share that power.

Hence, it follows that there is an element of predestination to every system created. After all, it is the vehicle to deliver the desired outcome. The promise of future technology is limited by the space from which it is created. How do you design the system, then, so it will produce results?

Due to the amount of time, people power, effort and capital that an organisation expends on creating the system, once complete it is not easily adjusted, altered or dissembled. So what happens when the new system doesn't actually serve its purpose?

Time, people power, effort and capital have been consumed. An outcome was promised, but not fulfilled. The usual cast of the smartest in the room – executives, MBAs, consultants, vendors, think tanks, gurus and shamans – had surely all but guaranteed success. Nothing negates the fact that the organisation has wasted enormous opportunity cost. Is the solution to attempt to modify the previously well-thought-out structure, or have the mistakes demonstrated sufficient dysfunction to scrap it all and start from scratch?

You know the inevitable moment of realisation that failure is imminent and a change is required when:

A new group of the smartest people in the room – executives, MBAs, consultants, vendors, think tanks, gurus and shamans – is appointed to uncover the problem and suggest a course of action. A post-mortem is arranged off-site. Failures must be translated into key areas for improvement and a profound learning opportunity. More than a few recommendations are made: key management shuffles, leadership changes, external hires or new consultants; perhaps implementing agile holacracy, flexible working, and/or enterprising social networks, platforms or artificial intelligence? Is there even a social media campaign? Can blockchain be applied here? Definitely hire some millennials, a few data scientists and install a ping-pong table or institute Hawaiian-shirt Friday.

Back in 1968, in his two-factor theory research Frederick Herzberg taught us that hygiene factors (process and system changes, pay, conditions, office space, policy changes, reward systems) all fail. They are all commoditised.

With renewed energy and vigour, the desired outcomes will be redefined, more practical teams and committees assembled, new processes readied for implementation, capital allocated and deadlines scribbled on a whiteboard.

A new group, usually eerily similar to the original cast of smartest people in the room – executives, MBAs, consultants, vendors, think tanks, gurus and shamans – promises manifest destiny due to their extensive learnings from prior failures. Now they have insight. Sit back and wait for the all but inevitable riches to pour in from their sure-to-be successful efforts.

Hasn't this movie played before? Failure has been analysed to the nth degree. Lessons have been learned. Everything *seems* to have changed before embarking on this new endeavour. But has anything *really* changed?

Conway posited that not much is likely to change this second time around either. The *people* weren't the problem per se, rather the organisation in which the people operate: the culture, hierarchy, politics, incentives, communications, reporting structures, account- ability and all the other elements that are difficult to measure and quantify but make an organisation, well, an organisation. The necessary human social structures have as much, if not more, impact on the outcome of a system design than the individuals who participate in the project. The individuals' behaviours are so heavily influenced by these factors that changing a few people is unlikely to be helpful. Actually, it is more likely to deliver either a similar or watered-down version of the previously desired outcome.

So how do we remove the ultimate obstacle to change? Modi- fications must move beyond superficial alterations and appointments of wise men to effectively create different outcomes. Achieving different results is very difficult; organisational cultures and histories are so woven into the fabric *of who we are* that certain change levers are never considered, or even brought to the table.

Herein lies the goal *Share* hopes to achieve. By laying out the challenges faced by modern organisations in a period of increasingly rapid change, a need may arise for an entirely new organisational mindset to be adopted in order to effectively conceive and implement a new system. In a period where competitors aren't just coming from the garages of Silicon Valley, but also from the classrooms of India and China and parts as yet unknown, the office parks of Lagos and Nairobi, the East End of London, the capitals of Europe and even the cornfields of the American Midwest, the projects and teams are global, and results are expected in dozens of countries by companies mired in a fight for market share in markets that don't even exist yet with business models as yet not imagined.

These are the challenges that the modern organisation faces. When confronted with the necessity to deliver outcomes, will the tendency to continue down the often flailing hierarchical power-centric pattern of history prevail, or will we open up and 'share' in the organisational power that delivers results in the twenty-first century?

TRIBES, CHANGE, FEAR AND MODERN LIFE

Stephen Hawking on…
  Diversity: 'We are all different. There is no such thing as a standard or run-of-the-mill human being, but we share the same human spirit.'
  Understanding and uniqueness: 'We are just an advanced breed of monkeys on a minor planet of a very average star. But we can understand the Universe. That makes us something very special.'
  Co-operation: 'We are in danger of destroying ourselves by our greed and stupidity. We cannot remain looking inwards at ourselves on a small and increasingly polluted and overcrowded planet.'

Diversity

Chris: I came late to Stephen Hawking. As I looked more and more into climate change, I found that I listened more and more. The three quotes from Hawking spoke to me as a way of summarising what this book was intended to be about and at the same time honour him and his forward thinking. The first quote is about diversity. I am fortunate enough to have travelled to nearly half the countries in the world, and I have found humans to be about the same everywhere. Differences are typically cultural in nature, but the core desires in life are the same: family, health, wealth, happiness – the best survival possible.

Human diversity reminds me of a garden of peacocks, each gorgeous in its own way but with a unique pattern that distinguishes itself from its fellow tribe member. I once stayed in a hotel somewhere in Asia where peacocks roamed in the garden. They strutted, they had unique character and proudly flaunted their individuality. Occasionally the garden would descend into avian chaos and violence as they competed to demonstrate who was the strongest or the prettiest. They were still a tribe of peacocks, but they weren't immune to competition for dominance to prove who was superior among them.

They shared the same garden but appeared focused on individual domination of that space. I couldn't help wondering what would happen if the garden suddenly became filled with smoke and they could no longer see one another. What if a fox showed up seeking a late-night snack? Would their displays of domination and strong individuality, their power issues, continue to serve their survival? Or is it inevitable that some should be culled? Could they shift their individuality into co-operation in order to survive? Should they? Can we?

Understanding and uniqueness

In the discipline of psychology an idea known as the Dunning–Kruger effect refers to research that found that the least competent people often believe they are the most competent because they 'lack the very expertise needed to recognize how badly they're doing'.[1] Similarly, in Ancient China Confucius told his students, 'Study without thought is labour lost; thought without study is dangerous.' Though considered one of the wisest men in the East of his age, Confucius did not believe any one person could possess the truth. He believed that through rational discussion the truth could be established somewhere between opposite positions, and that education and knowledge needed to spread as far as possible, to be shared by the many.

Further, do all get a *fair share* of the vote? Definitely not. Given the massive level of inequality, those who have power don't want to give it up. The hardest thing to acknowledge is that the elite do not have to give everything up for the world to be more balanced. Because you are here, now, reading this partly corporate book, you are likely to be among the world's educated, employed in corporates, non-profit organisations, government or consulting; and thus you are already different from most other people in the world. Most people don't have it as good as you.

Somewhere in these different ways of thinking, humanity limits or justifies the death of its members. Social constructs require people to compete, thus potentially killing this version of our planet, which all humans before us, who worked with so little in comparison, made for us through great sacrifice.

Family members who instructed us as children, or historical heroes we admire, dreamed that some of us would truly live our lives and have the power of the gods; we can learn from those mythical stories of the horrors that befall even gods when they fight among themselves in the face of hostility. Earth will continue, but there is a fear that, maybe through some elements of progress, humanity could either destroy itself or force itself backwards due to over-consumption of resources, devastating war and neglect of the planet.

It can already be seen to be taking place by the increasingly obvious divide between the *elite* and the *people*. For example, the top 10 per cent of global income earners are responsible for almost as much of the total greenhouse gas emissions as the bottom 90 per cent. Similarly, about half the world's population lives on less than $3 per day.[2] Most of us professionals probably identify ourselves as somewhere in between.

> **Chris:** I was one of those boys who grew up affiliated to some kind of tribe. In my formative years I identified myself as part of a tribal male group that sang, drank, hugged, travelled and hated together. In my case, identification was all about allegiance to a football team, Queens Park Rangers. Research has been undertaken as to why some males, maybe as they enter puberty, look to such groups for identification. I know that, through my football team, my friendships revolved around people who were generally from the same London postcodes and whose choice of colours and brand on a Saturday caused me to connect deeply with and defend such loyalty, and to expect the same from others. There was an unspoken belief about who we were.

> **Linda:** I grew up in pre-economic-reform China, where everyone was the same – same blue uniform with mandarin collars, same bicycle that carried a whole family, same salary for whatever job one had, be it in a factory or a hospital, same everything. It was not until I came to the West that I realised there are people referred to as the 'minority'. I then spent the next 20 years adapting to different ways to socialise, communicate and think because of the different cultures I chose to live in, to 'fit in'. Today, depending on what demographic, economic and social indicators one uses, I can be labelled in different 'minority' groups: women,

people of colour, Asian American, overseas Chinese...to name but a few. The constant feeling of being 'different' propelled me to consider what connects us as individuals, the need to differentiate one from another and how we choose to form and defend our own tribes.

As foreigners, the differences we've observed from living in the so-called Rust Belt of America and travelling to the tech-booming, money-rich coastal cities of the US stand out. The differences are more than fashion and diet, and permeate everything from work styles to relationships and values. We found we don't exactly belong to either group, but there are certain things that connect with both. We have an opportunity to apply the uniqueness of our learning right now.

Co-operation

Being inside a tribe is the default human experience. We have been around for 175,000 years, mostly in tribal clans. Until recently, most of us did not live to old age; we are wired through habits and our very senses to survive and function in biological, ancestral genes. We are trained at a biological level to behave as if tribes are natural. Though we live in our civilised world, and most of you, our readers, work in boxes of glass and steel, our bodies are wired chemically, neurologically and through behaviour for survival in a tribal context. Our civilised self is a very recent biological thing.

Pause to think about this: our brains are constantly scanning for danger. This is the primary purpose of the brain. The ways we interpret our fear for the stimuli in front of us determine adjustments such as the best fight/defence/flight response; this happens in a region of the brain called the amygdala. This process is dedicated to detecting the emotional salience of the stimuli – how much something stands out to us. This reaction is more pronounced with anger and fear. It also triggers the release of stress hormones and activates the sympathetic nervous system. We become more efficient when confronted by possible danger: blood flow and the stream of glucose to the skeletal muscles increase. Organs not vital to survival, such as the gastrointestinal system, slow down. A part of the brain called the hippocampus works with the amygdala. The hippocampus and prefrontal cortex help the brain interpret the perceived threat.

One of the primary things we look for in others is immediate signs of threat or confirmation – based on how much they may or may not look like us or others in our tribe. It comes as naturally to us as other bodily actions, such as breathing – we are constantly scanning for threats. For tens of thousands of years we lived in shared space, with relatively small, largely collective family teams, around 50 people sharing things, linked by genetics and a common language. We occupied our own familiar territory; we shared food and defended each other with our tribal allegiance...the most important things. We mostly had little or no real private property – everything was shared.

Things started to change for some of us relatively recently in the history of humankind. Chinese socialism is supposed to be built on sharing, but China is redeveloping private property rights. What about state-owned properties that fall into private hands as a result of corruption? During their administration (2003–13), President Hu Jintao and his premier, Wen Jiabao, appear to have sought a middle ground. Publicly, Hu promoted a 'harmonious society' that did a better job of distributing power and thus wealth equitably and that alleviated some of the excesses of pollution and corruption that accompanied rapid growth. Wen focused mainly on raising rural incomes and increasing social spending, especially on health and education.

Eventually, when we were under threat, a leader emerged from among our tribe. This is emergent leadership – conditions create a space for leadership. When leaders make us fear and sense danger, we seek strong direction and clarity. Many of our leaders today emerge because of fear. More information about the world around us and at our fingertips makes us more afraid. Best to trust the leader that makes us feel safe. That feels like our tribal default – one of us. This is what our brains tell us is best. The worst position to be in is one of uncertainty. We joined or conquered others, to grow our tribe. We created familiar stories of who we were and our history. It gave meaning to what we did every day. We instilled meaning into rituals and stories to share with our youngsters, so they retained who we were for the future. Being in tribes was critically important to us for survival. That's why it's still a natural default for many of our senses and responses. Being in a tribe meant strong cohesion with tribal members. Our first belief systems, religions and concepts of identity emerged precisely for the purpose of survival. It's quite a strong default.

Our earliest thoughts about our belief systems developed along the same lines globally. Indigenous people everywhere had different ideas about the supernatural and stories that created the non-tangible world show us that the worst threats were always the same: hunger, disease, natural disaster and defeat in war. These stories often implied cosmological relationships that, if broken, caused a threat. The relationship represented how we felt about the forces of Earth, or gods who controlled some aspect of the planet. Earth often came to be seen as an entity in itself – Mother Earth, or Mother Nature, in English. Today, this is often translated as the concept of Gaia. Things went badly if we humans did something wrong to Gaia.

In Chinese, the words combining 'Earth' and 'heaven' have the same meaning as 'world'. The Chinese emperor was called 'Son of Heaven' and he was also responsible for Earth. It was believed that the mood of heaven is directly connected with prosperity on Earth.

Both cultures stressed that we all interact with our surroundings on this planet to form reciprocity of systems and relationships that help to maintain and perpetuate the conditions for life on the planet.

Maybe our ancestors, as they developed their earliest ideas about belief systems, got this one right – really right. They learned from warnings perceived in the animals that survived the last time something went really wrong. Unfortunately, that seems to be how we learn best: through failure. Today, concepts within science focus on relationships; systems dominate our ideas of reciprocity and flow between systems. Our language now includes concepts of a biosphere, the system of all systems that govern our planet. The idea of this regulating system is that there is a neutrality, a balance, a harmony in order to maintain a status that produces the best conditions, for how we experience an Earth that is suitable for sustaining human life.

We also know that our thinking evolved to contradict principles of the concept of a biosphere and the ideas of a relationship between humans and the planet. Instead, we started to reject these ideas and to consider that our lives are best understood in the context of natural selection. That we as humans had dominion.

Natural selection, and the idea of not sharing, has held strong in the last 150 years of our existence. It allows us to believe that we, as the current incarnation of human beings, are smarter than those who came before us and therefore have made the most technical progress.

These core beliefs of superiority and competition were born in an age when some humans were starting to display enormous power in their ability to disrupt our planet and our human condition, in comparison with other times. In contrast, for thousands of years the Ancient Chinese believed everything – strong or weak – had a place in nature and justified its existence. Nature has immense power because it *contains* all of life, the same concept heavily referenced in the teachings of Confucius regarding leadership; to be able to lead, one has to be able to tolerate all differences and see good, or rotten. This idea that we use strength *and science* to justify what we do started at the beginning of the global colonisation on a large scale. These economies created the greatest discrepancies between the lives of the few rich and the lives of the many poor than at any other time in human history.

This is now, today, a time when we have more slavery, starvation and refugees than at any other time in recorded human history.

Back to the ancients and the consequence of disobeying a god: religion was fused with communal identity and purpose, integral to keeping the enterprise of a tribe afloat. The idea of people within a tribe believing in different gods, goals or belief systems was incomprehensible. Such a difference would threaten the lives of all the tribes and distract them from the hard stuff, such as staying alive every day. Such heretics would be killed.

The tribes that best survived – the so-called 'winners', our great-great-great...grandparents – were perhaps the most acutely aware of outsiders and potential foes. At this point, capitalism has for the first time in history seen a decline in the population. Not enough young people are paying for the old; job demand is shrinking, causing corporations to be unable to provide as many lifelong employment opportunities to young people in order to shed costs; young people are discontented, displaced and desperate, fuelling social instability. This is a vicious cycle.

Over the last 70 years of relative peace, at least in the West, many of us have forgotten what it is like to be afraid. Of course, we have television to help us imagine what horror can look like. We have had to create new bogey men in films and on TV because the sort of things that frightened our ancestors (e.g. not enough food) are not really scary to a lot of us, and even Halloween, with all its spooky connotations, has become increasingly commercialised.

And then we started to see the impacts of disharmony – lots of us being thrown together, across tribes, suddenly and globally, without a plan for change. Like Europe today. Like too many hastily built empires that no longer exist. Somehow, everywhere we go today we see and hear people from all walks of life and in every country talking about the same things. People are afraid of what the future may bring and think war or something equally bad is likely to happen.

So we speak to you, our reader, as a worker at whatever level in an organisation. You may work for a government or a non-profit, for a purpose or for profit. You are generally one of the elite in our world. We are educated, trained and prepared for organisational success; we are in a prime position to make a choice to share more, act differently, have a shared intent. This is an invitation.

Change management is an idea that seems hard to deny at the most basic level. Telling someone what is about to happen reduces his or her immobility feeling threatened. Having a plan for something where you think through the implications for all involved leads to overall better success in nearly every case. Over the past 150 years, the rapid growth of globalisation has seen a clash of cultures, with beliefs (religious and otherwise) challenged and not being replaced by new truths. Indeed, our only guarantee is that truth today is ever-changing.

We face ideological struggles concerning race, religion, political systems, geography, gender and so on. Perhaps the biggest struggle is the class war between the rich and poor.

Moore's Law tells us that science and the advance of technology will not proceed in a stairstep way. It does not move in an orderly fashion. It doubles.

Chris: I never really got the idea of an atomic reaction until I watched a programme that explained the power released by the doubling of an atom, and the doubling of that one, and on and on at tremendous speed. We cannot plan for the changes that we experience in our lifetimes. So without the ability to plan, in the context of the speed of change and scale of change around us we have this sense of a loss of control. A sense of danger. And so we are afraid. It is natural. We are chemically designed to be worried.

History is important because it gives us that meaningful glimpse into our ancestral pasts, how we got to where we are today. It gives us a sense of cultural belonging. That bad things happened before and that our ancestors made big decisions. We embrace identity, sharing the qualities, traditions and philosophies of what it means to be a community. Many of us – from so many backgrounds and in the context of all this change – either cling to the bits that make us feel safe, or as lost souls invent new principles all the time in a wave-wash of social media repugnance and latest shock value.

A sense of shared history tells us why our culture might do certain things and others do something else. History helps us understand change.

History includes triumphs and grave mistakes. It's rife with victories and tragedies, one thing leading to the next. Through a chain of events, one small occurrence sparks countless little incidents, or devastatingly large ones. So we can learn the nature of change from our ancient ancestors. More than 37 million people died in the First World War. The fact that the assassination of one fairly insignificant archduke could jump-start a war is fascinating, devastating and very important to understand.

History reveals patterns in our pasts. *History repeats itself*, as the saying goes. We have made so many mistakes throughout our history, and yet we always make exactly the same ones again. Why do you think that is? Maybe there aren't enough people interested in studying history, and really grasping its importance? Awareness of human nature in historical events helps us draw parallels between what happened then and what is happening now.

For you, our reader, we hope that a continued study of history raises your consciousness and provides you with a foundation for activism. Only by understanding history can we tackle the political or social reform that we may wish for.

We can consider how certain laws and societal standards came about, the effects on what kinds of people and the efforts taken by our ancestors who have been afraid at some point just as you might be right now, and who fought for exactly the thing you are fighting for today. Knowledge is power, and history makes us more empathetic. This is because we are able to learn the lesson of those who came before us from a safe distance. Thus, it can also provide a foundation for empathy across cultures. Fear and hatred of others is usually caused by ignorance. We're scared of the things we don't understand.

In some parts of the world, tribal conflict spawned by ethnic and linguistic differences has constructed systems of government designed to manage the consequences. They build cultures of compromise and of *sharing* – a neutral head of state, a constitutional monarch, or nonpartisan president – so legitimacy is less defined by one tribe or the other, with proportional representation making it impossible for one tribe to govern without coalition. Or mandatory inclusion of minority tribes to have a voice in government. They must share. They have learned, in deep pain, perhaps, that an inability to share is ultimately what can kill us most savagely. We seem to forget so fast; when the consequences are greater and the enemy plays for keeps, we don't get to play again.

Individual. Corporation. Society. Which tail wags which dog?

NOTES

1   Kruger, J., and D. Dunning. 'Unskilled and unaware of it: how difficulties in recognizing one's own incompetence lead to inflated self-assessments', *American Psychological Association Journal of Personality and Social Psychology*, 77 (6), 1999, pp. 1121–34.

2   Nuwer, R. 'How western civilisation could collapse', BBC 2017, http://www.bbc.com/future/story/20170418-how-western-civilisation-could-collapse. Accessed 10 April 2018.

2

HISTORY

'If you don't know history, then you don't know anything. You are a leaf that doesn't know it is part of a tree'

— Michael Crichton

'The most effective way to destroy people is to deny and obliterate their own understanding of their history'

— George Orwell

In this chapter:
- the importance of history on current times;
- the four industrial revolutions;
- the rebirth of nationalism and fascism as a predictable outcome of fast-paced change to society without regard to morals;
- the 'Darwin' mindset and social Darwinism may not serve us;
- a call to wake up and learn our history and challenge capitalism as we know it.

Without knowing where we come from, it is hard to know where to go. As children of immigration – forced (slavery) or economic (for education and opportunity) – we lose the signals of history around us. Even those of us who work in large corporations and stay in our host countries lose a sense of history of our homeland as we assume the short-term focus or the organisational rhythm of business.

These are times of both great promise and great peril for humanity. Billions of people and their tribes are connected through digital networks, the efficiency of organisations and the ability to regenerate the natural environment; every day we have the potential to undo the damage of the relentless exploitation that's been done for the sake of advancing industrial productivity in the past decades. The full impact of technology's unintended consequences is increasingly being acknowledged and addressed. The connections and integration of a re-found commitment to our collective survival does indeed show the promise of more opportunity to shape our lives with intent and with empathy.

TAYLOR'S 'SCIENTIFIC MANAGEMENT PRINCIPLES'

The past models of organisation that make up the best practices most of us grew up with have outdated leadership concepts centred around power and, thus, control and hierarchy. These models will not serve the needs of future organisations well. Many of our current organisational beliefs still have the shadow of the military or the Church hanging over them. During the first industrial revolution, corporations grew to sizes necessary to closely manage production scale and internal skills. Taylor's 'Scientific Management Principles' was born; how people do their best work became based on the mental model of that era, profoundly influenced by natural selection and competition – not only between industries and countries, but between workers and management. Ultimately, competition for limited resources determined the survival of the fittest: winner takes all.[1]

Today, there are calls for governments to do more in terms of regulations and laws in the face of disrupting new technologies. In reality, governments often lag behind, unable to process quickly enough to regulate new technologies and capture their benefits.

Unfortunately, in many cases the new technologies push industry and market systems into grey areas of morality and business ethics. Without regulation of some sort, there will be a host of new security concerns; inequality could continue to grow and societies further fragment. What ethics can govern the development of solutions in a global society when we are struggling with cultural and legislative differences, and find it hard to agree on what is a fact? Could we slip into a new type of colonialism, forcing a for-profit corporate culture into every aspect of private life and society, in effect having our personal lives shaped by those who design the artificial intelligence that will govern?

HISTORY NEVER REPEATS, BUT ALWAYS RHYMES

Without history, humankind will repeat mistakes in order to relearn what has been learned. Our vision becomes foggy. The historical impact of industrialisation will demonstrate patterns that show that our fears today are not only justified, but a real and present danger.

Throughout history, sharing has been a necessity; conversely, in the modern age wealth was created and accumulated by a few. The elite few justified their entitlement to more resources claiming they were stronger, smarter and harder-working; their (blue) blood was better, etc. They also carefully controlled the political machine to exert influences on the system so that their privileges would be sustained. The *people* didn't have a voice most of the time.

Not all elites are the same. Two types have existed throughout history, and we would argue are prevalent today: those who share and work for the people, and those who seek to protect their elite status. In the Roman historical elite, from which many of our political systems are modelled, there were two political tribes. The wealthy, privileged class were known as patricians, and claimed to trace their roots to the earliest tribes of Rome. They were split into two main political groups: the Populares and the Optimates. The Populares were for the cause of the plebeians (the commoners), particularly the urban poor. They supported laws to provide grain by the state at a subsidised price, land redistribution for the poor to farm and debt relief. They supported the extension of Roman citizenship to foreign allies. The Optimates supported the conservative interests of the aristocracy; they ran the Senate. The plebeian tribunes (representatives) and the Plebeian assembly clashed with the Senate. This led to the civil wars of the late Roman Republic: Sulla's first and second civil wars, Caesar's Civil War and others. The very same division essentially describes the political classes and systems today. Little will change unless we become more intentional and leverage the opportunity to create sustainable change.

Across our current corporate populations, there are also two types of leaders that embody those contrasting value systems: those who want to promote sharing and those who seek to safeguard their own.

This chapter will underscore the role our workplaces have played in changing the broader society in which they reside; in turn, we focus on how the development of our greater society influences the way our workplaces operate. Leaders who emerge through fear at such times need to be exposed in order to prevent unnecessary repetition. They present choices based on preservation, not progress. Informed choices and a well-balanced perspective make for sustainable decisions. We need to be empowered across our planet. The hope of the fourth industrial revolution is the empowerment of all.

The goals of the fourth industrial revolution are often analysed without looking through the lens that gives context to what has happened in the previous three, and why our current world was built in an iterative way. This is not only a story of applying technology to industry, but also the shaping of wealth distribution in communities. The future of our commerce and ultimate survival must be underpinned by ideas about how best to distribute power and create further wealth.

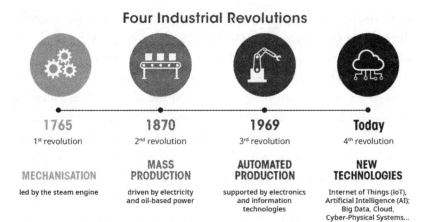

FIGURE 2.1   The four industrial revolutions

Sharing across the people is not new. (A sharing economy should not be confused with socialism.) It is in Greek history in the fables of kings and dictators and was central to Roman society. What we face today has been faced before. What have we learned?

THE FIRST THREE INDUSTRIAL REVOLUTIONS

During the late eighteenth and early nineteenth centuries, Britain led changes in many aspects of life through the Industrial Revolution. Scientific and technological innovations changed agricultural and industrial production, economic expansion and changes in living conditions.

This revolution created a sense of national identity and civic pride, spurring ideas of European nationalism and a *right* to rule the world. Across Europe and the US, rural areas became urban and industrialised, with massive growth. Wealth accumulated. New farming methods produced larger quantities of crops, allowing increased population, which in turn created consumer demand for manufactured goods. Mass production and the introduction of steam power was a final catalyst for the Industrial Revolution: machines that operated without human or animal power. New industries changed a country's infrastructure and transportation networks. This all happened over several decades, in the perspective of history a super-rapid change in human progress.

Similar to how we think about Moore's Law and the current pace of change in society, the first industrial revolution grew more powerful each year in a cumulative effect as new inventions and manufacturing processes added to the efficiency of machines and increased productivity. It continues today. We must remember that this is different from many political revolutions, which start and then are over. Technology and science build iteratively daily, and today, shape all aspects of global, national, local and political health, wealth and individual life choices. It is not really revolution, but progress – steady and over time.

Many factors helped bring about this revolution. Trade, most of all. Merchants had a supply of manufactured articles at a low price. Employment for all skilled workers who had no capital with which to start businesses for themselves. Salaries to pay for food. Lifting families out of poverty to consider possibilities of higher education.

There were new ideas that aided movement, such as scientific investigation and invention, the doctrine of *laissez-faire*. For centuries, the craft guilds and local governments had controlled localised industry to the minutest detail. Now business became regulated by the free play of supply and demand – laws were increasingly driven not by guilds but by the merchants at the national level who sought to harbour advantage. The government was hands-off and left businesses to drive and adopt new inventions and methods of production and the design of our societies as best suited them.

The second industrial revolution (from 1870 until the First World War) is notable for inventions in energy, materials, chemicals and medicine. There was a huge impact on production as a result of increased effectiveness of research and development in micro-inventive activity. Economic growth depended increasingly upon shared knowledge. This was a huge compilation of recipes, instructions and blueprints that constitute the techniques available to society. Science and technology refocused, including how to capture, share, compare and register scientific facts and regularities, as well as how to test hypotheses. The first industrial revolution had little or no scientific base. Engineering, medical technology and agriculture were pragmatic bodies of applied knowledge whose significance in terms of human stability was grossly undervalued. The second industrial revolution accelerated feedback loops between these two forms of knowledge and technology, asking, 'Why and how did we build what worked to help us get goods better, faster and cheaper?'

The second industrial revolution witnessed huge economies of scale. With the rise of the chemical industry, oil refining and other industries using containers, size began to matter more and more. Production technology influenced the rise of rail and telegraph networks, and in large cities, gas, water and sewage systems expanded enormously, with utilities such as electrical power and the telephone being the most important. Large technological systems moved from being the exception to the commonplace. Our lives became safer but more complex as we started to have more things – more machines in our daily lives, at home.

The limited liability corporation reduced risk to entrepreneurial activities. New sources of energy, new communication systems, new concepts of financial systems drove massive systemic change. We see these again today. The new energy source may be any imagined alternative forms of power. The new advances in our financial system, such as crowdfunding, bitcoin and blockchain, indicate a democratisation of finance.

In the third industrial revolution (starting in the 1980s), digitised communication created a super-*Internet of Things* infrastructure. Sensors are increasingly embedded into our machines and every device in our lives, allowing them to communicate with each other and leverage data to predict and shape the future. For example, your smartwatch is monitoring your BMI, blood pressure, glucose level and calorie consumption so if you have eaten an extra piece of pizza and have been skipping your workouts, it could instruct your fridge to refuse to accept ice cream. Also, sensors are now on warehouses, road systems, production lines, electrical grids, offices, homes, stores and vehicles, as well as being used to measure the flow of materials (liquids, solids, gases) – continually monitoring status and performance and feeding big data.

It is estimated that in the coming years there will be more than 100 trillion sensors connecting the human and natural environment in a global distributed intelligent network. Welcome to the Matrix. The entire human race can collaborate directly with one another, democratising economic life and raising risks and challenges such as preventing the creation of new corporate monopolies, protecting personal privacy, ensuring data security and thwarting cybercrime and cyberterrorism. Cameras on satellites would be able to detect chemical dumping at sea, knowing which ship and which chemical, all from space. There is heightened opportunity for regulation to drive ethical behaviour and for *privacy* to become an outdated term.

This expanded digital economy uses analytics to develop algorithms that speed efficiency, increase productivity and lower the cost of producing and distributing goods and services by predicting through shared data. Emerging digital generations can share music, videos, news, blogs for free, at zero-marginal cost.

THE FOURTH INDUSTRIAL REVOLUTION AND THE SHARING ECONOMY

Chris: A zero margin phenomenon is removing and creating new industries. When working at American Express I was involved in the downsizing of thousands of travel agencies as Internet travel companies emerged. We do not go into high-street shops to book our travel any more or buy vinyl, or get film printed. The same with insurance companies, which now use robots to underwrite policies and pricing risks, leveraging artificial intelligence. So, publishing, music, videos, photography, insurance, etc., all big industries, have all been completely disrupted. While many traditional industries have suffered, the zero-marginal-cost phenomena have created new entrepreneurial enterprises based on sharing information and creating communities. These new networks allow the creation of a new market exchange economy – what we call a sharing economy. It is based on the ideas of distribution and networks.

The evolving Internet of Things allows conventional business enterprises and millions of consumers to make and distribute their own renewable energy, use driverless vehicles in car-sharing services and manufacture 3D-printed physical products at very low marginal costs in the sharing economy. It transforms our city economics by changing concepts of where we can live and how our community is defined, impacting almost every conceivable aspect of life.

This transformation heralds the arrival of a fourth industrial revolution, characterised by velocity, distance, scope and systems impact. (The phrase 'fourth industrial revolution' was first coined by Klaus Schwab in 2016 and introduced the same year at the World Economic Forum.)[2] The speed of current breakthroughs based on Moore's Law has no historical precedent, even compared with the scale and pace of what we have already described. It gives us an opportunity for a shared vision on how we align societies and the world around us.

The fourth industrial revolution is evolving at an exponential pace, rather than being linear, and it disrupts *every industry at the same time*. The breadth and depth of these changes bring transformation of entire systems of production, management and self-governance. Can we imagine a world with little privacy, where shared space is so common that we must develop new mindsets to adapt to these intrusions?

It is an ever-evolving range of new technologies that fuse the physical, digital and biological worlds, impacting all disciplines, economies and industries, and even challenging ideas about what it means to be human. We create (and challenge) laws on things we did not know existed.

In developing new technologies, we are constrained and shaped by Conway's Law. This states that 'Organizations which design systems...are constrained to produce designs which are copies of the communication structures of these organizations.' Our organisational structures and our people are constrained by bias and the real-world concerns of the day, so the systems and technology are all connected.

STUMBLING BLOCKS

We are seemingly unable to leap to the next phase, which means thinking about the organisations that we work in as truly being purposeful towards enabling the world that we want to live in – and not simply contributing to the problem. We have to think big about the world we want to build, in parallel with driving the changes that excite us, and we need to be more intentional about things we cherish, or we might be driven into chaos. We have to have intent about what is possible for our technology to serve. It fills every aspect of our world today. All is transformed. We are now one shared computer, as humans. Do we realise this? How and where we drive, what we eat, what we watch, how we communicate – everything.

This is the time for opportunity. We have responsibility for ensuring that this technology serves all of us, and not just a few. For readers working in corporations: who are you serving, beyond the company? Who are you responsible for? What are you ethically responsible for? It seems mind-blowing, this power of technology to impact our lives now, and also the world that our children will inherit. It is the legacy that we will leave to those who come after us. It is happening faster than the speed at which we are accustomed to building our society.

An outdated capitalism

Capitalism has for the first time in history seen population decline – not enough young people are entering the workforce and paying for the retired. Most developed and developing countries have more people in the age bracket of 65 and above than any other age group, and we show no sign of changing that trend. Demand is shrinking, creating profit pressure, compounded by the ever more efficient technology. Corporations are replacing many jobs with robots and artificial intelligence. Lifelong employment is a long-gone thing of the past; even steady jobs are hard to come by. Young people are increasingly disillusioned by mounting student debt, bleak job prospects and rising living costs, especially in cities. They are discontented, displaced and desperate. Their sentiment is amplified by social media, fuelling social instability. It is a dangerous, vicious cycle.

This is why we are afraid. A lot of change is happening at the same time.

This fourth industrial revolution is ours to shape – if we are able to collaborate across geographies, sectors and disciplines to grasp the opportunities it presents in a way that speaks with empathy.

The fourth revolution is different from the previous three, which were characterised by advances in technology. These technologies have great potential to continue to connect billions more people to the Web, drastically improve the efficiency of business and organisations and help regenerate the natural environment through better asset management.

We do not have confidence in well-funded industry sectors whose ethics and contributions have records of overcoming naysayers' doubts. Governments – particularly democracies – will find it difficult to keep pace and regulate on behalf of society at the same pace as these changes. A technological breakthrough can occur in a cycle of two years. We will outline responses to these levels of changes later in the book, in the examples provided in Chapter 4 ('Luminous Cats').

The rebirth of populism, nationalism and fascism
At such times of significant change – when people are afraid – we often see a phenomenon sometimes referred to as the rise of the anti-intellectual, a mistrust of and hostility towards intellectuals. Even some educated people do not believe all the science; for example, we do not listen to the climatologists. It seems too big for some of us to fathom, too big for us to think about how we might have to share this planet in order for us all to get along.

We see more and more contempt for the power of education, philosophy and literature – of thinking and of the use of arts. Historically, a number of writers have cautioned us about anti-intellectualism. The historian Richard Hofstadter drew attention to this in *Anti-intellectualism in American Life* in 1966;[3] Susan Jacoby warned us in 2009 in her book, *The Age of American Unreason*;[4] and Tom Nichols announced *The Death of Expertise* in 2017.[5]

We see a rise in those who would give easy answers to the difficult questions of our time. They appeal to our tribal instincts not to trust the foreigner, not to trust anything complicated. They speak to nationalism, purely and often. They profess to talk in simple terms, to speak the language of the people, but for whom do they speak? Do they speak for you and all you hope for, or do they speak to your fear? Should our future be built from our fears?

They are populists, but unlike the Populares of Roman times they offer easy answers, the easy answers to complex problems and presenting themselves as champions of the common people. They can propose that the educated (that would be you) are a social class detached from the everyday concerns of the majority of the people, and that they dominate the arts, media and discourse…and, of course, education. History is littered with examples of totalitarian dictators, monarchs or world leaders who espoused anti-intellectualism.

Chris: One such example was Cambodia in the 1970s. I visited the Killing Fields and heard the stories of children leading their elders to slaughter. In the Spanish

Civil War, the White Terror campaign killed an estimated 200,000 civilians, heavily targeting writers, artists, teachers and professors.

Linda: In the decade-long Chinese Cultural Revolution, an estimated 500,000 to eight million intellectuals were persecuted or killed, committed suicide or were left permanently scarred. Intellectuals and scientists are seen as people whose occupations deal primarily with ideas as distinct from those who *do* things, who are more practical. This is a dangerous view, one that I have heard in almost every organisation that I have worked in. As humans we live in two worlds, the real tangible things that we touch and the world of ideas: laws, religions, belief systems, commerce. It is ideas and not real things that we often fear.

Populists say that we don't have time for long discussions about strategy, intent and ethics. *We have to do. We have to show our worth. Deliver. No time to think.* Fear of failure in our organisational contexts makes us criticise those who appear to think too much as 'theoretical', valuing pace and progress over thought. Even within our organisations we may consider that ideas, that *thinking*, is not practical; *execution* is more highly prized. Intellectuals can be accused of leading or writing terrible public policy, of playing with our lives. As such, even practitioners of human resources, change management and organisational development are sometimes viewed with suspicion: *can you execute what you are talking about? We need something simple, easy and fast.*

Populists today are the people who voice their opinion, usually a self-serving one, with no real knowledge and experience of the subject under discussion; what they *do* have is both the voice and the expertise to allow fear to shape our world.

We see today a strange juxtaposition of ideas about science. When I approached a Christian school in Illinois to which I was considering sending my child and asked about Charles Darwin, I was told, 'We protect our children from heresy'. They did not teach Darwin. So some aspects of education and science are accepted, but not all. I am able to detect a growing anti-science movement in the rhetoric of many of our emerging nationalist leaders, from the denial of evolution to the rejection of biotechnology and climate change. Regulations, trading practices, views on human rights and the repressive fear of litigation may drive scientific investigation towards being based on opinion rather than science. The idea of some news, some science, being 'fake' is nothing new. History tells us that 'fake news' was a term developed by the Nazi Party (specifically, Lügenpresse, or 'lying press') in order to discredit intellectuals. It was a core feature of the Nazi doctrine.

What causes this anti-intellectual, populist movement that we see in the world today? We see this as a direct impact of the third and fourth industrial revolutions:

1 Democratisation of information that is the direct result of the Internet – perhaps the most liberating and revolutionary invention of mankind – has a darker side. Anybody who has five minutes to kill on YouTube or WeChat believes that he or she can become an expert in anything. Consequently, people believe that their opinions are just as good as anybody else's, including those of experts.
2 Every important topic has been politicised by the unique views of those in power, based on their self-serving opinion. Acceptance or rejection of climate change itself has become a political litmus test.
3 It is easier to attack the integrity of the messenger than the content of the message.

Even though it may seem counter-intuitive, anti-intellectualism has little to do with challenging intelligence. It is, rather, a product of a culture driven by fear and emotion, not rational thinking. Many of the social problems we as a planet face are rooted in the rejection of critical thinking or the glorification of the emotional and the irrational. At its heart, it is fuelled by inequality – the widening economic gaps today created by the past industrial revolutions, which generate resentment. Resentment is now against reasoning.

Human rights exist to protect people from government abuse and neglect. A new generation of global populists claims to speak for *the people*; they treat rights as an impediment to their conception of the majority will. Discussion on human rights seems to have shifted away from being shared and universal. We no longer in our interpretations seek to protect individuals from the state, but ask our governments to defend our rights against *them*. One such perceived threat is migration, where concerns about cultural identity, economic opportunity and terrorism intersect.

Populists encourage this tribal, primal fear. It is perhaps human nature that it is harder to identify with people who differ from us and easier to accept violations of their rights. People take solace in the assumption that the selective enforcement of rights is possible – that the rights of others can be compromised while their own (this means you, dear reader) remain secure.

Martin Niemöller was a prominent Lutheran pastor who spent seven years in concentration camps for his opposition to the Nazification of German Protestant churches. He is best remembered for the following words:

First they came for the communists, and I did not speak out –
Because I was not a communist.
Then they came for the socialists, and I did not speak out –
Because I was not a socialist.
Then they came for the trade unionists, and I did not speak out –
Because I was not a trade unionist.

Then they came for the Jews, and I did not speak out –
Because I was not a Jew.
Then they came for me –
And there was no one left to speak out for me.[6]

Niemöller's message was clear: you may not like your neighbours, but if you sacrifice their rights today, if you do not see a shared need, you jeopardise your own tomorrow, because ultimately, rights are grounded on the duty to treat others as you would want to be treated.

This is the Golden Rule; treat others as you wish to be treated. It is this old tribal law of altruism that encouraged giving bread to strangers. The entire basis of Confucius and the Bible and every major philosophical teaching is based on the Golden Rule.

- Treat others as you would like others to treat you.
- Do not treat others in ways that you would not like to be treated.
- What you wish upon others, you wish upon yourself.

THE WAY FORWARD

Psychologically, the Golden Rule involves a person having empathy for others. We forget at our peril the demagogues of yesteryear who claimed privileged insight into the majority's interest, but ended up crushing the individual. When populists treat rights as an obstacle to their vision of the majority will, it is only a matter of time before they turn on those who disagree with their agenda. And this means instability – depression and war. All over the world we hear people speculating about the next depression or world war. After the Great Depression in the US in the 1930s, social welfare programmes were installed and a 70 per cent inheritance tax was introduced, ensuring that excessive wealth was not passed on to the next generation. Today, the pendulum has swung back, creating even greater income inequality and social instability than in the thirties. Hopefully, we won't have to rely on destruction and death to bring about change.

To counter these trends, a broad reaffirmation of human rights that starts in our corporations is needed – a discussion about what it means today to share our planet.

We hope that this rise of the populists leads to some soul-searching among you, our corporate citizens, in particular. You are among the most educated, and thus you have the most to be afraid of what populism can bring. Trade is threatened when populists defend national borders. Who will govern science and technology in these third and fourth industrial revolutions when it threatens our citizens by disrupting their workplaces, their communities and the future of their children?

When there is not a familiar tribe or tribal elder to speak with wisdom, what do we listen to? The fear of the crowd? Crowds lynch because of fear, not reasoning. When no one speaks up, the loudest voice prevails. The Web is full of populists who say, 'Follow me'. We reward them with marketing contracts.

If the appeal of the strongman and the voices of intolerance prevail, the world risks entering a dark era. We should never underestimate the tendency of demagogues who sacrifice the rights of others in our name today to jettison our rights tomorrow when their real priority – retaining their own power – is in jeopardy. This is one of the stark lessons of history.

We believe that there is a way forward through embracing principles of sharing at a most fundamental level. We believe that these circumstances have been brought about by ourselves and the organisations in which we work.

More critically, we believe that the solution for these organisations as powerful entities in our societies is to take a stronger collective leadership role in redirecting and reinventing what share-based economies, workplaces and communities mean. The corporation and the workplace have never played such an influential role in human history as now. Every aspect of our daily lives is more governed by a marketing team than by the government.

Can we totally rewire ourselves to make *sharing* a core mindset and guide for our practices so that people throughout the world can be one tribe? Can we move forward based on ideas about preserving and enriching, and not fear?

NOTES

1   Taylor, F. *Scientific Management* (includes 'Shop management', 1903, 'The principles of scientific management', 1911, and 'Testimony before the Special House Committee', 1912). New York: Routledge, 2003.

2   Schwab, K. 'The fourth industrial revolution', World Economic Forum, 11 January 2016. https://www.weforum.org/about/the-fourth-industrial-revolution-by-klaus-schwab. Accessed 24 April 2017.

3   Hofstadter, R. *Anti-intellectualism in American Life*. New York: Vintage Books, 1966.

4   Jacoby, S. *The Age of American Unreason*. New York: Vintage Books, 2009.

5   Nichols, T. *The Death of Expertise: The Campaign Against Established Knowledge and Why It Matters*. Oxford: Oxford University Press, 2017.

6   Mayer, M. *They Thought They Were Free*. Chicago: University of Chicago Press, 1955.

3

GOING GLOBAL

'Without accepting the fact that everything changes, we cannot find perfect composure. But unfortunately, although it is true, it is difficult for us to accept it. Because we cannot accept the truth of transience, we suffer'

— Shunryu Suzuki

In this chapter:
- what does global mean?
- personal reflections of global.

Chris: One of the reasons why I wrote *Rewire* in 2015 was that I felt at the time that people could see the start of a change in the world around them. And that they were becoming scared of that change. Fear was increasingly about the pace of change, the loss of control – and, as ever throughout history, the blame is often placed on those who are different.

One of the concepts that we talked about in the book was this fear, and that unless we appreciate how different we all are we will be led by a wave of populism across the planet.

Around the globe, we seem to be very afraid. I hear people in many parts of the world talking about the possibility of major war in our lifetime. Not just something that we watch on the news, but in our everyday lives. A war not fought in and confined to the lesser travelled parts of our planet.

It sounds dramatic spoken out loud, and as I write, I feel a little bit like the child in Hans Christian Andersen's *The Emperor's New Clothes*. Because it seems that I have been having this conversation with colleagues, strangers at airports, on the bus, with taxi drivers – in fact, everywhere that I go and experience humans. But this is not something discussed in the mass media and in social media we seem to pick sides early and not listen to each other. No place for sensible collective debate. It seems that, for all our advances, the most difficult one to achieve is the ability to have an adult conversation with empathy and with each other as a whole.

When we were a village, when we all knew each other and could agree about what to do, we would have this important discussion around the fire, or while eating. When I was in my football tribe, we would find time in a bar, on a train journey between cities, to commune before and after football matches with strangers about issues that impacted our lives. One of my favourite football tribe conversations was a vigorous debate about the best way to cook rice – and the conversations ranged over the years from world events to Brexit and animal rights. A tribal forum in bars and on trains.

Sharing our ideas with each other is something that we do when we feel safe within our tribes. I can be direct with my child or my nephew in my family tribe, I can criticise my football player within my football clan, I can challenge my leader in the closed room of my corporation and my country's politicians in my community hall meeting. Or I can resent the views of others, the intrusion of the other team's fans when they criticise our players, or the neighbour who offers unsolicited advice on how we might raise a child. We instinctively see things as a threat.

When we lived in small-town communities, a leader would gather us together to talk. But in the age of globally connected conversations, there is no market square (not one that we can trust) where we can all come together and have a dialogue about how scared we all might be of what might be about to happen.

A GLOBAL PERSPECTIVE

Linda: I was born in 1977, a year after the death of Chairman Mao. The young socialist nation was still closed to outsiders and it was run as a strong, state-controlled, planned economy. As a child, I would go once a month with my mother to buy sugar, rice and oil, using coupons issued according to the number of people in the household. There were three flavours of ice cream in the shop for about three months of the year: strawberry, vanilla and chocolate.

My parents are traditional Chinese who know nothing about the West. For some reason unknown to me, they insisted that I learn English. Their modest salaries – $8 a month – couldn't provide for a private tutor; instead, my dad, who was a chef, would cook for the tutor's family.

Whether through foresight or sheer good luck, I graduated at the time when multinational companies started to enter China. My English got me an analyst's job at one of the top-class consulting firms. After six months I was sent to the US for training. I clearly remember the first time I stepped into a Walmart, how overwhelmed I was by the endless selection of merchandise and the fact that I could freely pick up anything – touch it, smell it – instead of asking a long-faced assistant to get it for me from the shelf. I could have cried.

Twenty years have passed since then. I have lived in eight countries on three continents, have met a lot of people from various cultural and ethnic backgrounds and married one of them. My story is that of millions of others who have moved in the past 100 years with more freedom and opportunity across the national boundaries on the currency of their knowledge and skills. We are a part of and product of the second and third industrial revolutions. Our knowledge and capability are traded. They are a commodity. Compared to our parents' or grandparents' generations, who went abroad for similar reasons – for better lives and better education for their children – we do not rely on physical strength and hard work in low-paying jobs. My daughter is going to compete with everyone globally, even if she doesn't move. The world is now much smaller.

My classmates at London Business School came from more than 30 different countries, but all had a few things in common: good families, good health, good education and good jobs. After the first three months, we separated into two camps: one featured 'family business clubs' and weekend yachting or skiing trips; the other was dedicated to mock interviews and career coaching geared towards getting those exclusive internships and full-time positions at top consulting firms and banks. Unsurprisingly, plenty of romances occurred during those events.

I met my husband during the orientation and spent numerous hours hanging out at the Windsor Castle, the pub adjacent to the school, after going to the same lectures and clubs. At the time he seemed to me to be a nice boy from the Midwest of America, with the same interests and aspirations – a typical 'soulmate'.

Later, we had a beautiful daughter, who has the fashionable label 'ethnically ambiguous'. In my prenatal class, eight out of 10 couples were mixed race. Every baby looked unique, not exactly fitting into any classic 'box'. When Youjia was 15 months old, we moved back to America and initially settled in a medium-sized town in the Midwest. When she was about four, she began to notice how different she looked from other kids, being the only half-white, half-Asian in the nursery. She got really close with an Indian girl and the two hung out all the time, away from the others. This made me anxious. Was my daughter being sidelined for being different? Probably not, at least not consciously. But kids can be cruel.

We made a big decision to move back to the city, where all sorts of people mingle and she could be judged on her merits rather than her looks. Now she is thriving in an international school with pupils from all over the world. She has a big group of friends of various races who speak different languages at home. I am reassured that she is now on the right path to becoming a future global citizen.

Once we began to get acquainted with the school community and got to know other parents, it was fascinating to realise how much we had in common – many of us are political agnostics, we share the same gossip about the newest restaurants and wine pairings, and even have the same obsession over our kids' extracurricular accomplishments.

It dawned on me that we had entered another 'tribe', one that our education, experience and aspirations put us in. We represented a ubiquitous class of highly skilled, self-made professionals who are products of, and players in, the knowledge economy. To us, 'global' is not only a belief; it is our identity.

GLOBALLY CONSCIOUS

Chris: I was born in London, the child of a parent who left a British colony to pursue an education. I grew up in London, Georgetown, Guyana and New York City. I am not so different from many children from the Caribbean. Some children acquired an excellent education based on the old English grammar school system which has served India, Singapore and many other places well in the post-colonial world. I am a true transatlantic child. I have worked for numerous global companies, lived on four continents and travelled to around 100 countries. I feel like a global citizen.

My wife is what is called an African American but to me she is a typical American. She also grew up in the Midwest like Linda's husband. She did the 'good high school, small-town' thing, came from a well-educated family in a medium-sized city. She is from an American family that a few generations ago were slaves. She believes in things Americans typically believe in. Her family is large and centred in the Midwest across a few Northern States. They walked from Mississippi and Louisiana to be near the Canadian border, find work and escape living the people who once owned them. They mostly live in a circle of black friends, families and neighbourhood. They are good examples of the separate but equal post-segregation dream. When I have moved to cities in America, the local black middle-class network always reaches out in some way as support. It is a separate America. We met in a crazy bar one night in New York, in the year after 9/11, when the city was celebrating being alive. For those of us who were there on that day in Lower Manhattan, I find there is an extra level of shared beliefs about the importance of tasting life. Such horror rarely encroaches upon our corporate lives unless at a time of war.

For me, the history of being black, and the fact that at one point some of my own ancestors were slaves, gives a unique global perspective of the industrial age. Slavery was accelerated to enable the plantation system. This was a disruptor to the scale and industry of slavery and the societies that touched slavery from many perspectives. The Plantation system was a precursor of the technological changes, applied process management, of the first industrial revolution. It impacted the lives of millions, brought wealth to a few and misery to millions – common effects of technological change on society through history.

Perhaps like many others, I am aware of just how far we have come in a couple of generations. Marrying into a black American family brings an awareness about how unique 'we' are in the corporate office. It gives me a particular view on the world, as I am personally judged at times from the lens of my skin's history and how 'we' stand among others.

There is a uniquely African belief in ancestor worship that speaks about respecting your forebears and seeking their advice, as if they are standing alongside you. I am aware of the sacrifice of those people who helped me to be where I am today.

It seems incomprehensible that some ancestor on a slave ship, on a plantation, giving birth to a child that would be sold, would imagine that someday I'd be the child of their choice to live another day. My wife and I often think about the past and marvel at the world that has created such opportunities for us.

Now, my co-author and I sit with a different dream and perspective from the one our grandparents had – that our children be accepted into, and maybe even lead, *their* global world economy, and for both of us who write this – to compete with the best in the world. In the broad span of historical perspective, Linda and I have both come far in a couple of generations; it is extraordinary that we have even met each other and are now collaborating.

The global organisations that we work in today have made these stories possible.

When I listen to stories of travel, friendships and identity, I am aware that many of us increasingly have a unique perspective on this most global of times.

A new class is developing that is different from the traditional wealthy and middle class. We are increasingly global, connected and similar to each other in terms of thoughts and values, though we speak different languages. We share much and have more in common with each other in what we believe. We are different races, but we are also the same person. We work hard in order to acquire the kind of economic and physical freedom inconceivable to our parents; we are good citizens and try hard not to break the law. Like so many corporate workers, are we terrified that our privilege will be taken away by a change in the rules of the game, or that we will have to pay for other people's bad decisions? We are aware of how far we have come in one generation. We are 'firsts' in many cases: the first to go to college, or work in a corporation or for the government, to have an office job apart from my family, my village, my town, my street. Most of my football tribe can't believe that I work in the 'corporate world'.

Linda: I can never make my Chinese mother understand what I do for a living.

As a result, we can be viewed as 'politically neutral', or indifferent, deeming the country we are in to be 'the place of residence', rather than a permanent affiliation. It is not always polite to discuss what we think with our colleagues and neighbours: offence is taken easily.

We are all global citizens, you and I, aligned through birth into a nation with customs and practices, but able to look beyond the politics of the day or our locale. Our strength is that we have been able to adapt, to shift within the traditions of these organisations, to overcome cultural differences in our careers to be successful and accepted.

Back now to my husband and his background in the Midwest heart of America, southern Illinois – once called the Buckle of the Bible Belt.

In traditional organisations it was possible to work your way up. Even as a blue-collar worker you could get to a comfortable management position by accumulating years of experience. Your salary was decent enough to pay for a house in a respectable neighbourhood. Your wife took care of the house and kids. You worked hard and went bowling with the guys once or twice a week after work.

Companies were growing after the Second World War and making money. It used to be normal to expect living standards to continue to rise. Housing prices were guaranteed to rise. Suburban communities proliferated together with the growth of the middle class. Individualism and consumerism were celebrated, thanks to the promise of a lifetime pension. Neighbours would spend $800 on a snowplough that they used maybe twice a year, just so that they didn't have to bug their neighbours to borrow the damn thing. To many whose ancestors only one or two generations before had come from harder times – either because of war, farming or slavery – life was beautiful, as long as they did not cause trouble and respected their relationship with the company.

There was a natural paternalistic relationship with the big local employers for whom they worked. 'Paternalism', as defined by the *Concise Oxford English Dictionary*, means 'the policy of restricting the freedom and responsibilities of one's subordinates or dependants in their supposed best interest'. Put simply, the organisation acts as a dominant 'father' that makes decisions for you. There is an emotional relationship of loyalty and reciprocity. For employees, the workplace and the number of years on the job are part of who they are, and in many cases their organisation value (level/rank/seniority) also defines them socially in their small local community. This is exhibited in some way at every big corporation in which we have worked.

That was my experience when I first came to live in a mid-sized town in central Illinois – how much family and church is woven into the fabric of a workplace. The business is what defines the town.

The leaders of the company attended the same churches and were active as sponsors in all of the community events, local festivals, concerts, etc. The social life of the community and the workplace, church and personal relationships were intertwined. Company events embodied 'Midwestern nice' and family-focused culture at 'Play Days', Christmas celebrations and retirement ceremonies. Colleagues talked openly about expectations and of examples of the company 'taking care of' them and their families. Corporate decisions were personal and impacted families directly in the local and global communities. Decisions made for the local community were all in the context of the organisation. There was a high degree of social consciousness different from the big, city-based corporation. We see this experience as typical of the two societies being disrupted, the centre and traditional communities vs the growing cities where prices accelerate to meet new worker demand for new industries.

This picture that we paint looked good for several decades – it was the growth story that proved capitalism worked, and the growth engine of aspirations for many societies around the world. It took people from poverty to security. This was all okay, provided there was a context of sustained and constant growth. But that is hard in a global world, where there are limits. Boundaries.

A similar paternalistic mindset still prevails in many corporations that hail from the immediate post-war era. A senior executive in a global company with whom I worked commented, 'The sole purpose of the company's existence is to provide for pensions.'

I always wondered about the implications of such mutual loyalty. These cultures are centred on a principle of 'no fault': people are often unwilling to take risks, or to change the existing way of thinking and working. It is a type of social compliance and strong conformity. People are afraid of losing their jobs. Fear does strange things to people in corporations. In an institution, people become institutionalised. People are not as they are when outside the institution. They are programmed by organisations to behave in a peculiar way, adrift from normal human experiences.

Disruption at the workplace or the institution means causing disunity in other social contexts, such as the local church or the school PTA. Everyone is interrelated through either work or marriage. Citizenship is defined by the interests of the organisations, and loyalty is increasingly expected from senior members of the organisations.

To speak out from the workplace – to drive difference – is very hard; to speak up and be different is to challenge these cultures. Companies speak about innovation, but often nothing goes beyond statements from the management. Over time, workers, management and executives are rewarded for being good, which means following marching orders and not allowing open and involved dialogue.

For companies today, this way of working is increasingly floundering. The need to share, to collaborate, to have transparency, empathy and trust, to be an equal is difficult. Yet these are the words that typically litter the mission statements of our corporations.

My generation, Gen X, has grown cynical of our relationship with the corporate world, doubtful of the promise held by past generations, or following the rules and being looked after. We have personally worked to reduce local workforces, disrupt lives and ensure that organisational members compete globally to stay local for their next job. That promise has therefore been broken as corporations have had to change locations and business models and reduce workforces, all to ensure they meet targets of endless growth, and to ensure survival.

The third and fourth industrial revolutions bring new currency and language to define people and cultures through global competitive advantage. Our organisations live in a world of an outdated employee values proposition, remaining locked in cycles of behaviour from a past age.

We are now wise to enough to see this, to know the uneasiness of the corporate environment, however strong the benefits. How can we humanise this workplace, meaning being able to share more? How can these workplaces become more empathetic to the world around us beyond the service, product or function that we sell?

EMPATHY AND SHARING

Core to sharing is empathy. Core to inclusion is empathy. How can we build empathy and sharing into the default DNA of our organisational citizens so that our planet is thus guided?

We have noticed that sharing is perhaps a deeply embedded trait of communities in less developed or less affluent parts of the world – the still pre-industrial global planet. It is also present more in capital-restrictive corporations and sectors that we have worked in. We share if we gain – we know the dilemmas of prisoners, riddles and endless team-building activity. Somehow, this is all never enough to really learn. In times of scarce resources, we share. It was our default before we had such abundance.

In tribal times, some would go out to hunt or work in the fields, working *together* to kill to eat, kill to stay alive or offer *shared* labour to create food. Access to food was the baseline tribal resource and dominated categories of social class and wealth. Others would take care of the community; it was better to share time and effort to process food, care for the sick, educate and look after children, the unique and most undervalued of all human activity. Shared work communities were the default pattern of human existence through much of history, and until very recently.

The current focus on the role of the individual and competition in society, the way that we reward and treat people in corporations, contradicts values that are celebrated in popular culture about sharing – co-operation, fairness and reputation.

Such qualities are taught to children from a very young age through idioms and fables and Disney. Almost all Chinese children grow up on the story of 'Kong Rong Giving Up Pears'. Kong Rong

was the twentieth great-grandchild of Confucius and the sixth son
of Kong Zhou.

'KONG RONG GIVING UP PEARS'

When Kong Rong was four, on his father's sixtieth birthday
he was asked to share a plate of pears of different sizes with
his five elder brothers and one younger brother. Kong Rong
picked the smallest pear for himself, then gave the biggest pear
to the eldest brother, followed by the second biggest pear to the
second eldest brother and so on. When asked why he did this, he
answered, 'Trees follow the order of high to low, people follow
the order of elder to young – that is the ethics of respecting
elders!' His father was pleased, but asked again, 'But why did
your youngest brother get a bigger pear than yours despite you
are ahead of him by order?' Kong Rong said, 'I love and protect
my youngest brother, so he should have a bigger pear than me!'

For centuries, such stories established role models for how
one operates in a community and shares. Parents would 'test' if
the child was spontaneously sharing and took pride if he or she
exhibited such behaviours at an early age. Hardwiring 'share'
into behaviours is the only way that a populous but relatively
resource-poor community could thrive.

GLOBAL CITIZENS

Ironically, we are entering another age of scarcity compounded by
urbanisation and globalisation. There is a general and real decline
in tangible and financial resources across the world. Permanent
guaranteed growth is elusive for most industries.

Companies struggle to keep service provisions while driving
innovation. There is a global phenomenon of both forced and voluntary
migration of people towards cities and countries that are politically

and economically stable. Not only do we have to share public space, education, health care and employment, and find balance between public and private interest, but we must do this within an increasingly diverse context. As the US Army War College has coined it, we live in a volatile, uncertain, complex and ambiguous (VUCA) world.

On the positive side, we are adaptable social animals. There is hope. This is apparent from the fact that inhabitants of major cities have a much higher tolerance for difference compared with those living in small communities that haven't seen much population movement. Accepting difference also fosters curiosity and open-mindedness, which is lacking in suburban neighbourhoods where people seem to be 'self-sufficient' but lack the social connection that comes with 'sharing'. Of course, we also trade with each other. Trade, or sharing, brings peace. Trade requires peace. Trade enables the most significant advancements across societies. Trade builds a good life for many of us, but not all of us quickly enough. The way we trade is damaged by nationalism, driven by fear of the foreign.

It is easy to lose perspective. We see globalisation and the pace of technology as endless and in this we may be blinded. Our ancestors did not see the edges of this world, yet they thought the world was flat. The world is not flat. It is circular. With globalisation we have so many sharp elbows. People get hurt. Perspective and history should give us insight.

Another aspect of *Rewire* was this idea that Chris gleaned about the work of Simon Western in *Leadership: A Critical Text*. Western discusses aspects of leadership and organisational philosophy from three perspectives. He gives an analysis of the organisation through this recent industrial age of history. A central idea that he presents is that the experience of the individual worker or human in any given age is linked directly to the larger intent of the organisation and how the organisation thinks about that worker, linked to what is happening in the wider society.[1]

Technology now shapes society and links between the individual and the organisation seem obvious. This is an epoch of an unimagined digital age. In revolutions both civil and industrial, we saw mass disruption of society; people were drawn to towns and cities and the nature of the work of humans was transformed.

We have millions of refugees today. People just like us. But a solution seems a long way off because of a mix of *old-world thinking* – and an inability really to talk to each other. In order to resolve the refugee crisis, we must learn to trust each other, to accept our shared goals and to use empathy.

If we put a team together to decide on global trade, security, saving the planet – to lead the world towards a sustainable future – we would need to make some tough choices about how we compete ethically in business, but with a goal of doing it together. The team would create a shared code of ethics. No organisation would ignore this level of planning. All organisations dedicate some time to effectiveness, some mild to excessive team building. The board would address any nihilistic behaviour.

Where are there shared principles and big ideas today?

We believe that one way to start is to challenge the old paternalism and expectations of the corporations of the past. Instead, we could create an empathic, inclusive corporate culture which in turn enables an empathic approach to our planet and also best serves our own organisations, as they deal with the advent of transformational advances in technology.

We have on a global scale seen massive human advances in a short time. Through this period of the industrial age, birth rates and life expectancy improved. Overall, we experienced a life-changing epoch for all humans. With such a view of history, what a waste to suddenly take us backwards now.

NOTES
1   Western, S. *Leadership: A Critical Text* (2nd ed.). London: SAGE Publications 2013.

4

LUMINOUS CATS

'Instead of seeing what they want you to see, you gotta open your brain to the possibilities'

— Bumi in *Avatar: The Last Airbender*[1]

In this chapter:
- the impact of technology on society;
- the impact of small tech changes on our world.

Delving deeper into the idea of the links between our lives as global citizens and our workplaces, society and the planet are crucial to our success.

To illustrate the impact of this digital age, let's use the biological example of luminous kittens. Technical advances have allowed us to cross DNA strands between cats and jellyfish in order to research the HIV virus. Although not intentional, this remarkable configuration of science made it possible actually to create a luminous cat! Any child would want to be the first to own such a kitten.

Researcher Eric Poeschla produced three glowing genetically modified (GM) cats by using a virus to carry a gene called green fluorescent protein (GFP) into the eggs from which the animals eventually grew. This method of genetic modification is simpler and more efficient than traditional cloning techniques and results in the use of fewer animals in the process. The GFP gene, which has its origins in jellyfish, expresses proteins that fluoresce when illuminated with certain frequencies of light. Poeschla, of the Mayo Clinic, in Rochester, Minnesota, reported in the journal *Nature Methods* (2011) how he created a brand-new breed in an attempt to cure a disease.[2]

Conceptually applied to discrepancies and problems in corporate, governmental and social systems, the idea of using an entirely different organism to fix fundamental failings of another displays true outside-the-box thinking. Should society start to trade in luminous kittens just because it is possible to? Because we now have the technology, should we all be able to do it – globally? What if a start-up business were to sell luminous kittens, perhaps initially on the Dark Web and then by legitimate distribution? Glow-in-the-dark kittens could be ordered and delivered with a series of simple clicks. Soon a whole industry of luminous animals – a veritable cottage industry – would be bred around the country, decimating the demand for normal cats and quickly increasing the luminous cats per human ratio.

The price would go from very high to being commoditised almost immediately and a new business profit chain would be created, all because of luminous cats. More cat types (colours) might be designed for different market segments, features, etc.

The current speeds at which governments run – be they democratic, totalitarian, dictatorial, royal or by committee and CEO – are too slow for them to be able to react to the evolution of the fourth industrial revolution and the pace and possibilities of science. All current responses, however appropriate to science, seem cumbersome. There will be moral and theoretical arguments on multiple sides as to why no one should have consumer rights to buy luminous kittens.

It seems fanciful, but imagine morals and empathy were deeply inserted into how business was conducted. That it was a designed aspect that we focused on creating across our corporations. Decision-making at every level would be enabled in the simple assumption that more than a policy or a committee could be trusted. In fact, fewer decisions would need to be handed over to the committee overall.

Playing with biospheres, even simple ones, through introducing a new animal into the environment can have devastating consequences. Consider the impact in the local neighbourhood on foxes, birds and rodents from glow-in-the-dark cats.

Every business model we have is part of a larger system; regardless of the organisation you work in, you are likely to be impacting the future of our planet. How are we competing? What is the morality of the digital age? Surely sharing this planet's limited resources must be priority thinking going forward.

Where governments are concerned, who should they really serve and what should their functions be? Laws are passed to protect society, ideally through strong partnerships and shared knowledge. A revision of social norms and expectations could eliminate risk for the long term with perspective and co-operation. The old cycle of permanent competition with each other needs a change – borne of morality, necessity and culture, not only fear and punishment. Can we trust the individual in the street not to exploit the advance of science for his or her own selfish gain? Sadly, human nature can be weak and self-serving, and laws have been implemented since our earliest societies to protect us all from the selfishness within each one of us.

It is increasingly difficult, if not impossible, for governments to keep abreast of these changes and the new business models that run our planet. Our scientists seldom make the move to acquire roles within government. After all these centuries, blatant disparities still illustrate that humanity has not learned to share well. David Wallace-Wells points out the dangers of these disconnects in his eye-opening article about global warming, 'The Uninhabitable Earth':

> The fact that the country is dominated by a group of technocrats
> who believe any problem can be solved and an opposing culture
> that doesn't even see warming as a problem worth addressing;

the way that climate denialism has made scientists even more cautious in offering speculative warnings; the simple speed of change and, also, its slowness, such that we are only seeing effects now of warming from decades past; our uncertainty about uncertainty, which the climate writer Naomi Oreskes in particular has suggested stops us from preparing as though anything worse than a median outcome were even possible.[3]

All current models of government tend to direct and closely control science. But science should be considered non-competitive, as it needs no control to flourish. The market drives creation and the nature of human curiosity. To understand more of Earth's magnificent macrocosm is to thirst for even more knowledge of its complexities. A common thread running through history is that societies which have some of the fastest rates of technological growth through patents and inventions are those most under threat. Venice and other northern Italian cities that border the former Ottoman Empire and its friends drove an age of science. Israel currently holds a surprising number of patents and research firsts. Survival and purpose drive humans to perform and excel. Therefore, to create a planet that is for co-operation and against hostility is the way to promote a more productive future.

Democracy works through bureaucracy, cumbersome though it is in its present state, as mired as it is with so many special interests. Globally, we have lost trust in the political leaders and sacrificed our futures for the dull of entertainment media and self-interest. The new age requires *new*, transformative thinking leading to innovative behaviours and for organisations to more directly and positively shape society in a specific role alongside governments through shared morals, purpose and values-driven behaviour. Self-imposed best practices in business should at the same time display strength competitively to, in fact, adopt the transformative new ways of working and exhibit the agility required for sustainability and advancement.

In *The Uninhabitable Earth*, Wallace-Wells speaks not only of a rapidly warming planet, but of the implications of the changes occurring right now:

- *an absence of food*: for every degree of warming, yields decline by 10 per cent. Some estimates run as high as 15 or 17 per cent. This means that if the planet is five degrees warmer at the end of the century, we may have as many as 50 per cent more people to feed and 50 per cent less grain to give them;
- *plagues*: as the ice melts, experts caution that some long-dormant killers will survive; an eight-million-year-old bug was brought back to life in 2007. Warmer climates are necessary conditions for the return of such ancient plagues;
- *lack of breathable air*: the quantity of carbon dioxide in our air is growing; it just crossed 400 parts per million and high-end estimates extrapolating from current trends suggest it will hit 1,000 ppm by 2100, and, at that level, human cognitive ability declines by 21 per cent.
- *small increases in pollution capable of shortening lifespans by decades*: Americans will likely suffer a 70 per cent increase in unhealthy ozone smog, the National Center for Atmospheric Research has projected. By 2090, as many as two billion people globally will be breathing air above the WHO 'safe' level;
- *perpetual wars*: climate change produced a drought that contributed to the civil war in Syria; there is a relationship between temperature and violence. For every half-degree of warming, societies will see between a 10 and 20 per cent increase in the likelihood of armed conflict;
- *economic collapse*: 'fossil capitalism' argues that the entire history of swift economic growth, including the eighteenth-century industrial revolution, is not the result of

innovation, trade or the dynamics of global capitalism, but simply our discovery of fossil fuels and all their raw power. After we've burned all the fossil fuels, perhaps we will return to a 'steady state' global economy, where fewer of us live to be so old;

- *poisoned oceans*: a four-foot rise in sea levels, and possibly a 10-foot rise by the end of the century, will affect a third of the world's major coastal cities. More than a third of the world's carbon is sucked up by the oceans, resulting in what's called 'ocean acidification'; coral reefs – which support as much as a quarter of all marine life and supply food for half a billion people – die. Ocean acidification will remove fish populations directly; when the pH of human blood drops as much as that of the oceans has over the past generation, it will induce seizures, comas and sudden death.[4]

In a world six degrees warmer, the Earth's ecosystem will boil with natural disasters: out-of-control typhoons, tornadoes, floods and droughts – climate events that have destroyed entire civilisations. It may sound fanciful, but some of the catastrophic outcomes posited by scientists around the world seem more than plausible.

We often wonder if people at the end of a particular age knew that big change was imminent. Were our ancestors the Sapiens who left the cave when the mountain rumbled, leaving behind those who thought they would wait it out? The climate issue that society has been painfully aware of and failing to address for the past 100 years is escalating at an alarming rate. Little planning is taking place on a global level for the 42 per cent of the population around the world whose current industries are about to be impacted by digitisation. For these extended families, this is a terrifying age. Community and life as they know it is threatened. Do we really believe in survival of the fittest only, and winner takes all?

In southern Illinois, many see change in a lifetime of what seemed strongly cherished local traditions, churches and parades. There is no work where once there was plenty and the communities slowly starve to death. How do we build change that wins for all us? Do we blindly commit to pain or death for some of us?

Chris: One of the best stories I know regarding change comes from my time working at Caterpillar. At one point, the death of a person at work was considered part and parcel of the industrial heavy manufacturing business — it was unavoidable. Big machines moving around and hot metal cut and formed. Hard on flesh. They decided to protect each other and their communities, working towards a zero-incident safety journey where intent changed global behaviour. It is possible to bring systemic change to our climate if we have intent. We have the technology to do it...

The story was told to me by a factory supervisor in Northern Ireland, who had come in on a day off to show me proudly around 'his' factory. I was new and a visiting leader from HQ. He talked about the need for employees to have each other's backs from a point of safety; to think about those at home affected by the death of or injury to a fellow worker. This was personal. He urged me to think about the families, of the impact on the lives of the children of parents injured at work. He cared because he was part of the community and had empathy with his colleagues. When I too shared, I felt part of Caterpillar and responsible for having his back. So, when we share, we develop empathy.

We know that, through time, the advent of technology creates new jobs, new skills and, ultimately, a better world for all. At least that is the pattern so far — but it's not always smooth. Perhaps this calls for different social leadership from well-trained and well-informed corporate leaders who see tomorrow as being something they intentionally craft and who share common ideas about how we can best live together in harmony.

A case in point is the Old Order Amish, a Christian group that migrated to the United States from Switzerland in the early eighteenth century and is largely present in Pennsylvania today. The Amish are known for simple living, plain dress and reluctance to adopt many conveniences of modern technology. Whereas most of the modern world has embraced technological advances as a moral imperative, and struggled to come up with ways to absorb its impact on our families, communities and society, the Amish have largely stayed true to a way of agricultural living, circa 1850. They see what technology has done to the world outside the Amish community and come together to have a conversation about it. Every community then votes to decide if they will allow that technology to be adopted. If a person is diagnosed with cancer, for example, the community will admit that person to a modern hospital. But they have taken a very deliberate approach to reject two cornerstone technologies that have defined the better part of modern society: television and the automobile. The adoption of these two would render the community not 'Amish'. They are wise in two ways: first, they understand that technology is not value-free, and they carefully examine if the underlying purpose and value of creating that technology is aligned with their own values; second, they want to fully weigh the impact of that technology on their world beyond the initial big idea before fully diving into it. Most in the outside world, the world you and I live in, are completely unaware of those two considerations. It was only *after* the technology dominated us that we started debating regulating the ownership of guns or updating privacy agreements for Internet platform companies. It is one thing to set a family rule about no cell phone usage at the dinner table, but we can't construct rules as a society to prioritise what's valuable because of diversity.

Maybe it's just the company I keep, but in the past year I have seen European nation states advising citizens to collect enough materials and water to be able to stay indoors in case of a national security emergency. While visiting other countries, I have engaged in conversations with people – taxi drivers, local bar owners, shopkeepers, hotel workers, colleagues and friends. I hear people talk of the plans that they have in place when 'shit goes down' and this is a new conversation for people to be having. I did not hear this conversation 10, or even five, years ago. I hear of some people starting to stockpile food, getting weapons training or taking self-defence classes. But it seems strange to hear this vocalised. It is interesting to consider why we might be so unwilling to talk about these things openly. We cannot share a conversation globally.

There have been periods in history when it was important for nations or groups of citizens to have moral conviction about what was happening in the world around them that was greater than their individual needs. Should we in some way be ashamed about trying to hang on to what makes us feel safe? Maybe we should just accept future genocides and such horrors and instead simply enjoy the relative pleasures of our comfortable world today? Perhaps we should be satisfied with our immediate material pleasures and the security of the lives of our families, but I feel that for many of us reading this book, and with the mind to the next generation, we are faced with incredible challenges.

We have become so used to globalisation that perhaps we have not stopped to think about the implication of how we need to look after each other and our planet.

When we review history in chunks, we do not see one flat line of constant growth or peace. The line has peaks and troughs, hills and valleys, as it climbs through human history. There is often significant violence in the valleys of history, which we come to know as dark

ages. Periods of ethnic cleansing. I fear that we may be entering one
of those times again right now, unless we learn to share our Earth.

Could we, through how we live our daily lives, truly come
together as humans to make the world a better place? We know
the names of the heroes who have come before us. Those who have
driven or stood for positive change in the world. We also know that,
when they stood against or for something, and so shaped human
history, behind every hero there was a family or tribe or town or
even a city and nations of other people who stood with them.

But the quirk of history is that we know the story through the
voice of one individual hero. In the best stories, the hero comes
from the people, is not born to glory, but makes the choice to share
an idea, to live by ideals and purpose.

NOTES

1   *Avatar: The Last Airbender* [TV programme], Nickelodeon Studios,
    18 March 2005.
2   Wongsrikeao, P., et al. 'Antiviral restriction factor transgenesis in
    the domestic cat', *Nature Methods*, 8, 2011, pp. 853–9.
3   Wallace-Wells, D. 'The Uninhabitable Earth', *New York*, 10 July 2017,
    pp. 1–2.
4   Ibid., pp. 4–6.

5

A SHARE-BASED SYSTEM FOR ALL

'We cannot solve our problems with the same thinking we
used when we created them'

— Albert Einstein

In this chapter:
- closure on reflections on the need for change;
- the impact right now of our rapid progress on the world.

When we started thinking about this book, we were so excited about
the share-based economy. These models are the early examples of
the third industrial revolution, emergent, radical and thrilling.

It was like a new adventure of the economy. It seemed like a
shared space of new enterprise, a new commons. But it was a false
dawn. Power corrupts. It blinds us, makes us selfish, and power and
love of power consume us.

The issue with these sharing economy-based corporations was
that, while the business model was new, the internal congruence to
new ideas about ethics, governance, empathy and sharing as a way
of running the corporation was not there. As we have discussed in
previous chapters, our current models of organisations, and the way
we engage the most important aspect of organisations – people,
leave many unable to compete in new ways.

We propose a model of an empathy-based organisation. It starts with looking to create a shared intent and then building the structures, policies and practices to enable this new age of organisations.

THE SHARING ECONOMY'S FALSE DAWN

Chris: As I talked to friends who had leased out their personal space and met taxi drivers around the world who were now using their own cars, suddenly it all seemed to sound like yet another corporate effort that was exploiting people, and was in many ways regressive for workers' rights. Corners were cut to maximise profits. Health, safety and privacy were secondary priorities. It was a niche exploited to leverage the assets of others and release new economic value.

Some friends who at first seemed to value the newly found freedom of leaving their corporate careers, the early adopters of new Internet-based economic models, became bitter and cynical at having to become part of the gig economy. They compared their professional expertise to being bought like the assembly line worker who is paid on a per-piece-rate card. They worried about no longer having paid vacations, sick days, holidays or workers' compensation. Many crept back to the safety of the corporate world after a stint in the gig economy. The fear of life outside the 'comfort' of the organisation was too high. They felt exploited and not respected. In the absence of any intentional dialogue about how to treat people in your supply chain, such unintended consequences of new economic models arise.

The new sharing economy was meant to free people who wanted to become 'independent' and to be their own CEOs. In theory, the sharing economy allows us to *monetise our assets*: to use a brokerage website or app to rent out our house, our car, our labour, our driveway, our lawn mower – you get the idea... The companies benefited from treating convenience as a revolution. It sounded cool (it had a sexy, utopian feel), but in some cases was really a Trojan horse for a very basic model of exploitation.

The sharing economy has made it incredibly easy to hire freelancers, temps, contractors and part-timers. Companies can shave their labour costs by 30 per cent by not paying for an employee's health care, pensions and other benefits. Companies can leverage a workforce they can switch on and off. Management consulting firm McKinsey estimated that the gig economy now employs about 12 per cent of the American workforce and is growing fast.[1] It is predicted that the on-demand talent platform will be one of the top three workplace trends.

As a society, we learned from the past that technology is good. Technology is what pushed our economy forward, pushed productivity through the roof. So when an economic system promised seamless interactions to maximise the value of otherwise idle labour, home, vehicles, etc., we got extremely excited. We were not thinking about regulations or consequences once these new technologies started dominating us. We made them *special*. As Einstein predicted 100 years ago, technological advances are so much beyond human capabilities – we found ourselves once more ill prepared for the moral and ethical dilemmas that came with the rise of technological possibilities.

The early sharing economy models profess to be a share-based system but in reality can be based and run on the harshest of capitalist models, and in fact *backward* models, in terms of worker exploitation. There is unique opportunity right now for companies and governments to rethink how technology impacts human relations and society.

In the fourth industrial revolution, we look at machine learning and artificial intelligence as a path to a new future that enables us to string infinite data points together. As we build the ethics for AI, however, we face the question of whose ethics to choose. Is the choice and bias of the programmer a form of neo-colonialism, where the society which writes the code influences how such operate and the concepts of work for the whole planet? Is there a better path for shared wisdom across societies and organisations?

SUSTAINABLE SHARING

Some ideas about sharing are not new, but are, rather, inspired by the ideas of the old commons movement. Consider that the average power drill only gets used for six to 13 minutes in its lifetime. Think of all the resources it took to produce that drill and countless other products like it; sharing can begin to make perfect sense from an environmental standpoint. The concept of a commons-based society is about a shift in values and practices away from the heavily consumerist and 'me'-valued, purely market-based system that has dominated modern society, especially over the past 30 years. The foundation of the market is narrowly focused on private wealth for just a few, while the concept of the commons is built upon what we all share – air, water, public spaces, public health, public services, the Internet, cultural endowments and much more.

Is it possible to allow data to match what we have and what we need in ways and on a scale never before possible? Could we think about supply and demand, the relationship between buyers and sellers, being disrupted? 'Consumers' getting what they need from each other, value creation being reimagined by our governments and corporations, a broader 'collaborative economy', the macro paradigm shift that determines what our legacy will become – instead of war, famine and cruelty? I will continue to repeat the alternative and yes, it sounds dramatic but that's the point if we believe in science.

For a long-term and sustainable sharing ecosystem, we propose a focus on the following building blocks:

- *people and trust*: we have to agree on things like ethics and basic agreements about universal human rights and talk about such things in our workplaces. We must value and love each other – truly. Opinions and ideas should be respected. The same concepts need to be integrated into the business at all levels and across our business partners and our supply chain. Shared values. This hinges on open, shared, distributed, transparent decision-making process and governance systems – today enabled by our emergent technology; Elders are respected within our organisations because of their wisdom and not their political or financial power.

- *value creation and exchange*: a variety of forms of exchange, incentives and value creation must be considered; not only financial but wider economic and social value should be accounted for. Could our organisational systems embrace alternative currencies, local currencies, time banks, social investment and social capital (based on both the material and non-material) and social rewards to encourage efficient use of resources?

- *distribution*: could organisations sponsor the development of structures and policies to promote equitable and efficient distribution of resources at scale? Could idle resources be allocated or traded to create efficient, equitable, closed-loop or circular systems? Could recycling, upcycling and sharing the lifecycle of the product be introduced across corporations and communities? 'Waste' is essentially a resource in the wrong place;

- *design*: could products and services be designed for sustainability versus obsolescence, promoting the reuse of resources and creating goods and services that positively enhance the natural environment;

- *knowledge management*: information is shared and accessible. Transparency and open communications are essential. Information is distributed; knowledge and intelligence are widely accessible and easily obtained and can be used in a variety of different ways for myriad purposes;
- *culture*: we need a 'we'-based empathic sharing culture where sharing is a positive attribute, people who share are celebrated, encouraged and seen as role models. Where collaboration replaces competition and at the individual/local level is extended to that of neighbouring teams, communities and external bodies.

EVOLUTION

All this is not so far-fetched. We humans have the ability to transform an environment in our favour. It is not the most intelligent or the strongest who survive, but the ones who are open to the changes in their environment. We would argue that it is our *duty*, those of us who have awareness and who have ability (we have been trained in strong organisational skills by the corporations) to maintain a dynamic balance between the natural world around us and the human impact on that world. In this fourth industrial revolution, we certainly have the ability to do so. It is our responsibility to create an environment that can support our species and at the same time maintain the necessary planetary ecological balance.

Could we design a new type of a global society, with new types of corporations that are focused on improving the standard of living for all of us? Our current system reinforces dysfunctional institutionalisation. We cannot assume that such a functional share-based society could come about naturally. Discussing new ideas such as those we have presented to you so far is a difficult thing to take in – to rapidly transform a culture that is plagued with moral judgements about each other right now. We are moving towards a society with conditions that produce such behaviour. Our current technological progress is dependent on applying science and method towards a certain technical problem. We fail consistently – because of the effort involved, and our own bias preventing us from seeing the real big picture truthfully. Imagine that you sit on a balcony, above all in the world around us right now, and pause and reflect on what you want to do.

HUMAN BEHAVIOUR

Historically, the notion that humans behave according to universal laws has always been dismissed. Past philosophies have taught us that people have free will and that there are intrinsic factors, based on our localised shared imagination of a thing called society. Society is not a tangible thing. It is a construct created. These constructs essentially categorise us into 'good' or 'bad' people. There is also a very prevalent notion that people cannot change. These verbal and mental constructs have never been tested; therefore, it would be unwise for us to conclude that they are correct. To solve global social problems demands actions and new belief systems that are considered unthinkable and not practised today. We need to consider human and environmental welfare as an international priority. We cannot use the same old methods of thinking; if we do, this will result in the same problems we face today. We will have to intentionally seek or create new constructs.

TIPPING POINTS AND RISKS

The challenge when starting a new idea is moving from inspiring a few early adopters to a mass-market following, which is also the purpose of this book; our ambition is to be one of many sparks required to ignite the sharing society beyond the sharing economy. Initially, people were worried about security when buying things on the Internet. They then felt safe, only to have that confidence destroyed as their security was breached. Professional 'power sellers' now dominate peer-to-peer online marketplaces.

Good new-economy architecture must do two things that our present architecture doesn't do: protect vital ecosystems and broadly spread the fruits of our economy. The first is essential to preserving our planet, the second to assuring that all individuals and communities have the resources to become more secure and self-reliant.

Discussions about economic architecture tend to get stuck in the stale dichotomy of state versus market. Instead, the key to a new economy could lie in a third realm, the commons, or shared wealth. The commons is the source of human subsistence.

The most valuable forms of shared wealth today are natural ecosystems, such as our atmosphere, and socially built systems, such as our legal, financial, transportation and communications infrastructure, without which private enterprise couldn't flourish. Consider what would happen, for instance, if the Internet were to shut down; businesses that depend on the Internet would have little value on their own. The same is true for companies using other collectively built systems. In other words, *it is shared wealth that creates most of the value of private wealth*, yet we charge private owners almost nothing to use it.

The failure to charge for common wealth – for example, letting polluters dump freely into our atmosphere – leads to what economists call 'negative externalities'. Polluters don't pay the costs of pollution; the burden is shifted, and the transgressors are encouraged by economics and self-serving administrations to pollute nature and our future generations. And this market failure persists because no *living* individuals (or existing companies) would financially benefit from fixing it.

But imagine a system in which *everyone* benefits from fixing this tragic flaw. In this system, polluters would pay, and all living citizens, as joint beneficiaries and trustees of nature's gifts, would get dividends. The higher the price for using the commons, the larger the dividends and the lower the externalities. The health of nature's gifts would be directly linked to greater income for everyone. Sound revolutionary? It is possible – simple, really. Virtually everything described above can be done electronically, through corporate decisions, with little or no expansion of government.

The effects of this economic architecture would be multiple: identifying, protecting, and in some cases monetising common assets would accelerate the transition to a new economy and keep it on track for decades to come.

Think about that when you listen to the news about climate change, famine, war, epidemics of deadly diseases and environmental pollution that all contribute to the long list of global challenges we, as humans, need to address promptly before catastrophe swiftly becomes inevitable. Regardless of political philosophy, religious beliefs or social customs, all socio-economic systems ultimately depend upon natural resources, such as clean air and water, arable land and the necessary technology and personnel to maintain a high standard of living. Modern society has access to highly advanced technologies and can make available food, clothing, housing, medical care, a relevant educational system and a limitless supply of renewable, non-contaminating energy, such as geothermal, solar, wind and tidal.

It is now possible for everyone on the planet to enjoy a very high standard of living with all of the amenities that a prosperous civilisation can provide. This can be accomplished through the intelligent and humane application of science and technology.

Laws that demand maximum profit would, where possible, govern individuals and interest groups. These laws are inherent in the monetary system prevalent in most countries today. Exponential growth at all costs is only causing financial cataclysms.

We are separated by borders and beliefs, which make it impossible for us to arrive at relevant solutions while being divided ideologically. Most of our problems today are technical, but we are still looking for solutions through political means. We need to accept that eliminating these global threats requires the employment of science and method, with well-trained colleagues rather than personal or political opinions. With the level of crisis that we now face, if this were a movie, would you expect politicians to save the planet, or a group of expert heroes?

Overall failure to realise change management practices – building belief systems; finding common purpose and goals – results in long-term failure of politics and large-scale enterprises. We view the experiment of the European Union as a purely finance-driven one without the belief systems being put in place around identity. Where was the change management to build one common vision beyond currency, borders and economics?

For true change to stick, we need to have a shared vision and a belief in something beyond immediate gratification; if we don't have these, we feel hollow, incongruent, and there is *nothing*. We think the core failure of a ONE Europe experiment was the lack of change expertise applied: people who have fought wars against each other could not learn to share in weeks, and no thought was given to establishing the need for empathy for each other. A new shared identity needs more than a flag, a big building of mandarins and some balloons.

We ask you, the reader, to examine your own personal purpose and think about the difference that *you* can make.

Could we evolve from a purely market-based society to adopt some aspects of a commons-based society? One in which we value common assets, managing them for the benefit of everyone? Market-based solutions would be valuable tools in a commons-based society, as long as they didn't undermine the workings of the commons itself. Your first reaction is likely to be 'nice idea', but it is only a matter of time before a profound transformation starts in how technology creates efficiency and trust between us as we are required to become more transparent.

We will talk about how we establish an empathic, share-based corporation that competes better as we enter this new age, utilising

advanced technology to build a more shared world of resources in
an as yet unimagined new society.

NOTES
1   McKinsey Global Institute. 'Independent work: Choice, necessity and
    the gig economy', October 2016. https://www.mckinsey.com/~/
    media/McKinsey/Featured%20Insights/Employment%20and%20
    Growth/Independent%20work%20Choice%20necessity%20
    and%20the%20gig%20economy/Independent-Work-Choice-
    necessity-and-the-gig-economy-Executive-Summary.ashx. Accessed
    June 2018.

SECTION TWO

THE CURRENT SYSTEM
AND HR PRACTICES

6

CATCH UP, HR!

'I could either watch it happen, or be part of it'
— Elon Musk

In this chapter:
- the evolution of organisations and how it shaped society and opinions over the past decades;
- how HR theory and governance has failed to evolve in line with the external changes;
- why different frameworks and models are needed now.

Human resources has been trapped in the industrial age and there is now a moment of truth as we enter the digital age. There is an opportunity to keep up with the explosive change of business models and the speed at which they transform – with confidence. We see the proliferation of gig HR solutions, platforms and efforts on purpose and culture as being evidence of the failure of HR functions to adopt new practices internally. We (HR) either change our practices or we fail to deliver substance for the business changes ahead.

Telling the truth tends to be harder than telling white lies, or pretending the elephant in the room doesn't exist. We especially avoid truth in the corporate world, because it can be inconvenient. In this book, we want to force the conversations that we think necessary in the workplace, especially in the HR function. The modern workplace can be the forum where we enable individuals and society to learn and re-skill. To some extent, it has to be, because corporations are more powerful in our era than organised religions, mass movements, kingdoms and nation states.

> **Chris:** Some years ago, when taking a career break, I worked with a group of colleagues about bringing awareness to the issues of conflict minerals and the use of rape as a means of societal control in the Democratic Republic of Congo. Rape has been used as a weapon to subjugate that country's population for some time. I met a well-known BBC journalist who had created a documentary on the topic and asked him what I could do to help. He told me that the best thing I could do was to get back into an organisation and promote awareness from within. As with the palaces and temples of previous centuries, the average citizen could not get past the temple guards; today, it's the corporate security, the public relations department or company lawyers. In our role I can walk freely alongside decision makers, we talk in boardrooms. We sometimes have the luxury of access and privilege afforded to us as corporate insiders. Realise your own power, reader. Seize it. Speak truth to power.

PERIOD OF 'PERSONNEL MANAGEMENT' (1950s–1970s)
Since the Second World War, Western corporations have embraced the first wave of automation and the exponential productivity growth it unleashed. Large-scale manufacturing was the driving force. Instead of 'human resources' that we see today, imagine a 'personnel management' department where employees' details are kept on (paper) files in drawers. These drawers represented the power of management in most worker–employer conflicts. The personnel department had a special heavy door. A counter. You

were not invited in. It was a restricted area. Like the staffroom at school or a police station reception. It sat apart from the rest of the organisation. It held secrets about you. It was never a fair information exchange. They knew all the stuff about you. Stability, compliance and order in the first industrial age were everything. Procedures, policy manuals and hierarchies ruled. If asked to pick an avatar for HR – and given a choice among the social worker, the change agent, the police officer or the legal specialist – most employees would pick the police officer.

There was a post-war world in the West, where those who returned wanted to build a home fit for 'heroes'. Those who 'lost' in Germany and Japan adopted collectivist workplaces. These workers wanted to build better societies *everywhere*. They demanded safety equipment, better pay and other emerging concepts of worker rights (translation: citizens' rights). What happened in the workplace transformed the society around it.

In our discussion of how the individual, the organisation and wider society all work together to influence each other, this was a period where the role of individuals impacted how corporations grew and, in turn, shaped the world they had fought to build. Hopefully, a better world.

PERIOD OF 'RESOURCE MANAGEMENT' (1980s–2000s)

From the 1980s, technology (computer systems and the Internet) carried forward productivity growth such as enterprise resource planning (ERP), customer resource management (CRM) and global supply chain management. Expertise and internal know-hows were valued highly, such as Six Sigma (by GE), Total Quality Management (TQM, by Toyota), Balanced Scorecard (AT&T, IBM, Pfizer and others). Consequentially, organisational and HR practices became heavily reliant on processes.

At the same time, with the growth of computing technologies and data, knowledge and skills increasingly became the key forces that drove productivity, not muscle and adherence to company process and policy. To win in a knowledge-based economy, companies put into practice the phrase coined by McKinsey: they waged the 'war for talent'.[1] This meant that the richest and most educated people started to pay each other more and more, and salaries for the CEO and C Suite increasingly became multiples of the salary of the average worker in the company. It was all about the 'leadership' of the big man or the big brain, and the big specialists and organisations entered a fierce era: competing for critical skills, meticulously building talent 'pipelines' (see the machine metaphor language) and planning for leadership and technical succession. HR abandoned the sole role of 'police' and also adopted that of a 'seducer'.

There is an old HR joke: the chief human resources officer (CHRO) of a large corporate dies one day and goes to heaven. He is greeted and told that he can decide the destination of his soul: in heaven or hell. He is allowed to spend one day in each before deciding. He chooses to spend the first day in hell. It is a wild party and all his friends are there. He has a great time and hates to leave. The next day, he visits heaven. It is very quiet and peaceful. He is a little bored. He makes the decision to stay in hell for eternity. But on the first day, he is chained to a wall and tortured. 'What happened to the parties?!' he asks. He is told, 'That was recruitment! Now you are staff!'

This is the job of the personnel department: to coax and bid others to join them, again firmly representing the interests of the corporation and doing what is necessary to stay legal and protect the brand.

As organisational structures evolved, a further division of roles developed within HR. Thanks to the HR business partnering model most large corporations adopted, there is often an additional layer of gatekeepers to influence, each as strong, or sometimes stronger, than the CHRO. In some organisations, information is presented through writing formal papers or presentations. These papers or decks are edited multiple times by multiple people before going up to the executive floor, then travelling back down with remarks after months of prior work; often, this method of communications seems to be designed to ensure that it is hard to actually change anything – the process is effective at risk management versus change enablement. Instead of bringing all different elements of HR tools together to form an integrated solution, often the HR silos compete with each other for power, as all silos do, with compensation always the most powerful element at play. This is the easiest factor for a manufacturing organisation to understand, measure and apply. HR departments are often designed from the start for failure, for they are reflections of an earlier age.

PERIOD OF 'CHANGE MANAGEMENT' (2000s–THE PRESENT DAY)

The role of HR has changed dramatically since the days of 'personnel administration' in the 1950s. Particularly in the past decade, HR has been tapped to conduct a lot of unfamiliar tasks, including managing change, workforce transformation, defining and shifting culture, diversity and inclusion…the list goes on. Surveying Fortune 200 companies, we bet you will see wording similar to 'strategic adviser' and 'change enabler' in their HR mission and vision statements. Meanwhile, capability building has not matched the expectation. When there is a gap, a new business opportunity presents itself. Consultants go into these new sub-areas within HR, but they are not considered as mainstream HR. International companies complicate this further by setting up multiple layers of so-called centres of excellence often at the regional and global levels.

Bringing the change elements together is difficult. Because of the structure, the idea of developing effective organisations is good, but ownership of how to do this across silos is a challenge to define. Most HR functions are slow and compliant rather than inspiring and are resistant to change, even compared with other back-office functions. No other function has such narrow and artificial definitions for essentially the same job 'specialists' and 'generalists'. Not marketing, finance or risk. The specialists are often pigeonholed as 'internal consultants' in a so-called 'centre of excellence'. Too often they have excellence in administration. Rarely still does the head of HR have any sort of change, business or consulting background, which means there is often lack of confidence, curiosity, challenge and sufficient sponsorship from the top of HR. For an HR strategy team, often the same qualities that are prized in an external setting – being provocative, independent and insightful – can backfire when part of the HR management team and they run the risk of being ostracised. Knowledge doesn't change behaviours, relationships do. It takes enormous effort and time to find the right people to influence, work on their emotional conviction and build the confidence to change. Meanwhile, most employers demand to see big outcomes, and soon. When this happens, there is pressure to drum up the activities to show 'tangible results'.

The increasingly complicated matrix structure and inevitable politics in organisation make real change difficult currently instead of easy. Passive aggressiveness is easy to feel but difficult to overcome. People nod their heads, yet may not have the courage to follow through on agreed changes.

The change efforts that are sponsored are often shambolic: millions of dollars are spent to wage organisation-wide, top-down change campaigns that are designed within the ivory tower of a 'centre of excellence'. Those big-bang propaganda displays with banners and posters hardly change anything. The HR leaders who are spearheading the teams, rewarding behaviours and setting the culture locally change things or resist the change.

Most change approaches within HR are based on a set of fundamental values (such as democratic, inclusive, humanistic, etc.) that can seem like an out-of-touch utopia in modern corporate life. Concepts like change and organisational effectiveness have wide variations.

It has been a hard habit to break, until now, and maybe requires us to rethink our purpose as HR. Do we stand here to defend the organisation against the employee? Can we truly be trusted agents of change?

WHAT THIS ERA MEANS TO THE WIDER ORGANISATION

In the 2000s, most notably since 2007 – the year the iPhone was launched – technological advancement in both the corporate world and consumer industries has led the way, through the Internet of Things, big data, artificial intelligence; the list goes on and on. Most importantly, the mobile connectivity to the Internet and social media platforms has fundamentally changed the way we access information, express ourselves and collaborate with others. No longer do we need to look up and wait for a cascade of information from the top; our traditional hierarchical leaders don't necessarily have the experience or skills to teach us or give directions. We belong to various groups, networks and communities at work and outside work to gain knowledge, socialise and build relationships. We are fed data about the world and our own companies minute by minute – and directly to our devices. We now live in a world where we are constantly switched on and where there is a blurred boundary between the traditional sense of 'work', 'private life' and 'play' and where information comes from.

The pace of technology is having an unprecedented change on an unimagined scale. Where else to prepare us to cope and to manage this change? We need organisations that teach us – learning organisations enabled by HR processes to be agile and to share, to be curious and empathetic. To learn and be agile, we first need organisations to provide psychological safety to everyone within.

All this has significant implications for corporate organisation and the ways employees conduct themselves. Some changes are already taking place. Recruiters routinely search for candidates through profiling and professional networking sites, vetting them through social media. Prospective and current employees create live reviews and chats. Information is shared.

There is perhaps a deeper level of change that is happening. In the sharing economy, power is shifting from big, centralised institutions to distributed networks of individuals and communities. Power is moving from the top of the organisational hierarchy to the middle of the organisation, where the knowledge sits and success is assured. Yet that is not often for whom HR is set up to serve.

Chris: I remember the CEO of a company I worked for that was having a very hard time with digital transition. It was the mid-2000s, so it was actually before transparent technology became so relevant or popular. It was a relatively small, but very fast-growing privately held company, and the CEO was particularly interested in employee engagement. After almost three years of explosive growth, the idea of employee engagement became less appealing to him, because, in his words, 'It doesn't matter if they're engaged, we're making money hand over fist.' Even with that attitude, or maybe for appearance's sake, we did conduct an employee engagement survey. And it was no surprise it came back quite negative.

We are not necessarily fans of measuring employee engagement, anyway – mostly because it's a lagging indicator; once you find out people are disengaged, it's already too late. Regardless of how we measure it, it doesn't seem to change. In fact, Gallup research tells us that employee engagement has remained almost flat for the last 15 years, even though we are spending over $1 billion on it annually.[2]

So, this CEO wanted us to measure employee engagement, and we did. And when we got the results back, they showed a considerable lack of engagement across the entire organisation; it was not relegated to a specific division, leader or level – it was across the board.

My job was to communicate the results of the survey to the employees. I knew this was a tricky topic and it was all I could do not to say, 'I told you so'. Instead, I did what was expected and wrote an organisational email to come from the CEO that outlined the results of the survey, putting as much of a positive spin on it as I could, outlining all of the actions we were committed to taking and how seriously we took these results.

I gave the CEO the draft and after reading it he said, 'Can't we spin this further? Can't we make it seem like we are okay?' I was flabbergasted. Not that he had asked me to do it, but that he genuinely didn't understand that the employees would know if we were being less than honest; they were the ones who had completed the survey. They knew the results because they were the ones who wrote them. They were describing their feelings; they were being transparent.

I didn't work for that CEO much longer. I question how he is doing today with the level of transparency that is required to run a successful, innovative business. It's clear that generationally, it is more difficult for Baby Boomers and Generation X to be transparent, but if they can't get with the programme, they are going to miss out on the success that will be driven by the millennials and Gen Zers that demand it. Transparency is key here, and those who can successfully leverage the tools will win.

REIMAGINE HR

Large, established corporations already face the challenge that they must compete with start-ups for millennials and Generation Z; these generations see their peers become millionaires through IPOs before they even get married. Conversely, in the emergent 'gig economy', workers are interchangeable and disposable. Companies will need to rethink this approach as they use more freelancers for mission-critical tasks.

The world has changed, and is still changing. We see fear of rapid change leading to more radical politics and quick solutions. We believe that this relationship between the life of the individual, the society that they live in and the place where they work is never better demonstrated than in the complexities we face today. The role of HR now is to think beyond the process and the policing history of its past and truly build emergent practices that reshape how we define individual and corporate success.

As OD and HR practitioners, we need to be prepared to address a series of questions:

- what will the role of managers be if we rely on robots and algorithms to co-ordinate work and automate routine tasks such as performance evaluations?
- how does the whole concept of management evolve? If we want empathic learning organisations, then do we not need educationalists – and not managers – to create our workplaces?
- what are the impacts on vertical hierarchy and reporting structures when social media tools allow information to flow freely up, down and across the organisation? What if they also create a robust landscape of influence and power that is new and follows the rules of crowds?
- why invest in formal learning/coaching programmes if cloud-based learning is widespread across the company, with experts globally available and peer-to-peer coaching available 24/7 on an app?
- what happens to supervisor-driven performance management when self-diagnostic tools provide real-time feedback on productivity and team-based forums suggest continuous improvement ideas?

- why should I respect my supervisor if my work contract is flexible and I only expect a fleeting and passing relationship with the company? Rank, title and job level seem irrelevant. Why is so much of the HR function dedicated to continuing these elements?
- why not truly pay for performance and worth, and not reward hierarchy?
- would we even recruit full-time employees if expertise and capabilities could be sourced with a tap of a finger at a fraction of the cost?

How hard is it to reimagine an HR function for the digital age? Would we even call it human resources? It is about colleague enablement. But HR needs to enable itself first. Think of the concept of how to use your oxygen mask on flights: you must put your own mask on first before you can help others. HR teams need to act now and not be the barrier to be overcome. It is a decision point for each HR team to be professional and truly lead rather than simply follow.

NOTES

1   Michaels, E., et al. *The War for Talent*. Boston: Harvard Business Review Press, 2001.
2   Adkins, A. 'Employee engagement in U.S. stagnant in 2015', Gallup News, 2016. https://news.gallup.com/poll/188144/employee-engagement-stagnant-2015.aspx. Accessed 6 October 2016.

7

IT'S IN THE SYSTEM

'Those who were seen dancing were thought to be insane by those who could not hear the music'

— Friedrich Nietzsche

In this chapter:
- two foundational theories defining our time: complexity theory and systems theory;
- the need to look at business and the world differently in a systematic and dynamic way;
- our environment being volatile, uncertain, complex and ambiguous (VUCA) in the new digitally connected world and the impact on organisations and leaders.

In our work we often hear people express the feeling that they are 'out of control'. The information explosion is overwhelming. Apart from the data overload, leaders and managers today find it hard to plan and operate in an environment that is constantly changing. Often the entire organisation stays in a reactive mode that perpetuates stress and short-term focus.

What has changed from 30 years ago? In the next chapter we will talk about the digital disruption, the impact on the future workplace and the demand on the next generation of the workforce. At the same time, management science has progressed, as has all science. Yet we seem not to take notice and find it hard to adapt and adopt new habits.

We are creatures of habit and survive according to this. Our brain uses less energy when we establish habits and follow routines. Danger is minimised. Yet science tells us that the world around us is not habitual. It is in fact chaotic. We advance into the unknown – in which there are no rules. We continue to play this game as if there are constructs from recent times from which we have created habit. Yet, mostly they are just that – constructs.

BREAKING THE HABITS AND FINDING A NEW VOCABULARY

We recognise that we exist today in that VUCA world that we have been warned about for so long: connected chaos. We did not equip ourselves well for where we are today and we need to radically rewire our organisations to win for the future.

> **We focus on complexity theory and systems theory as base reasons for why we must break from current habits. Two reasons:**
> - management science: from the very start, when Frederick Winslow Taylor created this term at the turn of the last century in his work, *The Principle of Scientific Management*,[1] we have been heavily influenced by the view of a world determined by science as it was known at that time. Science has progressed, but our basic assumption of what management actually is has not;
> - organisations, like any other complex physical systems, follow certain rules and patterns of chaos – behaviours similar to those of biology, weather and the stock market – working as integrated systems and run by principles, not rules.

The reader may be familiar with Taylor's work in developing performance measures and driving work productivity. His obsession with solving 'awkward, inefficient or ill-directed movements of men' was profoundly influenced by Newton's laws of motion, used to calculate how machines could function with maximum efficiency. It used the machine as a metaphor for the organisation. We no longer see the organisation as one machine. Instead, we know that the organisation is a *system*.

The machine metaphor is everywhere in our day-to-day English language. We say, 'Things are humming like a well-oiled machine', 'They are rusty', 'I'm on autopilot', 'She's firing on all cylinders', 'The department is re-engineering' and 'They're just a cog in the wheel'. Viewing an organisation as a machine shapes how we think and act. We program and operate machines to do exactly what the organisation needs, in a precise way, repetitively, without variation, creating reliable results. To change machines, we create new blueprints and build to specifications. A machine does not participate. Unexpected results imply deficiency in design or execution. This is how we still think about organisations.

Constantly using data to make judgements is a problematic way of viewing organisations that are people-driven when we want to release very human concepts to be a point of innovation. Unlike machine parts, people think and care about their work.

> **Linda:** The machine ideal of repetition strongly encourages habits and precision. As humans, we are naturally curious, stimulated by new things. In fact, the biggest difference that sets *homo sapiens* apart from chimpanzees is the ability to imagine. Yuval Noah Harari, the renowned author of *Sapiens: A Brief History of Humankind*, exclaimed on his website, 'there are no gods in the universe, no nations, no money and no human rights – except in the common imagination of human beings.'[2] Managers working as the engineers in the metaphor of the machine do not realise our creative

capacity. I know that I dislike being told what to do without context. I am not a machine. However, we tend to avoid adapting to new ideas, because they are often associated with uncomfortable emotional responses. The machine model does not deal well with ideas and emotions.

The key approach that Taylor took involved breaking down the work processes into isolated parts in order to understand and better control them; this line of analysis followed the same deterministic thinking that prevailed in the world of science in the early 1900s. Basically, Taylor applied to organisations the same principles that scientists understood about the natural resources in the physical world.

Not too long after Taylor's book was published, Einstein's theory of relativity and his work on quantum mechanics challenged the laws of Newtonian physics. Randomness and unpredictability were observed at the extremes of space and time, from the entire universe to subatomic particles. Later, Edward Lorenz, an MIT meteorology professor, discovered that even the most minuscule change in sensitive initial conditions produces wildly different outcomes in the future; he did so by simulating weather patterns using 12 variables, including temperature, humidity and wind speed. His 1963 paper, 'Deterministic Nonperiodic Flow',[3] was cited merely three times outside meteorology in the next decade, yet his concept became the founding principles of chaos theory and spread into other fields, such as geology and biology, in the 1970s and 1980s. Thanks to the bestselling book Chaos: Making a New Science by James Gleick, published in 1987, the term 'butterfly effect' became known to the general public. Pop culture is fascinated with the shock effect brought about by the idea that 'the flap of a butterfly's wings in Brazil will cause a tornado in Texas'.[4] A proliferation of movies appeared based on the concept, including the thriller The Butterfly Effect in 2004.[5] It is both intuitive and scientifically proven that forecasting the future is nearly impossible.

Before you throw every management practice with 'planning'
out of the window in despair, chaos theory also addresses two
fundamental observations: first, there is order emerging from
chaos; second, complex systems often seek to settle in one
specific situation and this is called an 'attractor'. Such a situation
or equilibrium can also be dynamic, in which case it's called
'strange attractor'.

Linda: When writing this book, I had the luxury of sitting
down and reflecting on life events that ultimately positioned
me where I am today. One thing that struck me was how
random every turn was, mostly unplanned or completely
unpredicted. The best example is that my marriage and half
of my career have been literally a result of a wager.

At 28, I was a management consultant on the way to
becoming the youngest director with a reputable firm in
a buoyant emerging market. One day, I made a bet with
a friend over a beer whether I could get into a top-tier
business school 6,000 miles away. Next thing I knew, I took
two months' leave, crammed for the GMAT (Graduate
Management Admission Test), borrowed a bucketload of
money from the bank, sold everything I owned that couldn't
be packed into a suitcase and moved to London.

But did that truly happen by chance, on a whim, like
throwing dice, or is there an 'invisible hand' at work?
Although the individual incident looks random and strange,
when viewed as part of a series of events across time, it
makes sense.

Growing up in a populous country that was resource-
poor, I learned from a young age to take every opportunity
and exploit it. I saw that being action-oriented and risk-
taking were rewarded as China opened up and built an
insatiable appetite for change. In this case, the tendency
for how I think towards a certain situation acted as 'strange

attractor' and, over time, the pattern of life emerges. Just like my Chinese ancestors wisely advised in a proverb:

Be careful of your thoughts, for your thoughts become your words.
Be careful of your words, for your words become your actions.
Be careful of your actions, for your actions become your habits.
Be careful of your habits, for your habits become your character.
Be careful of your character, for your character becomes your destiny.

The quest for insights into how complex systems work sparked the discovery of two fundamental theories: systems theory and complexity theory. It is important to note that neither is a prescriptive management theory, nor does it provide a formula to solve management issues; instead, they attempt to widen the lens through which we examine and understand organisational behaviours – particularly valuable in today's VUCA world. In the rest of this chapter, we will discuss the implications of looking at business and the world differently in a systematic and dynamic way.

SYSTEMS THEORY

Systems theory promotes seeing organisations as living organisms that are constantly evolving and adapting – 'seeing the whole' – and particularly paying attention to the interconnections and interdependence of components (agents) within the system.

With the latest biotechnological breakthroughs, neuroscientists are able to understand how cells communicate with each other and molecules self-organise to accomplish extremely complex tasks such as reproduction and immune reactions in the absence of central intelligence or control. These tiny structures are the building blocks of every living thing around us. They have existed for millions of years and, without the self-regenerating and adaptation, our species would not exist. Scientists used to believe that the human body was a perfectly co-ordinated system, with our brains acting as the 'central command'; on the contrary, it is now proven through MRI scans that the millions of individual 'cells' or 'nodes' working somewhat independently formed an extensive network where there is a constant exchange of new information through billions of neurons. Most processing of information is decentralised.

In addition, there seem to be powerful feedback loops that send information back in reverse to alter how the brain works. Microbiomes, also called gut bacteria, were previously thought useless, but now we know that they have their own ways of receiving and processing information, forming 'The Third Brain'. They have lived inside human bodies for millions of years; at least a few of them have developed tactics to influence their hosts' behaviours for their own survival needs. For example, they can modify moods. Neuroscientist John Cryan pointed out in an interview in *The Atlantic* that 'happy people tend to be more social, and the more social we are, the more chances the microbes have to exchange and spread', hence increasing the microbes' chances of survival.[6] These are complex interactive systems.

Consider the example of a major financial services company: over the years it has built a massive and productive agent network that provides excellent customer service and comfortable profit margins. Suddenly, new technology enables competitors to set up online channels to sell to and serve customers directly, and at a much lower price. New channels appear with unusual new competitors, such as supermarkets selling basic financial products. The industry is disrupted, the product commoditised and the value chain disintermediated. Worst of all, customers, especially the younger generations who are Internet-savvy, embrace the change, ditching loyalty by shopping around and constantly switching for better deals.

The company decides to innovate and implement a similar online platform. A project is set up reporting to the CIO with an estimated budget of billions. To generate cash, the company hires more agents and pushes sales aggressively. Either due to the inexperience of new agents or the pressure of selling, customer profiles are not as closely scrutinised as before. More customers sign up, but because of the increased risks the company has taken on, there are more claims. The customer service department is not prepared and can't cope with the flood of claims; the results are long holding times, delays in the resolution cycle, poor quality service – and customer satisfaction scores monitored by industry watchdogs dip to the lowest in decades. Customers then leave, creating more pressure on agents to make up the numbers, but only for the short term. The company enters a period of volatile growth and damaged brand, and ultimately has to stop the innovation project, too.

You have probably gathered what was going on in this story – as sales grew, it became more and more difficult to maintain the same level of profit margin (premium revenue generated by customers minus the cost of agent commission, claims handling and providing service). What exacerbated the problem was the limitation of skill levels and experience in the organisation – massive hiring of new agents and new customer service reps without enough training. The two sides of the organisational system – sales and services – reported to different executives who buried their heads while solving their own issues but didn't talk with one another. As Peter Senge wrote in *The Fifth Discipline*:

> From a very early age, we are taught to break apart problems, to fragment the world. This apparently makes complex tasks and subjects more manageable, but we pay a hidden, enormous price. We can no longer see the consequences of our actions; we lose our intrinsic sense of connection to a larger whole.[7]

Systems theory directly challenges a few standard management practices that were, and still are, popular in large companies, such as fragmentation of work (v. end-to-end processes), separation of planning from execution (v. rapid development and simulation) and creation of pigeonholed 'expert' roles – all leading to rigid organisations with each part working in a silo and struggling to co-ordinate across functional parts. This should be the single biggest factor that contributes to what we said in the beginning of this chapter: leaders and people feel deeply frustrated and 'out of control'.

CAN MANAGERS TRULY HAVE 'CONTROL'?

The CEO at a European manufacturing company wanted to bring the federated company together as 'one' as his legacy before retiring. He hired a top-notch management consultancy to help transform the company's culture to overcome silos and enable collaboration. A huge amount of money was spent on bringing together the top 200 leaders across the globe on a retreat, reflecting on their leadership styles and impact on others, their relationships with each other and their deep-seated assumptions and mental models.

A good number of the executive leaders were enlightened and a few left the organisation. The CEO was satisfied with the energy and commitment the process generated.

Very soon after, it was the earnings report period and everyone got busy with meeting the numbers of their own profit and loss accounts. Very little changed in behaviours despite the initiatives. Another consultancy came along and pitched 'grassroots change', proposing that at the end of day it was the factory workers, customer service representatives and call centre agents who were affecting customers' perception about the 'one company' brand. Another wave of initiatives started with the goal of mobilising a large number of employees through networks of champions, lunch-and-learn sessions, peer coaching, etc. Again, great energy was generated – people were talking about the new direction at water coolers, in photocopying rooms and on the factory floor. Employee ideas about innovation were submitted every day. The CEO was excited. After another year and a few failed attempts at changing company work processes, champions of the ideas went back to their day jobs and the talk about 'change' quietened down.

What is happening here? One could simply say, 'Change is hard', but more introspective organisational psychologists have different theories. For example, Barry Oshry asserted, 'Structure shapes consciousness.'[8] The relationships we end up having in daily organisational life are the results of the structures we fall into and have nothing to do with individuals. In the above example, the 'top' team was preoccupied with complexity and accountability. They saw the opportunity of breaking silos and fostering greater connection. The 'bottom' team was concerned about job security and advancement. They, too, were excited about the prospect of a more connected workplace, more innovation and more responsibility for driving change instead of it being done to them. But the 'middle' was neglected, the middle managers who spent years climbing the greasy pole of the career ladder, who wanted to hold onto their existing territory and preserve the status quo. They felt depleted by being pulled in different directions, undervalued by their bosses and naturally competitive towards each other.

Unless the 'top', 'middle' and 'bottom' can work together to share information, build common vision and integrate with each other, there will always be disengagement and waste in organisation, and efforts to change things will fail.

Being able to see the system, to understand organisational behaviours and responses through a system lens is a critical first step towards any meaningful change.

COMPLEXITY THEORY

Also called complex adaptive systems (CAS), complexity theory is an interdisciplinary theory sometimes seen as an offshoot of the general systems theory from the 1960s. It has its roots in advancements in physics and biology that acknowledge and examine uncertainty and non-linearity. By the beginning of this century, the classic model of the organisation as 'machine' had long since been discredited, rejecting the idea that an organisational system could be analysed by understanding each part and that organisational behaviours could be predicted with accuracy; i.e. the *deterministic* and *reductionist* view.

In today's VUCA context, the linear relationship between inputs and outputs is broken. Planning has to be augmented by improvised change and agility. The traditional command-and-control hierarchy, top-down communication, rigid job profiles and specialisation have proven to be insufficient, if not backfiring.

Systems theory and complexity theory have become the dominant organisational models. Today's corporations are being swept up by social change, amplified by the Internet and social media at an unforeseen speed and scale. High-ranking executives are fired after making racially insensitive or sexist comments or displaying other ethical indiscretions.

Complexity theory suggests that organisational managers promote bringing their organisations to the 'edge of chaos', rather than troubleshooting, to trust workers to self-organise to solve problems, to encourage rather than banish informal communications networks, to 'go with the flow' rather than script procedures, to build in some redundancy and slack resources, and to induce a healthy level of tension and anxiety in the organisation to promote creativity and maximise effectiveness.

M. Mitchell Waldrop, author of *Complexity: The Emerging Science at the Edge of Order and Chaos*, contended that complex adaptive systems differ from 'complex systems' because of the potential of emerging order and learning through feedback from external environment in addition to 'self-organising'.[9] There is a growing interest in applying complexity theory to organisational studies. Managers are encouraged to take a step back from troubleshooting, to encourage and empower employees to set up informal communication networks and solve issues and to create conditions for creativity and improvement.

It is worth noting that complex adaptive systems are contrasted with command-and-control and chaotic systems because of the interrelationship among its members, as well as between members and the system. In a command-and-control system, there is a high level of constraint, meaning all member behaviour is limited to the rules of the system. In a chaotic system, each member is completely individualistic and does not change his or her behaviours because of others, or the system. With CAS, strong feedback loops exist to reinforce self-organising. This is how the organism learns and adapts.

APACHE AGILITY

We were excited to read the stories in the book *The Starfish and the Spider* by Ori Brafman and Rod Beckstrom. The central ideas were about the ability to be agile. My favourite is the story of the Spanish conquests of the Americas and the difference in the way that the Aztecs had been defeated, compared with the Apache nation. The former had a centralised control system with a big HQ and strong hierarchy. The Spanish surrounded them, cut communications and supplies, and defeated them relatively quickly. With the Apache, it was harder; when attacked in their dwellings, they became nomads, and when attacked in the mountains, they became desert people. When a 'leader' was killed, another emerged. For the Spanish, it meant attacking a fluid thing.[10]

Organisations need to become the Apache nation, embracing principles of competitive survival, such as understanding the context and systems within which they live and then dealing with the paradoxes of complexity. Even the smallest organisms operate by principles and not rules.

Survival in the face of the unexpected, for the digital world in which the rules have not yet been written means we need values and purpose, not rules and command. We need our organisations to operate on principles and morph anew. We need to build share-based systems within empathic organisations, where our people feel not threatened but part of something, beyond belonging to shared ideas, shared principles. Then we have agility.

The limited success of organisational change initiatives is due to the use of an outmoded conceptual model: the organisation as machine. The metaphor leads to unrealistic expectations of control and creates anxiety, blame and defensiveness when, inevitably, events do not proceed according to plan.

We propose an alternative: to view the organisation as a perpetual conversation. Always discovering. Enabled by *shared* purpose and psychological safety. An empathic system. This portrays an organisation not as an object, but as a self-organising pattern of curiosity, discovery, learning and sharing. This exists in the medium of human interaction in which we participate.

Principles of complexity have important implications:
- organisational change requires reflecting on and talking about what we are doing together, here and now;
- conscious involvement in new habits and new behaviours might interrupt old patterns or give rise to new ones;
- diversity and responsiveness favour the emergence of novel patterns;
- hold plans with equal value given to 'not knowing' and practise failure and redesign.

VUCA is here now. Are our organisations even aware of this? We need to change how we think about organisational change.

NOTES

1   Taylor, F.W. *The Principle of Scientific Management*. Loki's Publishing, 2017.

2   https://www.ynharari.com/topic/power-and-imagination/

3   Lorenz, E. 'Deterministic nonperiodic flow', *Journal of Atmospheric Sciences*, 20 (2), 1963, pp. 130–48.

4   Gleick, J. *Chaos: Making a New Science* (anniversary reprint ed.). London: Penguin Books, 1987.

5   *The Butterfly Effect* (2004), [film] Dir. Eric Bress and J. Mackye Gruber. USA/Canada: FilmEngine/BenderSpink/Katalyst.

6   Kohn, D. 'When gut bacteria change brain function', *The Atlantic*, 2015. https://www.theatlantic.com/health/archive/2015/06/gut-bacteria-on-the-brain/395918. Accessed 21 May 2018.

7   Senge, P. *The Fifth Discipline* (revised ed.). New York: Doubleday, 2016.

8   Oshry, B. (2015), 'Power and Love: A System Perspective', https://newstories.org/wp-content/uploads/2015/01/Power-and-Love.pdf

9   Waldrop, M.M. *Complexity: The Emerging Science at the Edge of Order and Chaos*. London: Penguin Books, 1994.

10 Brafman, O. and Beckstrom, R. *The Starfish and the Spider*. New York: Portfolio, 2007.

8

DIGITAL IMPLICATIONS

'People with advantages are loathe to believe that they just happen to be people with advantages. They come readily to define themselves as inherently worthy of what they possess; they come to believe themselves "naturally" elite; and, in fact, to imagine their possessions and their privileges as natural extensions of their own elite selves'
— C. Wright Mills, *The Power Elite*[1]

In this chapter:
- how digital and social media are changing societies and the role of ethics and corporations;
- why the current global systems of management that are protectionist and competitive will be hard to change;
- discussion of the future of work and workplace, and the demands from the future workforce.

Our current systems of government, be they internal to the corporation or in the wider social world, cannot deal with the digital future; they are still fixated on the physical world and fail to appreciate the fundamental change that has taken place across the industrial periods of the last 200 years to alter society towards more of a mass society.

We have failed to acknowledge as corporations that we own significant accountability in shaping our society that has been enhanced by the digital age. Today, corporations may possess the true power that can impact how our futures become reality. The real question is how to ensure that our corporate leadership thinks fundamentally differently from the past. In a mass society, how to manage the crowd, or the 'tyranny of the majority', as John Stuart Mill argues in his famous 1859 book *On Liberty*. And with what principles, whose ethics?

This ethics issue in a digital age is critical. We are in an age where all of our concepts of privacy are a mosaic. In the past, we thought of colonists in historic times as saviours or oppressors – either bringing civilisation to the 'barbarians' of the world or eroding old-world concepts with imperial aggression. Today, we face a new form of colonialism from those who run the platforms and those who decide the rules of machine learning and artificial algorithms – their bias and responsibility will impact the crowd at a bigger scale and impact our society more than any explorers in sailing ships.

DIVISION OF POWER IN A DIGITAL WORLD

Albert Einstein once commented, 'It has become appallingly obvious that our technology has exceeded our humanity.' We are reaching the point of 'singularity', at which point scientists don't know what will happen. It is not entirely inconceivable that the world we will be living in is what the movie *The Matrix Reloaded* imagined.[2] Most jobs across the middle levels have the highest economic value to be replaced by bots and at the bottom level humans will be working for robots. Uber drivers already take instructions from the app and don't necessarily interact with a human manager.

Think for a minute about most of the tasks an administrative assistant is doing: managing calendar invitations, making travel arrangements, submitting/approving holiday requests and so on. Digital bots can already do these efficiently. Bots can 'converse' with each other to collaborate and get things done. They can even 'refuse' to take a new appointment when they 'see' your workload has exceeded a sustainable level and 'decide' you should have a better balance by booking your yoga class instead.

Then think for a minute about the work you are doing: drafting a project plan, approving a budget, writing a report, deciding on an investment and so on. This work relies on experience and intuition. Big data and machine learning compute millions of scenarios in a second and propose the best solution without bias and mistakes.

Lastly, think about who you are working with. How old are they? Where are they located? Are they employees, contractors or consultants? Do they work flexibly with non-conventional work arrangements, like job share or compressed hours? Chances are, instead of 'going to work' you could get work from an online platform and develop a portfolio of 'employers', picking and choosing only the projects you are truly interested in, working around kids' schedules and living where you want to live.

The nature of work and the workplace is changing without us even realising it. We have read all the reports and listened to the futurists, but maybe the future is *now*, and maybe it is non-physical. Our failure to grasp this makes us victims of the change, and not shapers.

There are three technology driven forces that are rapidly transforming the nature of organisations:

1 Automation and robotics are not only possible, but economically beneficial for companies to do work without human involvement.

2 Big data, artificial intelligence and machine learning have proved that data-driven decision-making could be more effective and precise than human intuition and experience.

3 On-demand job platforms powered by aggregated personal data match tasks to the people who can best perform them, whether inside or outside the organisation, creating resource fluidity and challenging lifetime employment.

At the same time, our workforce and its expectation towards work is also changing. Ask many millennials about where they want to work and corporations don't rank high on that list. Some surveys show millennials' confidence towards corporations is lower than towards the Church or the military.[3] They are not alone. More experienced workers who hold traditional white-collar jobs would not choose to work full-time, or for one employer, but, rather, when and where they want, and these include people in all demographic brackets. Technology and the Internet enable virtual collaboration that typically was only achievable by co-locating, facilitating the rapid expansion of the so-called gig economy.

All the above has huge implications for companies in terms of managing flexible, non-employee types of resources; diversity and inclusion; intellectual capital; and the engagement and productivity of those who work in the organisation.

This is fantastic news for modern workers compared to previous generations who had to clock in, clock out, or even 10 years ago, when most work had to be done in the office. Then, our contribution was evaluated based largely on how much 'face time' one had with the supervisor; today, workers have a lot more options and flexibility.

Futurists were excited about the four-day working week and the possibility for most of the population to engage in creative or leisure activities because robots would be pulling all the weight. This did not turn out to be the case. Many of you will recall being told of the bright future that digital tech would bring us, but more leisure time never came. We are today permanently connected. Always on.

Even without such a drastic future in mind, most agree that current education and continuous education systems need to be fundamentally revamped to focus on *skills* instead of *qualifications*. Globally, higher and corporate education is breaking away from long-held traditions.

Today, the universal trend is towards a world where a majority is low-skilled and small parts of it are mid- and high-skilled.

This perpetuates the growing problem of income inequality and social division.

Across mature markets, corporations are challenged with upskilling and retraining employees because the labour landscape is completely different from the day they signed the contract with the company. If one considers government, companies and individuals as an ecosystem, a solution needs to be developed and tested with a similar macro perspective (e.g. companies and individuals are co-responsible for investing in and developing the necessary new skills in the gig economy).

If as a society we can develop more effective solutions to train our youth and employees, we could manage to significantly increase the skill level of most of the working population to avoid the tension of income inequality and social immobility.

We could 'share' the benefits brought by technology and improve wellbeing and living standards. Some forward-looking governments are already testing potential solutions to tackle singularity. The universal basic income is one of them. However, the road to utopia is not straightforward.

THE NEW POWER ELITE

Marc Andreessen, the technology entrepreneur and venture capitalist who co-founded Mosaic and Netscape and seed-invested in Facebook and Instagram, said: 'The spread of computers and the internet will put jobs in two categories. People who tell computers what to do, and people who are told by computers what to do.'

Two differences of this digital age characterised by AI and robotics stand out from past technological advances: one, not everyone benefits equally from the productivity gain through deploying technology. Those who are (a) smarter, (b) more flexible and (c) have better qualifications are rewarded disproportionally more than others. Two, those with capital who either built or invested in the platform are by far the most generously rewarded. Will there be a new elite class that rules the 'Matrix', while the rest of us will be working for the new feudal lords? What type of ethics system do we need to put in place to ensure fairness and sustainability of such a new world?

Some academics coined the term 'skill-biased' technological change based on this question. In 2013, labour economist David Autor warned that routine tasks – jobs like assembly-line manufacturing or traditional office work – were being automated.[4] These jobs use a lot of brain power, but in a predictable, repetitive way – exactly the kind of thing that computers can do better than humans. Even the traditional 'smart' jobs, those that involve data crunching and analysis, such as credit analysis and equity research, will not be necessary. Automation and artificial intelligence are allowing companies to complete these tasks using robots and computers instead, and with greater speed and accuracy. Achieving these utopian ideals in a digital age will require a new way of thinking. It forces a debate about the role of media manipulation and new concepts of corporate responsibility for those who have the funds to manage the opinions of the crowd.

Beyond profiting from the digital age, companies who own data and technological platforms have harnessed such power that no previous private, state or religious institution had ever possessed – without the public even being aware of it.

Our society is becoming networked due to social media permeating every part of our private and public lives. We are wrapped in a web of information from the minute we wake up. This shapes our perspectives about reality.

We have seen groups, corporations and politicians all over the world take advantage of this as they attempt to manipulate the citizens, from the Arab uprisings to the Indignados movement in Spain, from the Occupy Wall Street movement to the social protests in Turkey, Brazil and elsewhere.

Social media celebrities command the attention and mindset of millions for the benefit of wearing the company's products.

Consumers boycott the brand of the day for its transgressions. More recently, we have seen the spread of #MeToo and other digitally driven movements become the norm.

Manuel Castells, a Spanish sociologist, was famous for coining the term 'networked social movement' (NSM). He has developed a strong following which believes in free access to information, online communities and entrepreneurialism. Members of the movement meet at 'unconferences' (where delegates make up their own agenda) and 'hackerspaces' (originally, opportunities to tinker with electronics); their online forum of choice is typically something such as a wiki that all can contribute to and help to shape.

It might be intuitive to assume we are finally entering an evolutionary stage where people are coming together to collectively determine social agendas and solve societal challenges. But climate change still remains such an 'inconvenient truth' and the Davos celebrities, the brightest and most influential figures across the world, couldn't agree on seemingly basic issues such as intellectual property rights and net neutrality.

CORPORATE-RUN CROWDS

As we have said, we see corporations as the dominant forces directing and shaping our world, which is being driven towards a state of overconsumption. We could argue that planet Earth and our societies are increasingly run not by religious or national bureaucracies as before, but by a new energy that is held across the crowd, within data, and influenced by the corporation. The resources of the world consumed by us impact every living system and climate breakdown. We potentially see both of these elements leading to challenges to the stability of some societies and peace as we know it, within the present century.

We have always as humans entertained doomsday scenarios. Today, we have our climate change. We heard the world might end in the year 2000 (sigh), but here we are. What can you, as the reader, the individual citizen, really do to stop the apocalypse if you believe in science?

Small changes to our personal consumption patterns are important – e.g. recycle, buy organic, 'do what we can' – but are ultimately inconsequential compared with the impact of the transnational corporation to influence our world. They (we the corporates) now dominate our global economic and political system and almost every aspect of our daily life. Of the world's 100 largest economies, the vast majority, nearly 70 per cent, are corporations.

Political parties in democracies everywhere, in monarchies and collectivist worlds – and any other political system that we can see – are funded by billionaires, while government cabinet positions are staffed or influenced by corporate executives. Meanwhile, countries and cities compete with each other to beg the corporations for investment dollars, even if it means waiving legal protection for their own populations.

Environmental groups pressure corporations to improve practices by threatening to shame them publicly. Corporates are necessarily constrained by their very structure and purpose – they exist to bring return to shareholders, sometimes regardless of the unintended consequences; if unchecked, they may operate to monetise human activity and nature's abundance as rapidly and efficiently as possible. Think about your favourite animal or organism that is designed to do this – a creature that consumes something with endless growth as its only objective and think about what that creature does to its environment and the toll it takes on the environment. The Earth (and the system of sharing the space) always fights back, and wins.

A flourishing Earth or a viable future for all of us in the crowd is not a shared objective across the world's most powerful institutional force.

Could the transnationals, the national corporations and governments redirect their enormous power collectively towards a more sustainable path, considering the return that this would bring?

In law, a corporation is treated as though it were an individual – balanced but not equal. A corporation as a concept or entity alone can be devoid of any concern for the harm it causes or the consequence of the pursuit of its goals; if it were a human, we might call this psychopathy. But corporations are not unethical psychopaths. It is easier to change a corporation's values than those of a human psychopath. We could change the legal basis of its charter, making its explicit purpose to achieve a triple bottom line of financial, social and environmental outcomes – sometimes known as the 'triple Ps' of people, planet and profit. This would require the corporation to have the intention of having shared objectives and to be balanced and agile.

THE ROLE OF CORPORATIONS AND GOVERNMENT IN A 'SHARING' ECONOMY

In his book *Infrastructure: The Social Value of Shared Resources*, Brett Frischmann, a law professor based in New York, argues that digital infrastructure is often to some extent 'non-rival', meaning one person's use does not forestall another's. Limiting their use, for instance, by pricing them depending on who uses them and for what, can limit their value and slow down innovation.[5]

Big, established companies in recent years have almost all had some form of 'digital initiatives'. Some positive progress is being made: for example, integrating the digital workforce with the traditional workers, who previously saw new ways of working as a threat rather than an opportunity, thus making it difficult to materialise collaboration across business units and create value beyond pure marketing communications. Another is that top executives 'walk the talk' by embracing the hacker culture and transforming their own skills and behaviours.

We have seen a few companies start a wholesale culture change as a result of 'digitalisation'. Risk taking, failing fast and working across silos is 'sharing', which is a key to the concepts of innovation.

A big idea not shared is not an innovation – it is just an idea. It is also about adapting and taking – to share also means to be open to taking – it speaks to a lack of arrogance and an openness to learn from everyone.

As Montesquieu wrote, 'It should be noted that the main reason for the Romans becoming masters of the world was that, having fought successively against all peoples, they always gave up their own practices as soon as they found better ones.'[6]

Much of the philosophy of the current capitalist model of the organisation is based upon the element of competition – between executives and between employees. Much of the wasted energy and focus of the organisation is on the internal competition between employees, diverting energy from studying the external competition or servicing the customer.

It is fascinating to examine the psychological need for competition. The German expression *Schadenfreude*, 'feeling happy about other people's misfortune', illustrates that we like to feel we are doing better than the next person, because 'the fittest survives'. For example, in downsizing or other stressful situations, people hold back information or are reluctant to share ideas because they are scared and want to have a stronger chance of survival.

A more open, empathetic and sharing culture can bring about positive change. But, fundamentally, if companies continue to see digitalisation as simply a new source for profit, nothing will change. On the contrary, instead of making progress for humanity, we may be charting a course towards dangerous waters.

SHAPING THE CROWD
Since the earliest days of humanity, we have always sought to influence the crowd. Yet the crowd today is not a village square, a circle around a fire, or even a city state or nation. In this digital age, we are the ultimate mass crowd – producing data that are in

turn controlled by a few corporations, especially those who run the platforms.

Mass society is a concept built in the early days of the first industrial revolution; it describes a modern era defined by a mass culture across the entire population run by large-scale, impersonal, social institutions. A mass society was purported to be a society in which prosperity and the formal bureaucracy (functioning with a faceless lack of opinion) have weakened traditional social ties. It referenced the levelling tendencies in the period of the first industrial revolution that undermined traditional and class-based values. It was seen by philosophers in the early days as the erosion of beliefs, driven by the aristocracy and educated elite, who feared the 'tyranny of the mob'. Mob mentality. Mob politics.

We would argue that in the digital age we see the ultimate personification of that fear. A mass mob of data and people, tightly connected and cynically controlled. Émile Durkheim described society as a mass of undifferentiated, atomistic individuals held together by an industry of culture[7] – sports and fashion (and today, fake news and celebrity culture) – that serves the interests of capitalism.

Jung's exposition of the collective unconscious builds on the same classic issue in psychology and biology regarding *nature versus nurture*. If we accept that nature, or heredity, has some influence on the individual psyche, we must examine the question of how this influence takes hold in the real world to control the masses. They argue that we have 'primordial images', or 'archetypes', in the basic stock of our unconscious psyche, different from what we learn as we experience life. The existence of the collective unconscious means that individual consciousness is not immune to predetermining influences. It is in the highest degree influenced by inherited ideas if leveraged and we would argue that they *are* leveraged.

Herd behaviour describes how individuals in a group can act collectively without centralised direction. The term can refer to the behaviour of animals in herds, packs, flocks of birds, schools of fish and so on, as well as the behaviour of humans in demonstrations, riots and general strikes, sporting events, religious gatherings, episodes of mob violence and everyday decision-making, judgement and opinion forming – often conducted today in the digital space. We need to increasingly think of the world that we live in as not physical, but digital. Failure to realise this impedes organisational agility.

Our new digital communications technology contributes to 'the power of crowds' and so-called 'consumer choice'. We (consumers) have more access to opinions and information from those with opinions on platforms that have largely user-generated content. Leaders emerge through *popularity*.

Popularity is in turn seen as an indication of better quality. Popularity – the number of the masses that can be converted – is now, in the age of data, seen to be the truth. We have allowed digital concepts to influence truth in our crowds. If 1,000 people click 'like', does that make it the truth?

Online, likes may be more powerful than votes. We use the opinions of others on these digital platforms as a guide for products and brands that align with our self-perception of our 'peer'-based reality.

Our digital efforts as corporations are powerful tools in perpetuating and enabling herd behaviour. Social influence frames our attitudes towards brands. The strongest personalities are more engaged on consumer platforms and spread information through word of mouth more efficiently and effectively than any doorstep sales or political activity. Brands use 'brand ambassadors' as influencers to control that herd behaviour, to drive up sales and profits.

Marketing transcends commercial roots; it can be used to encourage action and opinion. Gustave Le Bon theorised that the new entity, the 'psychological crowd', which emerges from incorporating the assembled population, not only forms a new body, but also creates a collective 'unconsciousness' – similar to Jung.

As a group of people gather and coalesce to form a crowd, there is a 'magnetic influence given out by the crowd' that transmutes every individual's behaviour until it becomes governed by the 'group mind'.[8]

Le Bon detailed three key processes that create the psychological crowd: (a) anonymity, (b) contagion and (c) suggestibility. Anonymity provides rational individuals with a feeling of invincibility and the loss of personal responsibility. An individual becomes primitive, unreasoning, emotional.

This lack of self-restraint allows individuals to 'yield to instincts' and to accept the instinctual (primordial) drivers. The lowest base instincts. This 'contagion' is the very reason we fear crowds. Suggestibility is the mechanism through which the contagion is achieved; as the crowd coalesces into a singular mind, suggestions made by the strongest voices create a space for the worst of our unconscious to come to the forefront and guide behaviour. A psychological crowd – which is not physical, but invisible in the cloud – is thus created and becomes homogeneous and malleable to suggestions from its strongest members.

Recently, we have seen in elections all over the world, and in how our personal data is sold as a commodity to influence us – using psychological profiling – how potentially 'evil' companies and groups can be.

We cannot go backwards. We cannot unlearn and retrograde out of our digital space. Neither is the complete opposite a way forward. Activists make the mistake of demanding everything be shared and saying ownership need not matter at all, without addressing the underlying motives. Any first foray into technology is harsh. We exploit it for the meanest of motives and then find the power of that innovation to truly lift us up.

Where are our government and regulators? Unfortunately, governments are also systematically getting the balance of 'open' versus 'closed' and 'free' versus 'owned' wrong. Frischmann agreed that they are stuck in the physical world, where most goods are rivals and cannot be easily shared.

So we need to shift the 'ownership' mindset, not only within one company, but across the industry, even across whole societies – and with a good balance and a measured approach. Arun Sundararajan, a professor of business at New York University and author of *The Sharing Economy*, attributes the lack of preparedness to a physical-world mindset, which mistakenly assumes that if the company's product exists in the physical world it can't be digitally disrupted. He says, 'That's the wrong attitude. Any responsible company today should view digital technologies as a means to create a more efficient organization or a different form of customer engagement, irrespective of how physical the product may be.'[9]

We know that suggestion, the psychological process of priming and advertising, work. We know that companies now run the dialogues across our planet. How best to instil concepts of sharing, of empathy towards each other? For bad things to happen, the good just need to do nothing. Ultimately, failure to act by corporations could be the downfall of the society they seek to serve – so where does the impetus arise for the corporation to seize the opportunity and responsibility to serve its crowd?

NOTES

1 Mills, C.W. *The Power Elite*. New York: Oxford University Press, 1956.
2 *The Matrix Reloaded* (2003), [film] Dir. Lana Wachowski and Lilly Wachowski. USA: Warner Bros. et al.
3 KPMG (2017), 'Future of work survey of 1,200 millennials'. https:// assets.kpmg/content/dam/kpmg/fr/pdf/2017/05/fr-Future-Of-Work-report.pdf. Accessed 2 May 2018.
4 Autor, D. and Price, B. 'The changing task composition of the US labor market'. Cambridge: Massachusetts Institute of Technology, 2013.

5 Frischmann, B. *Infrastructure: The Social Value of Shared Resources.* Oxford: Oxford University Press, 2013.

6 Bowman, A.K., Garnsey, P. and Rathbone, D. (eds). *The Cambridge Ancient History*, Vol. XI. pp. 326–7. Cambridge: Cambridge University Press.

7 Durkheim, E. *Sociology and Philosophy.* Translated by D.F. Pocock, with an introduction by J.G. Peristiany. Toronto: The Free Press, 1974 [1953].

8 Le Bon, G. *Psychology of Crowds.* Southampton: Sparkling Books, 2009.

9 Sundararajan, A. *The Sharing Economy: The End of Employment and the Rise of Crowd-based Capitalism.* Cambridge: MIT Press, 2016.

9

THE EMPEROR HAS NO CLOTHES

'Concepts that have proven useful in ordering things easily achieve such authority over us that we forget their earthly origins and accept them as unalterable givens'

— Albert Einstein

In this chapter:
- challenging the accepted HR norms;
- a review of current organisational theories and practices in an analysis of traditional HR failings;
- attempts to blow up myths and challenge 'taken-for-granted' people and practices;
- redefining who HR serves.

With the assault on our senses of the constant digital stream in our hands, we are obsessed more than ever about the very next experience. It feels like throwing yourself into a crazy dance at a party, the most natural thing is to keep dancing. Yet, the moment you decide to take a break, walking out to the balcony and from there observing the crowd, you may develop different perspectives. We so often live in the day-to-day, we forget that everything around us was created in a time and context. It is not a given.

EATING SALT

> **Chris:** As I enter a new organisation, I often see things with the benefit of both experience and a fresh pair of eyes. Differences stand out for me. I have used such an analogy: say you invited me into your grand house to live with you. You asked me to sit down and eat with you. I find the first meal to be inedible, as the food is too salty. Do I point this out to you, my host? My first response typically is to act – because that's why you invited me in, to hear my views. To speak truth to power, to express. But it is hard for others who have a salty palate to taste the salt. They think this is normal. They are used to eating salty food. They are not only used to the taste of salt, they tell me that I will get used to it. Yet my role is to point out that the emperor is naked and say that the new clothes are not real. That the food is salty.

Many HR people practise in companies that were developed at different phases during the last 150 years. Each had a unique context of wider society, which drove the creation and adoption of HR practices in different eras. Today, what we often face is a mismatch of policies, ideas and processes across HR that do not always fit together or form a logical congruence.

The language that we use is important. Language is the construct by which we think about and assimilate in the world around us. In the strange institutions that we have built called organisations, we have adopted a set of practices and norms. Not all of these mindsets or constructs are still useful.

THE INVISIBLE INSTITUTION

We did a search on the concept of institutionalisation and we came up with:

> *in·sti·tu·tion·al·i·sa·tion*
> noun
> - the action of establishing something as a convention or norm in an organisation or culture;
> - the state of being placed or kept in a residential institution — *harmful effects such as apathy and loss of independence arising from spending a long time in an institution.*

We thought it was interesting that the two aspects of the definition reflected the points that we want to make in this chapter. The first is realising that things we take for granted are not actually what they appear to be, or even that they have to be. It is just that over time we developed a set of practices that became habits. We need to learn new habits. The idea of institutions became part of the post-industrial revolution thinking — that offices, factories and other common work environments would require a stylised set of routines in order to be effective, efficient and compliant with laws and regulations, and provide the benefit of a central language with which we can speak to each other. Each worker came from his or her own family and background, but each needed to learn a new style and approach — how to behave in this organisation.

The second definition is based on what we know about the impact of caged animals, which endlessly circle or sit in the same place all day; they lose the appetite for life, grow apathetic and unable to think for themselves. How best to change all our habits within an environment that is designed to conform to an already existing set of habits?

We have such preconceived ideas about employees that we see each other not as colleagues, but as differentiated groups. We live in separate groups, divided by words such as employees, workers, management and executives.

These ideas of separation work together with practices that are done *to* the employees. When we measure employee satisfaction, for example, we profess to listen to employees' feelings or opinions, yet we have employees in every organisation who do not trust managers or feel safe enough to tell the truth.

Why is that?
HR is the department that is placed in this no-win game, a game of shadows and half-truths driven by a clutter of policies and practices that have not passed the balcony test of congruence to an intentional purpose for our time today – a test for relevance.

Employees don't trust HR because HR is employed by the management to 'manage' that *difficult* space (people). HR reads trends from surveys and social media sites and makes incremental tweaks to employee practice. HR hires lawyers to defend the company against grievances, to protect the corporation and employees against random employee risk. Also, to manage the employee concept as a risk.

In our world we also place the police in a no-win situation. We ask them to come and save us, risk their lives, deal with the societal implications of our choices, act as agents for change for the poorest and uphold our property laws. It is a difficult job to carry out all those roles, which are morphed over time and not designed anew. Can the police play social worker and change agent at the same time for the organisational society, or are these really two different departments?

Can HR play police and change agent in our organisations? Or is it time for HR to acknowledge this mismatch and step back and refresh, reset and align process and policy to spoken intent?

PRIORITISING EMPATHY FOR THE EMPLOYEE
Studies of time spent at work, compliance adherence, breed a certain attitude towards employees as representing risk to the

organisation. This comes from the early days of people being considered less important than machines, an era and mindset when the worker was disposable – or at least more disposable than the machine.

Chris: I was once in the emergency room, facing a potentially fatal situation that was in the end just a scare. I was talking to the medical technician in the room with me. My health caretaker. He had once worked in a factory as a machinist. He told me a story that demonstrates this underlying mindset about how the employee can be viewed by the organisation as a relative risk. He told me that he had worked in a corner of the factory where there was a broken window. In the winter, his workspace was freezing. He repeatedly asked for the window to be mended and was told that it was not an essential repair at that time and not a priority for the maintenance crews. This continued for months, with the man having to wear full outdoor winter clothes, which made movement difficult and in turn his job harder and more dangerous to carry out. As winter wore on, the area got so cold that the oil in the machine became sluggish. Most hydraulic parts are made from iron or steel, which tend to be unaffected by ambient temperature. However, concern kicked in when these metal parts either rubbed against other metal parts, or the parts were attempting to push through fluid that was as thick as ketchup. The technical staff made a blanket for the machine to keep it warm and the window was fixed immediately. The care and empathy were for the machine and the process; within his company, organisational effectiveness determined that the human, the worker, was less important.

In the post-war West, with productivity being impacted less by the quality of machines, worker motivation became important. Studies of the process of person and machine interface search for the most competitive advantage. People practices developed accordingly.

I was once sent to a small call centre. The employee satisfaction scores had dipped sharply – an early warning sign in a place where employees were seen as the most crucial part of the business model. The workplace was non-unionised. Management saw great morale as the key determinant to a strong customer service orientation.

We found that the local management had taken to treating the employees like serfs: employees were asked to bring drinks or meals for managers and to run errands for them. There was zero flexibility for those with carer responsibilities in cases of unexpected absence. Employees were expected to supply their own stationery in order to save on office expenses.

When we visited the call centre, we were told a story. Only the previous day the department had been summoned to sing 'Happy Birthday' to the office manager. A large cake was pushed in on a trolley. Only certain senior staff grades were allowed to have any of the cake. It seems ridiculous that such an attitude might persist in a modern office. It reads like something from a Dickens novel.

As the result of our visit, the entire management team was dismissed from the company. In time, the company executives visited the office and apologised to the staff.

The worst example of employee satisfaction found in HR surveys I've experienced occurred when I was working with a financial services company. I visited a branch office in an Asian country with the highest-performing employee satisfaction scores. I wanted to discover their secret. I visited the pristine offices and was invited to shake hands with every team member in the office. As I did so, one of the local team members slipped a piece of paper into my palm. It said that they had been forced to fill in their employee scores in the presence of their manager and wrote what they were told for fear of losing their jobs. Here, the practice of caring about the employee was living in the process of having a survey. Yet the philosophy of seeing the employee as disposable was still alive in the mindset even if the processes themselves had evolved. The superficial process focus remains to drive the majority of employee tactics related to work culture today.

TIME AND CONTEXT

We measure time in organisations through production, pay and financial reporting cycles. Quarters drive the corporate mindset. This means that there is a short attention span. In contrast, most organisational change related to people practices takes a long time to be implemented. Organisational habits take decades, sometimes more than a century, to form.

> **Chris:** I signed up for a weight-loss programme in order to change my lifestyle. I was equipped with a nutritionist, fitness coach, therapist, physician and support group. A systemic change approach. The programme lasted ten months and was moderately successful in making some positive lifestyle changes regarding diet, exercise and sleep. In the end I was told I needed an additional 18-month programme to reinforce new habits and that it might take up to five years for me to really live a healthy lifestyle.

A short-term focus driven by in-year financial performance leads to impatience with any project over a year. Executive tenure in roles has been dramatically shortened in recent years, leading to a loss of sponsors to follow up investment or resources. Compounded with initiatives designed by siloed functions and an overwhelming list of 'urgent' issues, we get what we currently see in organisations:

a phenomenon of 'analysis paralysis' – reactive, poor decision-making and inaction in the face of current challenges.

Corporations in almost all cases exist for this sole, or most important, purpose: to make short-term profit. Societies see plenty of giant companies losing their 'soul' and existence as they grow. In contrast, the more successful ones consistently express strong and clear purposes that resonate with employees, customers, investors and the wider society. Many once-famous brands vanish from the 'top companies' lists every year as a result of being commoditised or overly focused on financial gain versus purpose. Only thinking about the short term and quick wins, rather than making the difficult choices to sustain customer empathy and loyalty is what ultimately kills a company.

TIME TO REIMAGINE WHO WE SERVE AS HR

We were once hunter-gatherers and farmers, later craftspeople and workers. Then machines entered the picture. That covers over 100,000 years of human history. In the last 150 years, with increasing cycles of relevance, we came to rely less on muscle and aggression to create, build and produce.

Today, we have machines as our muscle and at the dawn of quantum computing are ready to solve the things that we used only to imagine. A different set of people is maybe required in our new age. Those are people with great social skills, who know how to network, build communities and approach others with empathy, not power. They possess skills purposefully built for the digital age. Just for fun, let's call them women. Yet, where pay, benefits and policy are concerned, equality is not the norm.

In most developed markets, the HR frame, and thus, core policies and practices, are historically designed for the traditional family model with a sole breadwinner, normally male, and a homemaker. We have moved on from the 1950s *Good Wife's Guide*, as women stay in the workforce after motherhood, but childcare and seniorcare are yet to become staples of standard company reward practice. These are among the two biggest family responsibilities that often fall on women. Growing evidence suggests the '9-to-5' work culture is not motivating most millennials, does not fit with women juggling multiple roles and is an impediment to worker productivity.

In addition, with the issues of a multigenerational workforce and growing cultural diversity, it is no surprise that people management is cited as a substantial challenge facing companies over the next five to 10 years. Many issues sit with HR teams not being ready to evolve in the way they think about the employee. Many still see the worker, however skilled, to be a risk (to manage) and not an asset. We are obsessed with the new generations entering the workplace, but we have always had new generations coming into our workplaces – with new ideas and talents. This is not new. We are living longer. We will most probably have to work much longer, too. Multiple generations now coexist in the workplace for the first time in history. How to get the older 45-year-old to learn new habits? Einstein said, 'The measure of intelligence is the ability to change.' Change is undoubtedly hard. Can we even imagine what it might be like to rewire our mindsets, behaviours and habits to make a female-centred workplace?

HR has talked incessantly about wanting a 'seat at the table'. This metaphor is outdated, in part because the top HR leaders now *do* sit at the proverbial table in most organisations. Secondly, whose table is HR to sit at? Is HR best served by aligning with and focusing on what has always been seen as the 'top' table? Is the top table still the place of power and strategy that it has always been? In our new 'top table', there are actually hundreds of connection points across the middle of the organisation, run by what we today call middle managers. Success is about their empowerment. Is HR still focused on missing out on power at the top, when the real story of what is going on in the organisation is happening somewhere else?

We see four new emergent roles that HR needs to play, in parallel:

1 Compliance and control.
2 Coach/psychologist.
3 Change agent/catalyst/data analyst.
4 Strategist/functional broker.

It is difficult to be all of these at the same time. There is also a tangible integrity about the purpose of the company that requires someone across these roles to ensure they are aligned.

For each HR team, there is an opportunity to pause and reflect on which of their current practices and models truly align with their stated intent.

LEARNING TO LEARN DIFFERENTLY

Companies spend enormous amounts of money on employee training and education – but they seldom get a good return on their investment. For the most part, the learning doesn't lead to better organisational performance, because people soon revert to their old ways of doing things. Old habits die hard.

The way most companies approach learning is rigidly based on the job requirements, with minimal consideration of the individual learner. This creates a mentality of there being a single way to deliver the correct job performance and the company in turn seeks to shape the exact type of worker for the role, assuming that people are not innovative about the way they do their job. The reason for this, again, is that our thinking about learning is based on the mindset of the industrial age. Worker variation caused chaos, cost or legal action (risk). The times have mostly changed, but the way we teach organisational learning – even for new, complex concepts – has not.

Many companies traditionally train employees on a mandatory learning process regardless of roles and functions and seldom on *how* to learn. Those 'sheep dip' programmes are good at ensuring compliance and 'check the box' but are ineffective at enabling skill-building and completely useless in teaching values.

Another fallacy is to teach superficially – just the skills, but not the stuff that's below the surface of the iceberg (e.g. character, attributes).

> **Linda:** In the past, I visited West Point and Fort Leavensworth to understand how the military teach value-based leadership. I exchanged ideas with ex-officers from the British and Israeli armies. The director of the US Centre for Army Leadership once told me: 'I can teach anyone how to fire a machine gun within five minutes, but actually "making" a leader that is honest, courageous and intelligent, that takes years.'

Consistency of language and mindset works well in accelerating internal communication, because a consistent business language increases cohesion of decision-making. When everyone is indoctrinated into the same framework of reference, we lose the benefit of diverse perspectives and experience. New ideas struggle to surface or to be heard, because 'it doesn't work that way here'. A balance has to be found in how we teach learning from the perspective of the organisation (the machine) as well as of the individual. We have to reimagine how to learn.

One veteran military commander who transitioned to a company that is huge on Six Sigma and process improvement qualification was deeply frustrated. He commented on his own experience:

> Companies say they want leadership and organisational skills, and yet when they hired someone who has led at mass scale in difficult environments and battlefields, they are shaking their heads; 'you need to be a Six Sigma black belt' [in order to be an effective leader here].

The purpose of organisational training is too often to mould everyone into the same square. To conform and not release.

LEADERSHIP DEVELOPMENT CHALLENGE

If you don't have the right people capabilities in your organisation, it's very unlikely that you'll be successful in the execution of your business strategy. This is oft-quoted advice that you will hear from multiple corporate leaders and advisers.

The problem with the majority of current leadership development programmes is that either they are poorly designed, or poorly executed, leaving people with a temporary 'high' and some good ideas that are impossible to implement on the job; or they lack the overarching view of what types of organisational leaders will be effective in the specific operating context and culture; or they are simply not connected to the overall people strategy. The bottom line? It is not uncommon for a global corporation of a certain size to end up with hundreds, or thousands, of disjointed leadership programmes all trying to fix certain 'attributes' or provide skills that are hard to deploy in isolation.

These clumsy attempts at a culture of conformity respond to a different age of HR, the era of the great leaders, when we felt that we needed saviours to be heroes. This was in the 1980s and 1990s, when the West was threatened by Asian imports; like most humans in a crisis, we rushed to hold up heroes – CEOs who won. CEOs became celebrities. The most famous appeared on magazine covers. They mixed with politicians and stars of all stripes.

This focus on the 'great man' comes from the same era as a related HR challenge – the relatively recent in-vogue focus on leadership succession planning and 'talent'. This entire practice was borne from one book which coined the term 'war for talent'.[1] Is it really possible to regard people as the talent and yet have HR practices that treat the workforce essentially as a risk?

GENERATIONAL DIVIDE AND MIGRATION

Our civilisation has gone through countless changes over time. The context of mass population movement and the multiple diverse populations that work alongside each other is difficult to comprehend given the speed at which this has taken place. As we saw earlier, we also have multiple generations working together for the first time.

The Baby Boomer generation is the first to be able to carry on working well past traditional retirement age and most seem to want to do this. Even so, a lot of companies will feel vulnerable when the precious experience and skills go out of the door when the Boomers start to retire in droves in a few years' time. On the other hand, the millennials are not satisfied with the typical development path that might take 15 to 20 years. They turn around and see 26-year-old CEOs and start-ups that IPO for billions of dollars within seven years. When they get too frustrated, they leave, creating a vacuum in the leadership supply that exacerbates the reluctance of companies investing in developing the younger generations. Then there is the 'sandwiched' Generation X, which tends to be forgotten and polarised – a lucky few are able to join the executive club dominated by Boomers, while the majority will retire before they are even given a chance.

In countries with high youth unemployment rates, there are increased concerns that many young people will leave the workforce permanently, resulting in a lost generation. A friend of mine posted an advertisement on a popular au pair agency website for someone to look after her two young daughters. She never expected that her modest offer of accommodation in her south-east London apartment would generate more than 2,000 emails, mostly from Spain and Eastern Europe. Most were overqualified to be an au pair. Some wrote bluntly, 'There is no job here...I can look after your children while looking for a real job.' We have a migrant crisis on a scale never before seen in human history, with an over-abundance of skilled workers. We will see more. How best to access and enable a company that can make use of all these talented people?

HUMANISING PERFORMANCE MANAGEMENT

On most performance management (PM) blogs, the burning question is: 'PM has been largely the same for 50 years, but suddenly everyone hates it – why?'

What changed? Not only the generations (including millennials and their apparent need to not hear bad news) but the Internet, too. All generations now get immediate access to data and this gives us increasingly powerful intelligence.

It seems unnatural to have a formal conversation to share data once or twice a year. Employees expect managers to be working with them all of the time. To care, to have empathy – to treat them like family. We talk a lot about corporations wanting to feel like family. Appraisals are not a thing we do in families, at least not ours (try doing this with your spouse or kids – it doesn't work). We talk.

Corporations could also compare and assess their managers to discern if they know what they are talking about and if they are competent leaders themselves. The days of traditional respect of hierarchy are perhaps gone; the old model of guilds around the world – often associated with skilled trades, learning the trade from your supervisor – is increasingly irrelevant when information is easily distributed and available on the Internet. One Gallup study shows a strong correlation between likes for performance management systems and that for their supervisors.[2] At a recent PM conference, the moderator opened the morning by joking, 'For the past 50 years, companies have been using the same techniques and philosophies managing employee performance with no desire for change. Suddenly everyone is not happy with it and wants to throw it out of the window!' This is probably not too far from the truth.

A FALSE WAR FOR TALENT

The current talent management practices often stifle and frustrate instead of motivating and energising workers to realise their full potential. The company is hurt and the individual worker does not get a chance to use and develop his or her unique talent. The work by psychologist Carol Dweck has widely introduced the concepts of a growth mindset.[3] We know that we need to view everyone as talent. Is it really that simple?

Can we reimagine how we manage talent systems when every employee has the truly shared potential to become amazing? We wouldn't anxiously be searching for the next solution to motivate or 'engage' employees because they would be naturally and intrinsically 'self-engaged'. And research already proves that intrinsic motivation, rather than money or other forms of compensation, is much more effective and sustainable.[4]

The 40-hour week was first engineered to protect workers, allowing them to have sufficient rest away from manual labours in the industrial age. It might not be relevant and appropriate today because we are attached to our digital devices all the time anyway. Moonlighting, i.e. maintaining a side business, used to be scorned upon; today, it's encouraged and has a fashionable name 'personal branding'. It is entirely possible that in the future an individual can work for more than one company by offering a share of his talent. The company does not buy his whole time, but they buy the talent of his output. Shared talent will help solve the sense of 'shortage' by removing hoarding. Reimagined, this fundamentally breaks the very concepts of owned talent and talentship.

LOOKING AHEAD

In the past 20 years, most of the focus of the HR team has been on cost reduction, process improvements, business process re-engineering and other large-scale change investments. The goals are efficiency, cost and service improvements, and expanding how we conduct current HR models and practices. The current focus stops at making the function or process fairer, more effective or more empathic. We suggest that HR has a widespread opportunity to rethink the limitations of how and who it serves.

NOTES

1   Michaels, E., et al. *The War for Talent*. Boston: Harvard Business Review Press, 2001.

2   Gallup (2017), 'The state of the American workplace'. https://www.gallup.com/workplace/238085/state-american-workplace-report-2017.aspx. Accessed 18 June 2018.

3   Dweck, C. *Mindset: The New Psychology of Success* (reprint, updated ed.). New York: Ballantine Books, 2007.

4   Economic Policy Institute (2014), 'CEO Compensation Surged in 2017'. https://www.epi.org/publication/ceo-compensation-surged-in-2017/

MANAGING RISK

'An asteroid or a super volcano could certainly destroy us, but we also face risks the dinosaurs never saw: an engineered virus, nuclear war, inadvertent creation of a micro black hole, or some as-yet-unknown technology could spell the end of us'

— Elon Musk

In this chapter:
- risk as critical to work on culture;
- three circles of risk establishing congruence, agility and confidence in executives.

There are various forms of risk: operational, financial, reputational and systemic risk are just a few. The whole business of business in many ways is about the management of risk and the weighing up of factors to decide if this particular formula or idea, service, product, customer, timing will fit together to form a value proposition that will actually work.

Risk management, in our experience, is most often performed formally and overtly in more regulated organisations and woefully overlooked in other companies. We consider risk management to be an important targeted element in culture change. It is simply not understood or leveraged as a profession and a competitive capability. A weakness of strategy that we observe in those of most organisations is the failure to leverage risk models in order to manage scenario-based planning, and thus agility, and consequences of decisions.

We are faced with myriad decisions. Where to go next in our journey of life? We are presented with choices all the time. Sometimes we take the road less travelled; sometimes we take the more sensible path because of the stress or potential implications of an option. As we all look back at our lives, we see countless decisions that were weighed and measured and where the considerations of consequences inspired. Somehow, all too often in our corporate world, and in our wider society, we make big choices after listening to the wrong choices. Choices from fear. We need to be able to press pause and make decisions out of real choice. That is when we make our best decisions.

RISK IN A WORLD WITH AI

The use of AI and machine learning has totally transformed the way companies think about risk from a product development and forecasting perspective. The process of concept to development to testing and product launch used to take years; today, this can be modelled in weeks to months – with quantum computing, perhaps minutes.

We will be faced with more options, many paths and in real time. We are not used to this. We will focus on the dramatic time saving and cost saving to organisations, the opportunity to seek competitive advantage. This will lead to massive changes in how organisations think about their R&D. In the past, many such projects would be linked to failure, meaning losses on some projects of millions of dollars.

Companies have procedures, committees and policies to manage risk. With AI, money is freed up either for more lucrative projects or to test for projects previously considered too risky. Committees

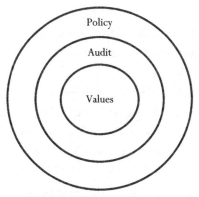

FIGURE 10.1 Three circles of risk.

are permitted less and less. AI allows scientists and executives to be more creative and to try out new ideas through modelling. This means that data will increasingly show how to mitigate risk significantly. Even so, we will find it hard to create new habits at the speed that the ability to multiply allows us through technology.

One question we struggle with is: what will our interaction with data and machines be in the world of the future, for the fourth industrial revolution? It is impossible to tell what the computing of the future will look like and where it will be powered/housed. We do not know the computing platforms of the future. We don't know what will happen. So how to plan for which scenario? Which approach brings the least risk?

THREE CIRCLES OF RISK

Chris: When I was working in one of the world's biggest financial houses, risk management dominated and was centred on three aspects of formal protection to the company: audit, policy and values. How these are purposefully used and understood is critical. The understanding of these and adherence to them drive *congruence*.

Congruence is everything. What we manage formally in the circles of risk tells us what is important. This chapter may seem basic to some, but it is a cornerstone missing in most change efforts and failure to adopt leads to error.

Proper risk management has values at its core. Too often, we think of values as something soft, but they are there to guide us in the most difficult of situations. We do not need values when things are easy. It is when we are faced with the unexpected – with multiple options, with the roads less travelled – that they are needed. In the moment of the practical decision, data gives you options. The decision in the context of consequences lies in principles.

In organisations, what we measure, where we spend time, is what is important. If sharing, empathy and behaviour are important in the organisation, how we manage decisions associated with these things becomes one of the most important aspects so as to move away from being another poorly executed change effort.

Audit

At the outer circle were the audit teams, each department in a cycle and reviewed for its adherence to policy and directive. Audit teams asked formal questions on behalf of the senior team or the non-executive directors (NEDs) and, when something was seen to go poorly in a particular department, they came in like a SWAT team or masked avengers to strike fear and reveal truth with impartiality.

They were often met in the same way as the internal affairs team on a police procedural matter: they are accepted as a necessary regulatory body but no one ever really understands the nuances of what they investigate and they accept the automatic responses of the managers and team members assigned to fill out the forms. There is an opportunity to turn risk assessment into internal consulting opportunities.

Policy

Policy is set as an aspect of risk management to ensure that there are clear guidelines and procedures in place in the case of a general systems failure. Policy offers guidance and sanction; it protects the organisation. When operating well, it provides:

- general guidance about the organisation's mission;
- specific guidance for implementing strategies to achieve the organisation's objectives;
- a mechanism to control the behaviour of the organisation.

Policies provide a framework and structure for the organisation. Congruent implications of breaking policy contribute strongly and set/define company culture. For an organisation to say that it has a strong policy on ethics will help instil the importance of integrity and ethical behaviours in employees.

Policies serve as a way for management to communicate behavioural expectations to employees. Guidelines should make clear the consequences for employees who violate certain policies, otherwise they lose validity. In many organisations there is mandatory training on policies. Most executives have additional accountability. In the most congruent organisations, these sessions are taken seriously. In one organisation, employment contracts stipulated that all employees had to complete the required training by year end. Those who did not received a polite note regretting that they had decided to leave the company. Every year, those who failed to complete the training saw their contracts terminated. It seems extreme, but the point was made: people knew that, at this company, a policy had teeth.

Policy and adherence to policy are of huge importance. When it comes to safety policies, local interpretations of law or government intent are enforced in a mixed way across organisations. Take fire drills, for example: is every team well trained on exactly where to go? Are there impromptu evacuation drills that disrupt business routine and allow real-time rehearsal? If not, why not? And what is the risk that the organisation is playing with?

In many cases, the disruptions cost risk and the risk of annoying an executive is deemed too high in comparison to the risk of the death of employees. Employee safety — enshrined in policy — is less valuable in this version of congruence than risk to business continuation. What message does such enforcement of policy demonstrate to the congruence of culture? It's important to think this through as these are the types of things employees point to when indicating an organisation's failure to follow through on intent of promise.

Values

The third circle of risk focuses on the individual. It is about articulating values that should pop up at the right time. Values are about doing the right thing: they are about integrity. All values at their core, no matter which words are chosen, are about the values of integrity. Knowing the right thing to do in the moment depends on the ability to judge the consequence of the decision. This is something that can be articulated, taught and practised. We see this as the most important aspect of risk management.

The focus on the individual employee is the one aspect that will protect the organisation in a VUCA world — a world where the organisation will encounter aspects of change that are as yet unknown and with no rules to follow. Audit and policy respond to what is known; rules cannot be set for what is unknown. By instilling strong values in the individual, we count on them to make the right decision. To create the organisation that is truly empathic and share-based, think about the core value(s) that need to be in place.

Take this simple experiment: you go to an ATM and find $5 has been left in the machine. It is the evening and the bank is closed.

What do you do? Do you take the money back the next day? What if it were $50? Or $200, or $500 – at which point does your decision change? *Would* your decision change?

Instilling strong values is critical and provides organisational agility. The old concept of principle-based decision-making from the total quality management (TQM) movement is useful to consider here. The point is that it is valuable to instil *principles* of action versus hard rules. The unique situation, the one-off, the decision at the point of invention, makes it hard to know what to do. When faced with the unexpected in life, we pause and ask for expert advice – from our family, accountant, lawyer, priest, shaman, friend or therapist. At work, this means escalating to your boss and talking to colleagues. On the contrary, we often delegate our power to a committee or an executive to sign off. There is not much trust in organisations.

When values are part of an organisation's risk management, the individual is empowered to make a call, to follow the principle. To ask for forgiveness and not permission. It challenges the individual to do the right thing as part of the employment relationship. A practice in one bank was to require executives to take an uninterrupted two-week vacation, during which time they were not allowed to contact the office. The point of this was that if you were running some kind of fraud or other practice that was illegal or broke policy, it might drop in the time that you were away. Furthermore, a colleague would most likely notice any flaw. However, for that person actually to say something would require courage and values. It speaks to the intrinsic (rational and emotional) motivations of the individual. It also acts as a mechanism to deal with and evaluate the hard systems. It aligns across cultures and national states and languages when done well. It delivers a consistent expectation of quality of behaviour and decision-making – regardless of language barriers. There is an economy of scale as everyone speaks the language; there is an operational agility benefit.

CONGRUENCE BREEDS CONFIDENCE

It is so basic but maybe one of the most important themes in the book. Will you do what you say, will you deliver on the promise, do you mean what you say? Will you act on the things that you say are important and take the pain of the decision when it means discomfort?

> **Chris:** At the time of writing, I was facing a challenging life decision involving some close family friends which required me to look at and question the values I hold dear and won't compromise on. At work, I had a new major phase of a project approaching. I had a choice of how I led this piece of work: how should I involve others, with whom I shared power and information? How should I best make that decision? How should I lead my team? If I didn't share power, I might get it done faster and get it right. What should I do?
>
> Critical-analytic, data-based decisions only get us so far. At the end of the day, our values, principles, who we are, guides whatever the right answer is. If we pay attention to the decisions that the organisation and its individuals make, and the values that they imply, we practise effective risk.

This realisation of values as part of an essential risk framework is vital to grasp. It underpins the congruence required for long-term culture enablement. The lack of attention to the relative importance of thinking through aspects of risk builds a lack of belief or thoughts in what future work will mean. In this case, we want a share-based organisation, one that is empathic and provides the basic promises of protection and safety; and where employees can and will share freely. To uphold policy to do well rests on the voice of the executive in particular to think through risk and manage effectively. Failure to do so completely undermines all the speeches, the fine words, the posters and campaign mugs created in typical change efforts.

When there is alignment of risk considerations with cultural intent, it starts to breed confidence across all sectors:
- the individual worker;
- the team;
- the government (regulators);
- the customers and clients;
- the public;
- society at large.

If there is consistency in what you promise and what you actually do, this is always enabled by values as a core part of risk management. It can restore confidence to deal with the luminous cat scenario – this is the only way to ensure that confidence is given back to sectors of industry that progress quickly with technology.

Values are at the heart of all that we do when we make decisions. They mitigate risk. They build reputation and brand. They act as a safeguard for executives and management and the non-executive directors as *the* core safeguard against rogue behaviour. Good risk management enables the brand promise.

Risk management is weakly practised and, unfortunately, seldom associated with effective change practices.

SECTION THREE

CASE THEORY

STRATEGY

'没有规矩，不成方圆' (Nothing can be accomplished without norms or standards)

— Mencius, 372–289 BC

'Any company that embraces the status quo is on a collision course with time'

— Howard Schultz, former CEO of Starbucks

In this chapter:
- why the 'how' of strategy is as important as the outcome;
- strategy as a network and not hierarchy approach.

To envision a workplace that is truly based on 'shared' principles, we chose the STAR Model, one of the popular organisational design models by Jay Galbraith, to illustrate key elements of a new type of organisation.[1] There are many models that offer a systemic approach to designing an effective organisation, but we think this is the simplest. These models align the structure, rewards, behaviours, processes and strategies – they guide us holistically as we seek to create a share-based organisation.

We decided to group the *tangible*, often rational elements – strategy, structure and processes – into this chapter; and talk about the *intangible*, sometimes people-centric elements, such as reward, in a separate one (see Chapter 14).

RETHINKING THE TOP-DOWN STRUCTURE

Linda: I was at a company's annual strategic planning offsite event where one of the topics was about developing new product for urban-minded millennial customers. It was obvious that the majority of the senior management team, who were white, male, in their fifties and had always lived in the suburbans, found it difficult to relate to the very customers they desperately wanted to attract (urban, diverse, mobile, Gen Y and Gen Z). Those executives had spent decades working together through the ranks of their company. They knew each other's views and positions so well that they could almost finish each other's sentences. They stopped challenging certain long-held assumptions because 'It is just the way we do business.'

This probably sounds familiar. The overall direction of a company is often created by a small team of senior executives and experts who are supposed to know better than the ordinary employees. Annual strategic planning, where this is still done, is a ritual and expansive exercise that involves only those at the top of the corporate food chain. In some instances, the invitation to the exclusive group becomes a status symbol – one company I know calls it 'Chairman's Circle', and people openly judge others by whether or not they belong to the 'in group'.

There is a basic assumption in this approach that the hierarchy of titles represents the hierarchy of information, so the bosses know better through aggregating all the information from underneath. After all, the higher you go, the farther you see, no?

However, in a digital age, when information is coming from everywhere and the vast majority of information is often neglected due to overload, employees at all levels can access and process the same intelligence, with a more immediate and direct perspective. They are also connected more than ever to converse, exchange and collaborate through networks, online platforms and virtual workgroups. As Sun Tzu observed in *The Art of War*, 'Three cobblers together are smarter than a genius strategy.'[2] This is an age of democratised information.

We have an image in our minds of what it means to have information and data in our new possibility: it is a cloud filled with endless individual nodes of lights. What all management books, gurus and models have functioned to create to date has been on the premise of the vertical organisation. Power running up and down, a hierarchy. A more effective pyramid has been the goal. Now we need to imagine that each node of light can be empowered to shine, through the power of its connections and influence. We instead look at the power of networks. We think of this as a 'Galaxy' model, each node a star in a system that needs to be ignited.

A network is the anchor point of future structure design. This is not a straight shift. The current model and associated power memes have been in place for our entire organisational history. It will be disrupted. We see the old structures disrupted around us through social media that enables the horizontal and not just the hierarchical. The shift to a new state of structure will follow experiments and many failures until it provides as effective a system as the current model of hierarchy power to drive efficiency. We enter a period of transitions in structures. We will be in chaos for a period. So how we think about strategy being a thing that is top down has to change first, and maybe before any other aspect of how we do things.

> **There are three ways companies can adjust their top-down strategic planning process:**
> 1 Look for 'bright spots' in unusual places.
> 2 Add diversity into the mix.
> 3 Create the right environment.

'Bright spots' and 'unusual suspects'
Let's start with the periphery of the enterprise. Often undeterred by red tape and politics, driven by a lack of resources and thus the need to improvise, those places become hotbeds for entrepreneurial inclinations and innovative ideas. In fact, multiple evidence suggests that the most brilliant ideas are generated from unexpected places (mailroom, call centre, far-flung post in a small country, etc.).

Diversity in decision-making
The City Council of Barcelona used a collaborative approach and crowdsourced a sharing economy policy framework co-working with a range of stakeholders, including municipal officials, residents and sectors (socially inclusive co-operatives, foundations and enterprises based on open source or open data). Four hundred people attending a three-day event generated 120 policy recommendations, 80 per cent of which were selected by *Decidim Barcelona*, a participatory democratic platform for citizens to provide feedback to municipal policies and became Barcelona's collaborative economic plan. For a city with a long-held tradition of democracy, it seems a no-brainer that all citizens should be included and have their voices heard in policy formation. Can companies learn from this?

Some companies recognised the collective power of brains and tried to reap the benefits by extending an open invitation to employees into the process. Open-source software development companies are pioneers in this regard. In his 1990 book *The Cathedral & the Bazaar*, Eric S. Raymond compared different software development methods and proclaimed Linus's Law:[3] 'Given enough eyeballs, all bugs are shallow'; in other words, the more widely available the source code is for public testing, scrutiny and experimentation, the more rapidly all forms of bugs will be discovered.

Other companies have purposefully invited the opinions of minority groups such as Gen X and Y and new joiners. Multinational companies with a pressing need for international business expansion in particular need to hear from the periphery of the company – where people tend to be more creative due to fewer resources but also are less likely to reject ideas that don't immediately fit with the company's dominant framework of thinking. As the old Chinese saying goes: 'A general out on a mission has to adapt the orders from the emperor.'

Create the right environment
Just bringing the outside views in is not enough. Senior executives must ensure they create the conditions for the different perspectives to be truly heard and incorporated into strategy making.

> **Linda:** I was once involved in a study of future industry trends for a large company. Seventeen young leaders across different businesses spent months on a presentation to the top executive team. Following the presentation, instead of asking questions or engaging in a discussion, the executives judged the findings as 'impractical' and 'not solving the company's top issues' and they dismissed them summarily. It was no surprise that after that people went back to their old ways of doing things and there was no 'future' talk any more.

What happened here? The fixed mindset of much established management has wasted a great opportunity to discover and unleash the creativity within their organisations. As Gary Hamel, a professor at London Business School, who has written extensively on the topic of strategic planning, said: 'Democracy is not simply about the right to be heard; it is about the opportunity to influence opinion and action.'[4] So don't let your impulse of 'That wouldn't work' or 'That's not the way we do things here' stop you.

Similarly, in any organisation there will be internal noises and even disapproval about the 'chaos' a non-traditional approach espouses. We believe that a pattern always arises from the apparent chaos.

> **Chris:** I was an only child growing up in Guyana. You learn to play on your own. Many days, I would sit and listen to the forest birds, the monkeys, the dogs and the unseen things that rustle. After sitting in a forest for a while – and many of you who venture into woods will know this – you start to hear the rhythm and the conversations happening around you. It's the same if you sit in a park in the city or a busy railway station: you see the flow and hear what the world is talking about. To begin any strategy, to become something different, it is important to immerse yourself in the environment that you want to change and understand it. We are then able to fully listen to all of our senses and use the collective shared wisdom from the randomness of our environment to understand the emerging patterns.

Though it is impossible to see the end from the beginning, an open and inclusive process of strategy creation substantially lessens the challenge of implementation. Because only a handful of people have been involved in the creation of strategy and only a few key executives share a conviction about the way forward, implementation is often more difficult than it need be. Thus, *planning* and *intent* are required to mitigate that risk.

Multiple extra steps are often added to a project (e.g. getting 'buy-in' and building an 'advocate' group), all geared towards getting what is in the heads of the bosses into the heads of the workers. In contrast, when several hundred employees share the task of identifying and synthesising a set of unconventional strategic options, the conclusions become almost inevitable. In such a process, the senior managers' task is less to 'sell' the strategy than to ensure that the organisation acts on the convictions that emerge. The participants start to share their new insight and conviction virally. How often does the planning process start with senior executives asking what the rest of the organisation can teach them (share) about the future? Not often enough.

BEYOND STRATEGY

Some companies have gone even further to extrapolate the 'open' approach to determine who runs the company. One example is Red Hat, a software company founded by the ex-CEO of Delta Airlines, Jim Whitehurst. At Red Hat, instead of automatically deferring to managers high up in the chain of command to decide the direction the company is going in, they opt for transparent processes, open feedback from everyone and decision-making as a group. Meritocracy is part of the everyday business language and underpins every people-related decision. Employees who earn the right to be listened to can develop a career of 'achievement' (vs. 'advancement') and can act as informal influencers who set company strategy.

We encourage the ongoing dialogue about the direction of the organisation not to be an annual process linked to the calendar or the budget, but, rather, a continuous process where information is shared, where people are involved and listened to. This process will look different in every organisation, but the core principle is the same: *share and be agile*. Or consciously choose not to be – but be aware that that is a choice that you can make without going to the expense of employing consultants.

NOTES

1 Galbraith, J.R., and A. Kates. *Designing Your Organization: Using the STAR Model to Solve 5 Critical Design Challenges*. San Francisco: Jossey-Bass, 2007.

2 Sun Tzu. *The Art of War – Special Edition* (1st annotated English ed.) (L. Giles, trans.). El Paso: Digital Pulse Inc., 2007.

3 Raymond, E.S. *The Cathedral & the Bazaar: Musings on Linus and Open Source by an Accidental Revolutionary*. Sebastopol: O'Reilly Media, 2001.

4 Hamel, G. 'Strategy as revolution', *Harvard Business Review,* July–Aug 1996, pp. 70–75.

STRUCTURE

'If I negate powdered wigs, I am still left with unpowdered wigs'

– Karl Marx[1]

> **In this chapter:**
> • context and trends in organisational structures and the impact that structure has on relationships, mindset and ways of working;
> • imagery, imagination and the move from 'pyramids' to 'cells'.

In Chapter 7 we reviewed Barry Oshry's thesis on 'top-middle-bottom' in its simplest term of organisational structure. Most modern corporations are much more complex than that – but still, in our experience, they all fall into this hierarchy. The key insight is that how I see you is the reflective result of the relationships we fall into.

HIERARCHY AND MATRIX MODELS

The traditional organisational structure that is still predominant today was based on models from the Roman army, which formalised ranks in a hierarchical structure. In the first industrial revolution, the

Church and Navy were held up as predominant models of how people thought about organising. In this structure, employees usually have clearly defined tasks and accumulate experience from performing those tasks again and again, developing functional 'expertise' or 'competencies'. Titles and job levels denote differences in power and authority.

Decision-making strictly follows the protocol of 'decision rights', i.e. who gets to decide, approve and provide inputs, or simply who is to be informed. To co-ordinate across units or functions, processes are put in place and paperwork mounts, hence the bureaucracy. Such a system requires clarity, communication and precision in execution; even then, exceptions or mistakes happen, thus slowing down decision-making or creating bottlenecks.

Dedicated business units are responsible for a company's products and markets. Independent functional departments co-ordinate pools of specialists who are in theory 'assigned' to and 'partnering' with business units, but in reality are often handcuffed by their own functional agendas in the name of 'standards' and 'consistency'.

The problem is that the hierarchical model naturally disempowers individuals and reinforces the 'boss' culture. When large corporations started going global in the 1970s, to deal with the complexity brought by managing resources and operations across a portfolio of products, functions and countries, a single chain of command proved to be insufficient to ensure that managers balanced multiple priorities and conflicting interests. Many enterprises then adopted the matrix organisation structure.

In projecting its organisation over the next 10 years, GE management stated in its *Organization Planning Bulletin* (September 1976)[2]:

We've highlighted matrix organization. Not because it's a bandwagon that we want you all to jump on, but rather that it's a complex, difficult, and sometimes frustrating form of organization to live with. It's also, however, a bellwether of things to come. But, when implemented well, it does offer much of the best of both worlds. And all of us are going to have to learn how to utilize organization to prepare managers to increasingly deal with high levels of complexity and ambiguity in situations where they have to get results from people and components not under their direct control.

GE was right – matrixes often do not work, because of the nature of 'dual command'. The frequently observed problems that plague most matrix organisations include power struggles, too much layering, excessive overheads – all negatively affecting decision-making speed and quality. In times of economic downturns or fast-changing competition, these organisations often fail to respond quickly, ultimately leading to severe consequences.

Most senior individuals in organisations today grew up in and lead these structures, with all of the associated conception of what power and hierarchy means to them. The majority of management jargon is developed in the context of managing such organisations in a predictable, steady-paced environment; for example, 'peers' and 'superiors' implies a level relative to the position of the incumbent.

These organisations were not built for a VUCA world, or to be fast and agile. They are not designed for constant challenge to reinforce accountability through a general sense of limited control. Employees wait for orders instead of being released or empowered; they feel like a cog in the machine, with individual freedom, equality and cultural vitality absent. At a higher management level, a bureaucratic and rigid coalition is often observed that generates lowest-common-denominator outcomes.

Under such conditions, where there are abundant problems to solve, people grumble and voice opinions a lot, but no one lifts a finger to do anything different from what they are told.

There is also a limit to the size and complexity such structure can handle. According to Jay Galbraith, one of the founding fathers of matrix organisation design, matrix seems to function better

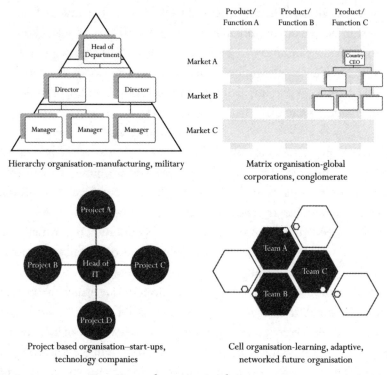

Hierarchy organisation-manufacturing, military

Matrix organisation-global
corporations, conglomerate

Project based organisation–start-ups,
technology companies

Cell organisation-learning, adaptive,
networked future organisation

FIGURE 12.1   Four types of organisational structure.

when no more than 500 managers are involved in dual-reporting lines. This figure coincides with the number of people with whom, anthropologists suggest, humans can develop personal relationships to effectively carry out communication and perform collective tasks.[3]

PROJECT-BASED MODEL

In recent decades, to overcome the inevitable slow pace of hierarchical or matrix structures and their strong tendency towards internal stability, companies started to rely on project *teams* to get things done. Inspiration was drawn from NASA's moon-shot project as a textbook example of co-ordinated functional, geographic and divisional response to deliver a spectacular success.

It is possible to foster a meritocracy-based culture, which is empathic to the individual and the team. Teams could be given a degree of freedom and empowerment with project leads being the central person to cut through bureaucracy. As long as most decisions could be made at the lowest level, things worked and progress was made much faster, especially when there was a clear mission and roles that were most central to delivering the mission were clearly defined and properly resourced.

This is evidently true in early-stage start-ups and some technology companies. It is difficult to realise the full benefit of teams in most established industries because of the inherent complexity and territorial mindset. Even in start-ups, as the teams proliferated, the sense of urgency began to evaporate, teams began to get in each other's way and progress stalled.

CELL MODEL

The future of organised structure will be more like the cellular structure that mimics what happens in biological systems in nature.

In the process, researchers at the Santa Fe Institute have developed some basic rules for 'complex adaptive systems'[4] (see Chapter 7). These systems are among the most successful in nature. Some examples include the ecology of tropical rainforests, colonies of ants and even the human brain.

These systems have several characteristics in common. First, they are 'self-managed' – that is, they consist of a network of 'agents' that act independently of one another and without guidance from any central control. For example, each one of the brain's roughly 100 billion neurons is a kind of miniature chemical computer that follows its own independent pattern of behaviour. Take a neuron out of the brain and it can still function. There is no 'master neuron' or central area of the brain that controls what each neuron does.

Yet these agents are capable of engaging in co-operative behaviour. They can form groups or 'communities' that co-operate in producing higher-order behaviours that no single agent could accomplish on its own. In the brain, each neuron is connected to millions of others. Some communities of neurons, clustered in particular areas of the brain, specialise in functions such as language or visual recognition. It is precisely the *interactions* among neurons that produce human intelligence. For example, the structural difference between individual squid neurons and human neurons is relatively small. However, a human brain not only contains many more neurons than a squid's but also the organisation of its neurons is much more complex and interwoven.

A particular kind of feedback makes self-management possible. In a sense, self-organising systems are learning systems, but of a specific sort. Capable of 'learning' through feedback from the external environment, they also 'embed' that learning in their actual structure. For instance, the more a set of neurons is involved in some piece of mental work – like recognising a face or solving a mathematical problem – the stronger the actual chemical connection among the neurons (and the easier for the brain to make the connection the next time). Indeed, the human brain is for ever reconfiguring the connections between neurons in response to external and internal stimuli.

In this way, self-organising systems constantly rearrange themselves as the effects of previous actions or changes in external conditions ripple through the system. Information is embedded in structure. As external conditions change, the structure of the system automatically changes. In this condition, principles, values and precedence rather than hard and fast rules are the key to success. They account for the new and complex and allow freedom of movement. An inflexible rule brings an impasse when faced with the novel.

Finally, self-management and learning through feedback allow these systems to operate by 'flexible specialisation'. Self-organising systems usually contain an array of specialised behavioural niches occupied by specific agents or groups of agents. However, old niches constantly disappear and new ones are created as the external environment changes. Therefore, agents aren't permanently locked into previously useful behaviours that have since become obsolete, which helps the system as a whole adapt to change. Waldrop notes that self-organising systems tend to change so rapidly and so completely that it becomes meaningless to talk about agents or groups of agents 'optimising' (a term redolent of the nineteenth-century focus on efficiency) their behaviour. Rather, such systems are characterised by what Waldrop calls 'perpetual novelty'.[5]

In general, the complex adaptive systems found in nature contain individual agents that network to create self-managed but highly organised behaviour; respond to feedback from the environment and adjust their behaviour accordingly; learn from experience and embed that learning in the very structure of the system; and enjoy the advantages of specialisation without getting stuck in rigidity. If these characteristics sound familiar, it's because they so closely match the new kind of organisation many managers are struggling to create in order to cope with a more uncertain – and frequently chaotic – business environment.

A PATTERN OF NETWORKS

In a digital environment, being 'Big' is actually a disadvantage, because it means being less agile, less flexible and a bigger target to attack. Small towns across America that have benefited from the rise of corporations have faced grim futures as the same organisations that provided secure employment, comfortable living standards and pensions are grappling with the challenges and baggage that smaller rivals don't have to deal with.

Networks will bring the current computer technology to the next level. One prominent example is Microsoft's $26 billion acquisition of LinkedIn. In an interview with Microsoft CEO Satya Nadella in *Fast Company*, Harry McCracken writes, 'Melding together Microsoft productivity tools with LinkedIn's data about people and their work could make all the services involved richer, [Nadella] says. One example: Microsoft's Dynamics 365 CRM would be a far more potent prospecting tool if it was hooked directly into a salesperson's LinkedIn network.'[6]

Formal and informal networks exist in every organisation. Harnessing these networks in new and different ways can drive dramatic results. This includes identifying 'informal influencers' – those exert disproportionate influence over others regardless of formal titles and job levels.

> **Chris:** In a workforce transformation initiative I was involved in, we met significant resistance. It's one thing to advocate the business case of the transformation objectives, but quite another when an employee impacted by relocation decisions has to go home and tell their children to say goodbye to their best friends.
>
> One thing that finally made a difference in that case was the use of informal influencers to evaluate communication messages and broadcast personal stories and experience that were inspiring to others. Establishing a mechanism (either virtual or in person) whereby people within networks can regularly share experiences and provide two-way real-time feedback on how we were doing also proved to be invaluable.

Leveraging these informal networks effectively can build momentum and energy and even drive self-organisation. We've seen a few advocate groups emerging spontaneously. One team of product managers in an IT function self-organised with a much flatter structure. They built wiki pages to explain their different ways of working and are inviting people from other areas of the organisation in to see how they are doing it and the results that they are getting.

Understanding the consequence of making organisations inefficient or even 'soulless', several prominent management thinkers proposed 'adhocracy' several decades ago as a flexible and informal alternative to bureaucracy:

'Democracy is Inevitable...(Democracy) is the only system that can successfully cope with the changing demands of contemporary civilization' – Warren Bennis and Philip Slater[7]

'In an era of accelerating change, organizations, and national economies, most likely to succeed are those with the ability to adjust and adapt. Robert H. Waterman Jr...shows how and what this sort of innovation must become a way of life for business organizations across the board. What is needed is an environment that fosters the use of an ad-hoc problem-solving technique, in effect an adhocracy that functions outside the often initiative-stifling bureaucracy' – Summary for Robert Waterman Jr's *Adhocracy:The Power to Change*[8]

When comparing adhocracy with a meritocracy-based organisation model, the key differences lie between priorities and personal motivation for workers. Meritocracy encourages the free flow of ideas through debate and discussion; adhocracy focuses on actionable opportunities or problems. Meritocracy creates experts of the subject through personal mastery, while adhocracy recognises the importance of trial and error and team effort.[9] In an information-overload age, a meritocratic approach of collecting more and more data endlessly in search of perfectly informed decisions is more detrimental than the bureaucratic approach of deferring to a senior colleague; because time is of the essence in today's world, the test-learn-adjust cycle is vital in order to respond to fickle customer demands and fast-moving market trends. Using real-time and widely sourced data to experiment – to try a course of action, receive feedback, make changes and review progress.

Legendary GE CEO Jack Welch wrote in the company's 1990 annual report, 'Our dream for the 1990s is a boundary less company...where we knock down the walls that separate us from each other on the inside and from our key constituencies on the outside.' Thirty years later, any company with the help of technology could transform itself by removing communication barriers among traditional functions, sharing resources and capabilities between domestic and foreign operations, and ignoring or erasing group labels such as 'management', 'salaried' or 'hourly', which get in the way of people working together. The same is true for every large organisation.[10]

A group of companies is turning to self-governing via committees and consensus, including Compagnie Financière Richemont, whose businesses include Cartier and Van Cleef & Arpels; DPR Construction and Peakon, a new human-resources software company. DPR's 4,000 employees feel free to propose ideas and make decisions on their own. Veteran leaders – like Doug Woods, now a board member – rotate off its eight-member management committee gradually and continue to advise current members, keeping the direction of the company consistent.

'Putting in hierarchy reduces collaboration,' said Daniel Rogers, a co-founder of Peakon, a two-year-old human-resources technology company with offices in Copenhagen and London.[11] Leaders there felt that bestowing the CEO title upon one person could breed infighting among junior employees or stall the flow of ideas. Instead, a six-person management team meets regularly to settle big issues facing the company.

Earlier in 2016, a crowdsourced investment fund called DAO, an acronym for a decentralised autonomous organisation, launched as a fully autonomous business without human leaders. Instead, investors put up digital currency in exchange for special tokens allowing them to vote where to allocate money. The fund raised $252 million in the spring, but shut down in June after a hacker siphoned off $55 million. The funds were eventually recovered and investors got all their money back, said Stephan Tual, CEO of Slock. it, the German tech company that helped write the code for DAO.

SUMMARY

Hierarchies used to dominate the corporate world, but the landscape is fast changing. Most companies have informal teams and networks to supplement that traditional top-down structure. Others formalise teams of teams as a way of connecting, communicating and collaborating.

The world we are entering into is increasingly complex with all these legacy, hybrid and innovative structures co-existing. The implications for leaders and executives are far-flung. It requires them to develop new skills such as constantly scanning for the unexpected, negotiating complex agreements, accelerating learning curves and learning from mistakes or failures, and becoming adept at fostering trusting relationships across diverse groups and among established and temporary teams. Central to the effective functioning of teams is this idea of perpetual feedback and the seeking of perspective. The role of the individuals and leaders is most critical, so the organisational design practice of simply changing the structure without considering the change in behaviour and perception required is doomed.

We suggest the following to enable the share-based, empathic organisation:

- ensure that middle managers have values and principles well established in their mind and not hard and fast rules – this has to be linked to a sense of higher purpose;
- build curiosity and feedback skills;
- work to mitigate power issues directly where they obviously arise in the design of any new structure;
- design organisations as cells and networks rather than pyramids. The very act of drawing from a mindset of sharing and information flow and not power and hierarchy as the key principle for creating different pictures. Then think about how to make that pretty pattern of networks work.

NOTES

1 Marx, K. *Introduction to Critique of Hegel's Philosophy of Right*, 1844.

2 Stanley, M.D. and Lawrence, P.R. 'Problems of matrix organizations', *Harvard Business Review*, May 1978.

3 Galbraith, J.R. 'The Star Model'. http://www.jaygalbraith.com/images/pdfs/StarModel.pdf. Accessed 28 January 2016.

4 Waldrop, M.M. *Complexity: The Emerging Science at the Edge of Order and Chaos*. New York: Simon & Schuster, 1992.

5 Ibid.

6 McCracken, H. 'Satya Nadella on Microsoft's new age of intelligence', *Fast Company*, 2016. https://www.fastcompany.com/3064030/satya-nadella-on-microsofts-new-age-of-intelligence. Accessed 11 November 2017.

7 Slater, P., and Bennis, W. 'Democracy is inevitable', *Harvard Business Review*, September/October 1990.

8 Waterman, R.H. *Adhocracy: The Power to Change* (book summary). New York: W. W. Norton, 1993.

9 Birkinshaw, J., and Ridderstråle, J. 'Adhocracy for an agile age', *McKinsey Quarterly*, December 2015. https://www.mckinsey.com/business-functions/organization/our-insights/adhocracy-for-an-agile-age. Accessed 5 February 2016.

10 Davis, S.M., and Lawrence, P.R. 'Problems of matrix organizations', *Harvard Business Review*, 1 May 1978, p. 1.

11 Feintzeig, R. 'Companies manage with no CEO', *Wall Street Journal*, 13 December 2016. https://www.wsj.com/articles/companies-manage-with-no-ceo-1481641203. Accessed 20 March 2017.

13

CAPABILITIES

'十年植树，百年育人' (It takes 10 years to plant a tree and it takes a hundred years to teach a person)
— Chinese proverb

In this chapter:
- the importance of building new capabilities in a networked organisation;
- why the conventional approach of simply setting the vision is not enough to enable widespread change;
- examples of developing hands-on capabilities in actions confirmed by neuroscience.

Linda: This is my favourite chapter, not only because of my profession and geeky interest in the topic, but also because of my self-identity as a lifelong learner and student of leadership. I've worked for some great organisations with longevity — collectively, the most recent four companies have been around for more than 500 years. They are in different industries and headquartered in different countries. They all share two important traits: investment in people and focus on knowledge development.

In the age we are now in, when AI is set to replace between 30 and 50 per cent of jobs, yet governments, educational institutions and corporates have not come together to find solutions for re-skilling our current workforce, talking about capabilities carries added urgency.

INTERPLAY OF PEOPLE, CULTURE AND ORGANISATION

This link between people capability, culture (the way we do and talk about things) and organisational capability is taken by many organisational scholars to be the true engine that delivers sustainable competitive advantage. The premise is that the way a company organises internally, including its people practices, is much harder for competitors to copy than pricing and marketing. The key is to be deliberate about which capabilities a company invests in and develops to meet changing customer demand and also aligns processes from recruitment to reward, from talent identification to continuous learning, etc. – all geared towards developing those differentiating capabilities. When we think back on ancient civilisations, we think of their practices, art and conquests as interplay. What we do, how we do it and how we talk about it are all the same thing.

Though this concept was raised in the nineties, it is still relevant in today's gig economy context, if not more so. Two economists, Lawrence F. Katz and Alan B. Krueger, found that all net employment growth in the United States since 2005 appears to have come from what they termed 'alternative work' – that is, contract and freelance work, which has ballooned by more than 50 per cent over the last decade. When most basic standard capabilities can be bought, companies need to be extra clear about what differentiates.[1]

> **Linda:** I led a digital transformation effort for a large financial services company. The first step the project team took was a culture survey filled by executives, middle managers and front-line leaders. We asked them to reflect on current

prevailing leadership styles, how their teams responded to those leadership behaviours, and to propose where they would like to see change in order to adapt to an agile way of working and faster-paced decision making. All three groups identified a significant gap lay in the mindset and soft skills.

We identified six cultural skills that represented the gap between where we are and where we want to be:
- *risk acceptance/mitigation*. To understand and capture opportunities, not to use as an aversion technique;
- *data-driven decisions*. Our business is increasingly being disrupted by predictive analysis and data insights at an aggregated level, thanks to the Internet of Things. Our gut and experience are no longer enough;
- *flexibility*. Things change and so must we. Past performance is not indicative of future results;
- *prioritisation*. We can't do everything, so where do we focus attention?
- *measurement and monitoring*. We need to know the desired outcome so that we can monitor achievement;
- *talent management*. The right people with the right behaviours in the right roles.

These were the skills that the company leaders were not confident they had. These were the cultural reflexes (habits), the capability that we needed to exhibit quickly. It was difficult to quantify – it became the focus of the leadership team's attention when they sought to change behaviours and culture. That was by far the most difficult part of any change programme and required a strong execution paradigm to have a chance of success. Over time, the new leadership styles and behaviours enabled a fast-sharing environment where stories were told and concepts shaped.

Assuming we have clarified which capabilities to develop, there is often a strong desire to jump into solutioning. In the past, HR, particularly learning functions, has developed an unhelpful reputation for being the 'order takers'; i.e. we can be too tied down by 'learning objectives' and 'needs analysis'; once we figure those out, we either develop the training ourselves or call a vendor we know to get it done. We are the experts, aren't we?

Take the example of HR transforming itself in recent years – we know solving this is not as simple as having an expert standing in front of the room and telling everyone, 'You all need to think more strategically about the business'; or providing a series of processes or a slick tool to suddenly change the way we think or partner with business leaders. Although these sound attractive, they only solve the superficial layer of the problem.

A different way to approach learning and capability development is to go back to basics by focusing on the end users through design thinking – who are we developing the learning experience for? And in implementation, heavily leverage imagination and habits – two of the most powerful ways human brains are wired to learn and to improve performance.

DESIGN THINKING
If you are hosting a dinner, you start with an understanding of your guests – who they are, where they are from, what kinds of flavours they prefer, what they do or don't eat, and so on. Once you determine a cuisine that will delight your guests' taste, a main dish and complementary side dishes, you will probably check your fridge and decide what you need to buy, or swap. Developing people solutions shouldn't be any different. When it comes to developing new solutions for on-boarding, learning, performance support and engagement, more and more companies find simply asking their employees 'Are you happy with the (current) programmes?' or 'What do you want in the (new) programmes?' is not effective.

A big trend is borrowing the concept of *design thinking* from the art industry to deepen the understanding of the users – in this case, employees – and their profiles, needs, challenges and assumptions.

There are two eminent features in design thinking: empathetic and iterative.

Empathetic

Design thinking focuses on users and their day-to-day experience with deep empathy and genuine interest in understanding their world and challenges versus telling them what to do differently.

> **Linda:** A large professional services firm that I worked for grappled with engagement and retention challenges at lower tenure levels. The attrition was much higher for employees who joined the firm within two years than other groups. After some focus groups, the management determined to redesign its employee on-boarding programme. The project team started with the mindset such as 'Our current programme doesn't do a good job of "selling" the organisation to new joiners. We want people to understand the opportunities they have if they stay with us.'
>
> It conducted empathy interviews by asking questions like:
>
> - what do you say when friends or family ask you what you do?
> - what did you have to learn the 'hard way'?
> - how soon did you understand what it would take for you to succeed in the company?
>
> The stories surprised everyone. It was evident that new employees were so focused on staffing and chargeability that they were missing opportunities to create their own long-term success in the organisation. The focus of the programme changed from selling the benefits of the

organisation to better setting expectations for how new employees could create a niche, build a legitimate network and seek out ways to gradually affect the business, instead of immediately going after project work.

Iterative

Have you ever been in a situation where you felt that to a hammer every problem is a nail? Or been in a brainstorming session but felt every proposed 'idea' was the solution you knew would be implemented from the start? Or someone said something dramatically differently, the room went silent, then people brushed the idea aside because it would take too much time to discuss it?

There are certain unconscious biases that neuroscience has proved our brains tend to fall prey to, including *confirmation bias* (reverse-rationalising a known result), *recency bias* (what happened last time?) and *consensus bias* that leads to group thinking. Settling into consensus too early in the process or endlessly searching for the perfect answer can compromise the quality of decisions, whereas an iterative approach consisting of several short 'sprints' could be more effective.

TACTICAL TIPS – LINDA

In the past, I facilitated design-thinking sessions for leadership development. The first session went well, with a group of pre-selected high-performing, high-potential leaders. For the second session, we didn't apply the filters of performance rating and nine-box rating while pulling out the name list from the HR management system and ended up with a much more mixed audience. This session was more challenging – at times, I felt that we hit dead ends or I was running out of ways to lift the negativity and help people see a way forward, but in the end we exposed more systemic challenges than the previous session when 'things go well', such as lack of transparency in performance evaluation, micromanaging...Other tactical tips include:

- *structure exercises to encourage safe sharing of ideas.* I ask participants to talk with their neighbours before reporting back to the whole group; sometimes, they interview other participants in a 'speed dating' fashion and report back themes – anything that minimises the awkwardness of public speaking and fear of being wrong is happily tried;
- *keep a high level of energy.* I use music, set time limits and encourage physical movements to keep the ideas flowing. This is really a volume play, so the focus is on speed, not quality (that comes later);
- *avoid 'expert opinions'.* The key to innovation is resisting judgement. I tell the participants several times throughout the session that there is no right or wrong answer.

SIMULATION

In a 1998 report designed to train officers for the twenty-first century, the US Army War College presaged a world that is 'volatile, uncertain, complex, and ambiguous' (VUCA).[2] Simulation was also created by the military as a cornerstone of executing strategic goals effectively – what does it entail to take that hill? What if the enemy has a countermove? – all played out in a scenario and practised again and again.

Thomas Hout, a former partner at the Boston Consulting Group, cited celebrated fighter pilot John Boyd's work on developing strategy as a continuous mental loop he called OODA (observe, orient, decide, act), describing how winning pilots sized up the dynamics of each new encounter, read its opportunities, decided what to do and acted before their opponents could. As a result, they could take control of the dogfight, pre-empt the opposition's

moves and throw the enemy plane into a confused reactive spiral.[3]
By adopting his mindset (with a particular emphasis on the two Os,
given our turbulent context), we can get much better at making
learning effective through a series of experiments.

Have you ever watched kids in the process of learning? They pick
up toys and objects and naturally start putting them together and
testing how they can use their new creation. If it falls apart, they
have at least learned something and will try a different approach.
They also love to 'tell' other kids what they have learned and share
their experience. David Kolb's experiential learning theory (ELT)
defined an individual's learning process as the combination of
experience, cognition, behaviour and perception. By putting the
learner in an active role and involving them in sharing, collaborating
and joint problem solving, they not only learn faster but also enjoy
the process, which leads to sustained interest levels and prolonged
memory of the new knowledge.[4]

We all know people who swear by 'learning by doing'. Now it
is proven by science that this could be one of the best ways for
people to learn. Adding the social aspect to it, this is a powerful
formula. Interacting with one another is collaboration; it is a fact
that co-operation enhances knowledge, resources and capabilities
to perform tasks.

> **Linda:** A technology service company I once consulted for
> had a series of client skill programmes that everyone loved.
> It used heavy role-playing of simulated client scenarios.
> When it was first launched, they even videotaped role play
> and would play it back in feedback sessions. Huge impact.
> The execs believed the client scenarios were the most
> valuable part of the programmes, so in a cost-cutting
> exercise it transformed that content into virtual learning
> materials and provided it to employees online. The uptake
> and satisfaction of learners significantly dropped. A quick
> survey uncovered that what people enjoyed the most was

coming together and being immersed in peer coaching – the opportunity of learning from each other while building commandership and their networks. Past participants vividly described their experience as, 'looking at each other in the eye and telling the uncomfortable truth to help the other person grow.'

HABITS

Habits shape our lives across work, home and play. Many daily 'decisions' are based on habit versus conscious thought. Habits help the brain conserve energy by running on 'autopilot' so it can be freed up for other logical activities. Habits create a reward in the brain that makes them compelling.

> **Linda:** Growing up, I was a chubby kid and was bullied at school. Now I'm 30 pounds lighter than when I was 13. Most of my body transformation was no secret – swap cookies for fruit, eat smaller portions, do some form of exercise on most days...It took me 10 years to form the right habits so that my food choices and workout regime became second nature.
>
> Take digitalisation as another example. Some executives admit, 'Digitalisation creates incredible opportunities but also incredible fear inside the organisation.' Others wonder 'How do you make everyone feel there is a real revolution going on? Constructive destruction.' So, a deeper question is: 'What is your people's role in the future, and how do you break it down into bite-size actions and repeat those over a long period of time for small actions to turn into big results?'
>
> Yet, longer-term initiatives, such as branding, slipped through the cracks as the management team focused on immediate matters, such as sales numbers. Sometimes a

CEO with a special mandate is hired to keep the management team on track, compile metrics and structure the team's meetings. Does this ring a bell? When was the last time you obsessed with the number on the scale when embarking on a weight-loss programme instead of focusing on long-term wellbeing?

Unless there is transfer of knowledge that results in sustained behavioural change, we cannot say that learning has occurred. But in order for people to learn, we have also to deal with the phenomenon of forgetting.

USE THE CROWD

By breaking a habit down to several micro-behaviours, crowd-sourcing micro-behaviours through hackathon interventions and developing a list of micro-behaviours that link to leadership principle and support company culture, businesses have dialogues to determine what they want to focus on and practise. In their standing business meetings they have further dialogues about how they are achieving as a team.

We believe in listening to the crowd. The crowd will say the things that you don't want to hear. It is better to know than to not know. One of the gifts that data from crowdsourced solutions brings is an ability to move the focus from the leader to the group. When a group is able to identify the issues, the solutions and own the actions in a shared manner, we see significantly better results.

DRIVING BEHAVIOURS

Bad habits can block the way of transformation. One regional business had a hackathon to discuss 'What got you here won't get you there!' These are not flaws of skills, intelligence or personality.

Most of those that were identified were interpersonal or leadership behaviours, such as collaboration overload, passing judgement, lack of active listening, punishing the messenger. The talent and learning team then ran a weekly podcast on each behaviour to explain the negative consequences and the tactics required to recognise and overcome unproductive behaviour.

If we were asked to build a strategy for an organisation, the first thing to consider is what is a capability. It is habit, a competence, a body of knowledge or the way that particularly works with something. In the case of driving a more empathic and sharing culture, we have to be as rigorous and deliberate in picking the right habits to enable the new needed capability as we would a sales or CRM process.

If asked to create a new habit, we would not design a training programme. We know from clinical practice in the resolution of bad habit formation (drug and alcohol abuse, phobias) what tends to work. We now have the benefit of advances in neuroscience that enable us to make long-term habitual change to members of our society that need help. It is not the purpose of this book to provide a robust overview of the constantly adapting work from clinical practice or neuroscience. It is to point a large arrow to that body of work and suggest strongly that change practice in organisations (and wider societies).

Why would organisations not directly pursue new practices that work better? *Cui bono* (who benefits) is the concept used in criminal and financial crime. Who benefits from capability not being exploited in the most direct way and with the latest that science and practice has to offer? It does not appear to be in the interests of any of the stakeholders. In English criminal law, there are the concepts of *mens rea* (criminal intent or knowledge) and *actus reus* (wrongful act) – both have to be proven for crime to be proven. The guilt of the act without the intention is criminal negligence. Given that the importance of creating competitive capability and driving behaviours is so neglected, it is in our opinion negligent on the part of those charged with creating new competitive capability for their organisations to survive. We know the language seems strong, but the neglect of good practice in this area seems 'criminal'.

NOTES

1   Katz, L.F. et al. *The Rise and Nature of Alternative Work Arrangements in the United States*. Princeton: Princeton University and NBER, 2016.

2   Bennett, N., and G.J. Lemoine. 'What VUCA really means for you', *Harvard Business Review*, January/February 2014, pp. 3–4.

3   Hammonds, K.H. 'The strategy of the fighter pilot', *Fast Company*, June 2002.

4   Sternberg, R.J., and Zhang, L.F. (eds). *Perspectives on Cognitive, Learning and Thinking Styles*. Mahwah, NJ: Lawrence Erlbaum, 2000.

14

REWARD

'There is more hunger for love and appreciation in this world than for bread'

— Mother Teresa

'Brains, like hearts, go where they are appreciated'
— Robert McNamara, former US Secretary of Defence

In this chapter:
- greed and inequality exacerbated by current trends in executive compensation and the concept of reward;
- trend in gender pay gap;
- reward strategy in a share-based economy.

It is difficult to believe that 'initiative' and 'incentive' are actually quite old management concepts. They were both invented at the same time that Frederick Taylor declared management itself should be a science. An Internet search on 'pay for performance' generates over 200 million results. An enormous amount of research has been developed to understand what really makes employees tick, not to mention all the money that has been spent on crafting and fine-tuning incentive systems to drive differentiated employee effort and performance results.

There has been a constant tension and shift in thinking between directly influencing those outcomes through careful design of performance metrics or influencing the 'hearts' of employees so that they are self-motivated to do more. Traditional management by and large held the view that managers should exercise coercion; for example, in Taylor's opinion, part of managers' responsibilities was to understand the processes of how work gets done by breaking them down into isolated parts (the 'scientific' way of management) and regularly raising piece rates once most workers met them, in order to boost productivity. But once workers realised his intent, they quickly became smarter – they intentionally limited their output in order not to keep the established output stable, and they learned to work in large groups to exert more negotiating power over management. We still see this in frequent industrial actions in heavily unionised industries such as manufacturing, transport and public services.

After the last industrial revolution, productivity soared and the pay gap between those with or without a college education widened quickly. Professional, white-collar jobs mushroomed to support new industries heavily reliant on the creativity and knowledge power of those jobholders. For the next half century or so, our society inculcated in us this belief that if we are smart, ambitious and hard-working enough, we should be 'successful'; and 'success' is largely determined by how big the pay cheque is. It becomes okay for someone who is managing other people's work to be paid significantly more than those who actually create the output.

EXECUTIVE COMPENSATION

Traditional executive compensation pays for loyalty and longevity. Often this is known as golden handcuffs. For a long period after the Second World War, the majority of executives, regardless of their seniority, were paid similarly; the key differentiator is tenure. In the

1990s, it started to benchmark with external markets, driving up executive pay significantly. From 1978 to 2017, CEO compensation increased 979 per cent (based on stock options granted) or 1,070 per cent (based on stock options realised); a rise more than double stock market growth and substantially greater than the 11.2 per cent growth in a typical worker's compensation over the same period, according to Economic Policy Institute, a liberal think tank[1]. Other executive pay packages follow suit with that of CEOs and increasingly have a higher portion of stock options; nowadays the average is about 60 per cent.

There is a fundamental problem with paying top executives not based on how well their *companies* are doing, but how well the *stock markets* are doing. Resent research identifies a strong correlation between 'the CEO's concerns for the current stock price to reductions in real investment'.[2] In other words, executives and shareholders are more interesting in *vesting (equity)* v. *investing*.

The most outrageous practice is stock buybacks. US companies spend billions of dollars buying back their own shares to artificially create demand thus drive the price up. This means less funds available for investing in research and development, training for employees or increasing salaries and wages. The damage is double-folded, i.e. less investment to drive productivity and exacerbating income inequality, one that is the worst the US has seen in the last 30 years since the Great Depression.

Two Duke University economists, Philip Cook and Robert Frank, documented the growing prevalence of the 'winner-take-all markets'. They explained that these are 'markets in which a handful of top performers walk away with the lion's share of total rewards'. This may always have been common in entertainment and professional sport, but in the last 20 years or so it has permeated many other industries, particularly those knowledge-based professions that are the backbone of the modern economy, including law, journalism, consultancy, investment banking, creative design and even academia.

Within companies, this uneven distribution of wealth further creates psychological illusion, a phenomenon called 'reality distortion field'. Those at the top think they must be capable, because they are paid so much. They disconnect with people/front-line leaders, who are disappointed with perceived unfairness and favouritism, etc. 'Loyalty' becomes 'fealty' – the old feudal tenant practice of swearing unswerving loyalty to their lord. People are not compelled to put their best ideas forward if it means challenging the status quo or putting their jobs at risk. Change becomes even more difficult.

PAY TRANSPARENCY AND FAIRNESS

Traditionally, pay scale is designed by a small group of people who have power (top executives and the HR team) – it is an entirely elite-led approach. Companies also invest in industry benchmarks; for example, Mercer's pay database costs tens of thousands to access. It is considered 'best practice' to determine where the company wants to be – top quartile, median, etc., but this is assuming employees have all the market information on pay and can/want to make rational decisions, which rarely happens. Once they've joined the company, employees are disadvantaged in terms of having influence or control over what they are worth and what they are paid. It is completely at the discretion of the core group that is in power and has the most influence.

> The core group Art Kleiner's Who Really Matters: The Core Group Theory of Power, Privilege and Success states that this is a group of people in any company whose interests and priorities are taken into account by people who make decisions. Organisations may espouse all sorts of values and ideals, from enhancing shareholder value to fostering a better workplace or making a better world, but when the chips are down, they'll move first and foremost to help the core group.[3]

Even if one can obtain the exact pay information through contacts or other channels and might feel a (false) sense of control via pay negotiation or job hopping, it is still an illusion for the broader workforce to become better off. In the past 30 years, American productivity has increased by 72 per cent; however, wages increased by only 8 per cent[4] – individual workers never reap the majority of the benefits from the productivity gain. Plainly, it is always a masked exploitation. Considering it is such an 'inconvenient truth', no wonder most employers are reluctant to provide full transparency on pay. Employees are discouraged from sharing pay information with colleagues (or even forbidden to share it), because ultimately, it is impossible to be 'fair' and the core group finds it hard to defend their subjective decisions. In fact, the level of public scrutiny towards executive comp has put off high-growth start-ups from listing.

Thanks to social media and the younger generation's tendency to share internal memos with the external world almost instantaneously, a lot more previously 'confidential' company policies have been exposed. People's attitude towards pay secrecy is also changing. Thus, it's not surprising how much salary information they are willing to share with strangers on websites such as Glassdoor and Salary Ladder. Increasingly, research has suggested that being open about pay information and providing opportunities to explain pay decisions drives positive employee experience. In *Under New Management*, David Burkus observes that the number of pay-transparent companies continues to grow – from technology start-ups like Buffer and SumAll to big established companies like Whole Foods, where both pay and performance data are shared openly on the company intranet. In each case, after the initial novelty of knowing everybody's salary wears off, the information is conducive to having productive conversations about how to improve the fairness of pay scale and how to improve individual performance to move up it.[5]

CO-OPERATION

Transparency in pay and reward has another huge advantage: it facilitates co-operation. Biologists argue that most human endeavours, whether tool making or language or warfare, are not that distinct from those of other animals, whereas they agree that the success of human evolution is closely linked to our sociality. The ability to co-operate, to make individuals subordinate their strong sense of self-interest to the needs of the group, lies at the root of human achievement. A large social network can generate knowledge and adopt innovations far more easily than a cluster of small, hostile groups constantly at war with each other, the default state of chimpanzee society.

At the same time, psychologists have discovered that very young children have an urge to help others and toddlers as young as 18 months demonstrate 'sharing' behaviours without being prompted. Michael Tomasello, a developmental psychologist at the Max Planck Institute for Evolutionary Anthropology in Leipzig, Germany, contended, 'A system of cooperative bands provides the kind of social infrastructure that can really get things going.' One of these skills is what he calls 'shared intentionality', the ability to form a plan with others to accomplish a joint endeavour. Children (but not chimps) will point at things to convey information, will intuit others' intentions from the direction of their gaze and will help others achieve a goal.[6]

> **Linda:** I found this fascinating, because our educational systems seem to contradict human nature. The same goes for extracurricular activities. The focus tends to be on external rewards and individual success. My daughter was six and she loved dancing and swimming. Once, she came back from swimming practice with a gold medal. I asked her if she had won a race. 'No,' she answered, 'but who cares? Everyone got a medal.' Another time, she did a great job at a dance performance at school and we were all proud

of her. But she was upset because she didn't get a flower or trophy like some of her peers did.

In these scenarios, the goal of instilling the sense of 'reward' in our children, rather than celebrating the learning process, is mistaken. My daughter's teacher and her friends' parents missed an opportunity to build *intrinsic motivation* through (a) enjoying completing a task and (b) acquiring new skills — both of which would have provided more *sustained* satisfaction.

Children naturally help each other with homework and teach when left alone. In fact, it seems easier to learn from a peer, something that I have seen operating successfully at some of the more 'progressive' schools that my daughter has attended.

A WAY FORWARD

In a way, the societal focus on individual success, the fear of missing out (FOMO) and the over-emphasis on winning showed how much we have lost our way — including why we work and how we should work together. In the future, people will increasingly have a voice in what makes sense for them — and this has to come from inside themselves. Since payroll is not an intrinsic motivation, it 'forces' people to look for a deeper reason to work and to choose meaningful work.

At the same time, transparency is enabled by various platforms filled with user-provided data. Within companies, everyone can see which job has experience/training requirements. Workday and other new-generation human resource management systems already enable this. At any given career point, one is presented with the next possible positions. If they fulfil those requirements, they could get the job and associated pay. Externally, market-based pricing will make people aware of how other companies would pay for similar roles/work experience as theirs. This could lead to the elimination of recruitment agencies/headhunters as middlemen with unnecessary agency cost. It moves to a highly individualised system where employees can choose the pensions/pay/rewards that they want. Company loyalty and the constant guessing game of 'Where do I stand?' will be a thing of the past.

NOTES

1   Economic Policy Institute (2014), 'CEO Compensation Surged in 2017'. https://www.epi.org/publication/ceo-compensation-surged-in-2017/

2   Alex Edmans, A. et al. 'Equity Vesting and Investment', *The Review of Financial Studies*, Volume 30, Issue 7, July 2017, pp. 2229–2271. https://doi.org/10.1093/rfs/hhx018

3   Kleiner, A. *Who Really Matters: The Core Group Theory of Power, Privilege, and Success*. New York: Currency/Doubleday, 2003.

4   Economic Policy Institute, 'The productivity–pay gap', 2018. https://www.epi.org/productivity-pay-gap. Accessed 5 September 2017.

5   Burkus, D. *Under New Management: How Leading Organizations are Upending Business as Usual*. Boston and New York: Houghton Mifflin Harcourt, 2016.

6   Tomasello, M. *A Natural History of Human Thinking*. Cambridge: Harvard University Press, 2014.

15

LEADERSHIP AND CULTURE

'When a prince's personal conduct is correct, his government is effective without the issuing of orders. If his personal conduct is not correct, he may issue orders, but they will not be followed'

— from *The Analects of Confucius*

'Even the smallest person can change the course of the future'
— J.R.R. Tolkien, *The Lord of the Rings:*
The Fellowship of the Ring

In this chapter:
- from ladder rungs to network nodes;
- definition of leadership;
- evolution of popular leadership theories;
- leadership and culture in a shared context.

In the Machine Age, leaders climbed a ladder. People fell down the slippery slope. 'When one rises, we all rise' was an aspirational idea. All these concepts were confined to the idea of a vertical. The dominant structure of the organisation was the pyramid.

LEADERS OF THE GALAXY!

Yet it is now, or about to be, the age of the Internet of Things. Instead of the pyramid corporate, imagine instead a galaxy (see Chapter 11). An endless network of stars. It is not flat – it has no 'shape' at all. It is a network, a web. Across silos, partner organisations, dealerships, suppliers, agencies, suppliers of suppliers. We all operate in a B2B2B2B2C environment. It is not effective to manage relationships with a service-level agreement. At the core must be trust, shared values, shared aspirations, something relating to a belief in the other party to deliver; agreement. And the core of such relationships is an individual human being. A node in the network. A leader.

This is the shape of the future organisations: a network of cells, relationships and influence. In this age, hierarchical power will be important in the same way. A hierarchical structure, as we mainly currently understand it, is important to keep others down and to ascend to power. Or to be as 'safe' as you can be. One of the big impacts of our fourth industrial age is on organisational form. If we accept that the organisational form will change, then the nature of leadership and the concept we have called management are also disrupted.

Governments and other organisations will have significantly more power to monitor work, production and regulation. It is all connected. The system will be able to monitor almost all aspects of work. Productivity is in an immediate feedback loop. In most robotic-enabled factories today, there is no foreman walking around checking up on employees and telling them what to do. The walks by the management are often safety prioritised to protect the humans. In the offices, people work autonomously. We do not need humans checking the accountability of other humans in the same way that we did in the Machine Age. We have to be in the process of figuring out what the new dominant model will be. It can and should replace much of the current language, ideas and concepts.

The very word *manager* fails to encompass the needs of the networked age. In a network, vertical power models are neither relevant nor effective. As humans will increasingly be 'monitored', our frontline is not to drive accountability, but to ensure privacy in our governance as leaders – a battle for every scenario that humans will face in a system run by networks.

Imagine trying to reach a node in a network instead of a direct report. You are trying to inspire that node to come alive, to shine bright, to act. The leader's role is to encourage, finding a passion for that node to shine without direct power based on fear. Convincing others in every direction instead creates power. To make influence across a network, you must have a viral power. Inspiration is contagious.

The servant–leadership models imply service to a thing. It still is based on an idea that is in essence hierarchy. We propose that true leadership is about *you*. Your choices. You as the node *are* the system, and you must identify what actions you can and should take.

CONTROL

Everything around us is changing at the same time. The speed of the evolution of things is dynamic. Consider other things that are ever-changing: water, weather, a crowd. Ideas of controlling, of hierarchy power, are passé. You either have to constantly adapt your means of control, which takes huge effort (energy and cost), or you learn to live in a new way in harmony with the element, in a new environment. Most of us are stressed by daily work because we deal with a lot of uncertainty. Change is stressful. Our prefrontal cortex, the thin operating centre which takes a disproportionately high amount of energy when under stress to compete and to deal with everything. Stress kills. We know this medically. With such effort, we are physically exhausted more quickly. How can we be inspired to work differently?

We see inspiration and purpose as lights from within that ignite others again and again. A source of energy. Literally to empower. *To pass power.* You yourself must be like a battery. You will need to be constantly replenished. If you are able to share your power, then your wisdom and energy will ignite others. It is a different age and a different model, and a new idea is needed.

Leadership has always been seen as the golden chalice, the holy grail of organisational and people development, yet there has not yet been a clear, universally agreed upon definition of what good leadership looks like in the context of the future. The very words *manager* and *leader* are redundant to us as they both describe a relationship of hierarchy and control. Their context is not a network and their currency is power, not relationships.

LEADERSHIP DEFINED

How we think about leadership changes as we evolve as humans and is shaped by our environment. Until very recently, leadership and the associated privileges were about the bloodline. We knew that we could breed cattle and other animals to shape behaviour and capabilities, so why not humans? It is the rationale behind royalty.

An officer class in most countries meant just that: a class of people bred to lead the rest of us. It was only after the First World War that we started to differentiate leaders based on personal traits and to have more objective discussions about leadership standards. But the influence is still heavy.

Leadership is also in the eye of the beholder. Take China as an example. For almost 3,000 years it had been an empire. Modern leadership thinking bears the imprint of the teachings of ancient Chinese historians and scholars who used to serve the rulers. Chinese wisdom had it that time and situation 'mould' leaders; in other words, leadership is highly contextual. There are three key tenets of the Chinese philosophy of leadership:

民本 (empathy with people)
正己 (integrity with self)
谋势 (visionary with strategy)

The last principle originated from Sun Tzu's *The Art of War* (孙子兵法) and is completely dependent on timing (天时), strengths (地利) and team (人和). In 94 BC, Sima Qian, Grand Astrologer to the Imperial Court, wrote in the *Records of the Grand Historian* (also known by its Chinese name Shiji), '善战者，因其势而利导之', which means 'The best generals who are great at winning wars understand the situation and take full advantage'.

So is it possible to say that the most brilliant leadership is not about 'execution', which we often value above all else, but is more about insight of all elements in the environment, including those that can be controlled (e.g. team) and those that can't be controlled (e.g. timing), as well as mastery of orchestration – conducting, directing, to the desired outcome?

> **Chris:** One of my proudest leadership moments came when I was working for the National Health Service in the United Kingdom. I worked with a medical scientist who showed the potential to become more senior in the organisation. I was coaching her as she worked through a management diploma while still in full-time work. At home, her husband totally controlled all aspects of her life. One day she came in and told me that for the first time in her life she had put petrol in her car. It was her first big breakthrough, an act of defiance on her part. Prior to this, I had only talked to her as a colleague, but here I was given the contextual space almost to transfer my energy to enable her to act differently. It was a powerful feeling.

Since the mid-2000s, increasingly people associate strong leadership with the ability to drive change. The hardest change is probably behavioural, such as culture change that involves a whole organisation changing the way it acts and interacts. Peter Northouse, in reviewing leadership theory, identified four common themes: (1) Leadership is a process. (2) Leadership involves influence. (3) Leadership occurs in a group context. (4) Leadership involves goal attainment.[1]

How we think about leadership is the core of any organisation's culture. An organisation lives in the shadow of its founders and core group members and how they lead. They are really inseparable. As Edgar Schein states, the *founder* of any organisation sets the tone for many aspects, including leadership.[2] The organisation is often a reflection of the founder's personal style. For some organisations, the sheer importance of leadership is too often overlooked. It is not seen as paramount early on in the start-up culture – it's more of an afterthought to define and train, and set by the founders too late, thus sometimes dooming the enterprise to repeat their human flaws.

THE EVOLUTION OF LEADERSHIP DISCOURSE
In *Leadership: A Critical Text,* Simon Western argues there are three main leadership discourses: Controller, Therapist and Messiah. He also promotes a new discourse, called 'Eco-Leadership' (see Figure 15.1).[3] In Chapter 6, we reflected on the three periods of HR evolution (personnel management, resource management and change management); it is not surprising that leadership has followed a similar pattern that coincides with the previous three industrial revolutions.

Controller
The first leadership discourse, 'Controller', reflects Taylor's work on scientific management. Both promoted an extremely rational approach and ignored emotional needs in the workplace. In his ruthless chase of 'efficiency', Taylor treated workers as another

The Discourses of Leadership

| 1900 | 1960 | 1980 | 2005 |

Controller
Scientific
Management

Therapist
Human Relations
movement

Messiah
Transformational
leadership/culture control

Eco-Leader

Therapist continues via coaching and emotional intelligence and is still popular in HR and public sector leadership

Controller still found following the mode of production,
particularly in manufacturing and in China/Asia

FIGURE 15.1 Approximate timeline of leadership discourses (Western, S. *Leadership: A Critical Text*, 2013).

resource to be utilised to the fullest, similar to machines. He advocated work to be broken apart and workers to be de-skilled and kept disposable, instead of developing craftsman skills or expertise. The Taylorist approach brought about huge economic success in the post-war industrial revolution and factories. The management style was one of 'utilitarian control', where power was based on a system of 'carrot and stick'. Workers were motivated only by the basic level of material needs. Tension between management and workers was high. Union actions, walkouts and other labour disputes took place regularly and rarely improved actual working conditions for workers at a sustained level. We measure using metrics and control the processes relating to human asset in the context of a machine here, from an HR mindset.

Therapist
According to Western, the second leadership discourse, 'Therapist', emerged from the influences of post-Freudian psychology and the post-war democratising effort in the workplace. Workers returning from the two world wars demanded better working conditions and better social integration. The 'command-and-control' style

of leadership was not working. The leadership focus moved from coercion and control to engagement of the workforce. Leaders were expected to understand what was going on in workers' lives and focus on better workplace dynamics and relationships. Typical leadership skills required at this stage included social skills such as emotional intelligence and coaching. This created engagement surveys, models of motivation theories, benefits and occupational health and safety concepts.

Messiah

The third leadership discourse, 'Messiah', focused on trans-formation, vision and mission and shaping workplace culture. This emerged at the same time as globalisation was taking place. One huge influence was the Japanese management philosophy and approach, e.g. total quality management (TQM) and *kaizen* (continuous improvement), which instil a strong work culture that emphasises quality, service, flexibility and teams that operate like families. These values have been ingrained in Japanese society for thousands of years and became the biggest competitive advantage of Japanese car manufacturers in the 1980s.

Schein wrote, 'Leadership is partly a cultural phenomenon and must be analysed within a given cultural, political and socio-economic context'.[4] In Western countries, transformational leaders are often charismatic and visionary, using a range of tools (symbols, ritual and language) to lead and influence. They focus on reshaping company cultures, rewiring how their followers think and behave to accomplish disruptive ideas and goals. The 1980s was the period when CEOs started to become celebrities, heroic figures come to save the day from the Japanese. 'Talent' systems were created, as it was so important to find the next 'great man' leader to save us. Succession became important, as if in a time and place of royalty.

Although Simon Western plotted the three leadership discourses along an approximate timeline (1900, 1960 and 1980), in fact the

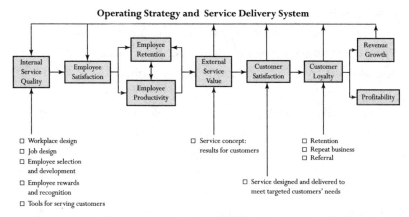

Operating Strategy and Service Delivery System

FIGURE 15.2   The service-profit chain (Heskett, J. L., et al. 'Putting the service-profit chain to work', *Harvard Business Review*, July–August 2008).

three still exist, in parallel, in different types of organisations and can still be relevant and effective.

Most Chinese manufacturing industries still rely heavily on 'Controller' leadership to drive cost efficiency. In the professional services industry, 'Therapist' leadership is favoured because most of the cost is in 'people cost', so putting people first and reducing turnover is important; the same goes for most service industries, where the service-profit chain drives revenue (see Figure 15.2).

Industries being seriously disrupted by digital and newly emergent technologies and automation (logistics and financial services) often seek and promote 'Messiah' leaders. These companies constantly need to be saved from the rapid change, so leadership here is all about vision and agility, which are necessary to revive the companies or rebuild the business models again and again.

Eco-leadership
Eco-leadership is the fourth discourse, which Western argues is happening now. It speaks to the need for ethical and moral leadership, which is distributed through a horizontal rather than a hierarchical context. The context is networks, teams and lateral

co-ordinating relationships – where the boundaries of organisation are fluid. Eco-leadership speaks to the need to consider the wider community as stakeholder and have ethics and personal code aligned to purpose. In this interconnected age, credibility is everything.

Western also discusses the concepts of emergent leadership in the new networks and non-hierarchical leadership systems. This is displayed in political action groups and global movements. Here, leaders step up when required; aligned to purpose and sparked by opportunity, they emerge from the crowd to take a lead on an aspect for which they have passion, skill, knowledge or proximity. They then sink back into the crowd. They are followed because their purpose is aligned and resonates with their skill, knowledge, etc.

SERVANT-LEADERSHIP

Aligning with purpose has also been a major feature of what is called 'servant-leadership'. This model evolved in the context of those who work in military, health and government departments – that is, for us. Many commercial organisations that have a founder or core group with a strong faith association align with the servant-leadership model: others before self. Larry Spears described the model:

> As we near the end of the twentieth century, we are beginning to see that traditional autocratic and hierarchical modes of leadership are slowly yielding to a newer model – one that attempts to simultaneously enhance the personal growth of workers and improve the quality and caring of our many institutions through a combination of teamwork and community, personal involvement in decision making, and ethical and caring behaviour. This emerging approach to leadership and service is called servant-leadership.[5]

The effectiveness of this leadership model is about the congruence with the nature of the industry, the business model and processes, and how it reflects the work and the societal environment. It is still located in the idea of hierarchy. The leader still sits above or below, and not everywhere.

INDIVIDUAL V. CONTEXTUAL LEADERSHIP

Linda: Most current leadership assessment and development focuses on individual traits and competencies. Through business schools, many adopted such texts as Douglas McGregor's work on the Theory X and Y types of managers. The key assumptions:

TABLE 15.1 Theories X and Y, created by Douglas McGregor while working at MIT Sloan School of Management in the 1950s and 1960s.

Theory X	Theory Y
People inherently dislike work and will avoid it if at all possible	Work is natural and people will exercise self-direction
Most people must be co-erced, controlled, directed and threatened with punishment to put adequate effort into the achievement of organisational objectives	Individuals seek responsibility and development and the average person's potential is not being fully used

The INSEAD Global Leadership Centre once tried simplifying common traits into *conscientiousness, extraversion, dominance, self-confidence, energy, agreeableness, intelligence, openness to experience and emotional stability*. The major criticism of the individualistic camp of leadership is the lack of context and over-promotion of a one-size-fits-all approach.[6]

Fred Fiedler's contingency approach argues that effective leaders need to adopt different styles based on the situation. It adds some parameters to acknowledge the different social context a leader or manager might be in, e.g. organisational size; whether influencing individuals one on one, in a small team or in a large group; and organisational culture, including environmental, political and psycho-social dynamics. It is noted the underlying model is still two-dimensional, i.e. relationship versus task. Task-centred leaders focus on accomplishing the tasks rather than focusing on the people. Their leadership style tends to be more directive, pace-setting and tactical. Relationship-centred leaders care more about people engagement and development and are more inclined to take a coaching and participative approach even in the short term; they have to sacrifice task completion.[7]

Chris: Here is one story to illustrate the point. At a football match, my friend Dave and I were once chased by a gang of Birmingham City fans. In the days of football fan rivalry, their group was (and still is) known as the Zulu Warriors. We were cornered on a housing estate with our backs to the wall. They were led by a large red-haired man; he was about to hurt us very badly when a brown-skinned man stepped up from among them and said, 'Let's leave these two.' He eyed the redhead and the redhead backed down. Then he turned to me and winked. Dave (who was blond) was grateful that he was with me. There was a relationship/purpose affinity here beyond the task. The task was to hurt us, but an emergent leader stepped in, at some personal risk to himself, to lead the group in the moment for their own unique psycho-dynamic. Why did I not get hurt? Why did the man come to my aid? The answer is not in a two-factor model but in a multi-dynamic context where purpose and values provoke emergence.

Neither situational nor contingency leadership theory takes into consideration the complexity of power and relationships, a context of networks and the impact on leadership. They are focused on power and co-ordination for the purposes of execution.

POWER AND AUTHORITY

We know that as humans we defer to authority. Power is important to human groups. Power comes in multiple forms in organisations. Today, we see this well-known theme being challenged in some of them. Some industries lack traditionally harsh competition; due to market dominance, today they are suddenly being digitally disrupted.

Some such companies have developed democratic, egalitarian versions of a leadership ideal. This is because the core group has been together for some time. These companies rarely hire externally at senior levels and are stable. This could prevent leaders from taking up their authority and effectively driving change.

At a long-standing successful financial services firm, its members aspired to consensual decision-making, yet a strict management hierarchy restricted this. Over the years, it had put a considerable number of procedures and controls in place. Secure employment and long tenure made preserving relationships paramount at all levels. As a result, it is difficult for such companies to move forward to meet the new digital challenges until everyone is on board. The mantra of teamwork and collaboration moves to such an extreme that too many stakeholders get involved but no clear owner for pretty much anything emerges.

The Web becomes so big that everyone can hide and also be both visible and invisible at the same time. So, understanding that these are the cultural root causes for (a) diffused accountability, (b) slow speed to act, and (c) lack of results orientation helps us to recognise what needs to be changed. How to allow leadership to emerge and not control it?

A NEW TYPE OF 'LEADERLESS ORGANISATION'

In the 2017 survey 'Transitioning to the future of work and the workplace', we saw that over 40 per cent of C Suite executives say that they will 'increasingly place more focus on facilitating the flow and exchange of ideas and providing greater autonomy at team and individual levels. This shift from "top-down" to what we might see as "alongside" is a crucial component of the equation.'[8] In the highly networked, more fluid organisations of the future, leaders will need new ways to communicate with employees and keep a finger on the pulse of their organisation.

In Chinese the word *leader* is made up of two words:

领 lead ahead of you, handholding
导 coach and direct.

The role of leader is balancing and directing – much like Qi Gong and balancing of yin and yang. Effective leaders observe, converse and discover the different containers/segments within one system. They must sense where there is imbalance or tension and direct. It requires high levels of self-awareness and interpersonal skills. It is different from the traditional problem solver or the charismatic cheerleader stereotype of leadership.

In their 2006 book, *The Starfish and the Spider*, Ori Brafman and Rod Beckstrom wrote about the 'leaderless organization', where organisational boundaries are blurred and information exchange across silos become a key driver for quality, speed to change and innovation. The spider and starfish analogies are used to describe hierarchical versus decentralised institutions. The spider, with its brain, head and body, represents conventional order. Although it looks scary and powerful, if you cut off one of its limbs it will die within days. In contrast, the starfish represents a network. If it loses a part of its body, the rest can still function, will eventually regenerate and the starfish will survive.[9]

Brafman and Beckstrom point out that some modern organisations are adapting a hybrid model to capture the benefits of both worlds. In addition to decentralising certain functions such as customer experience, the key is to promote smaller teams versus overgrown departments, to encourage networking across different areas, understanding that chaos is a natural part of creativity, super-focused on knowledge development and participation from everyone. The leadership that wins in tomorrow's workplace is moving from managing individuals to designing and enabling the environment through values and culture code with a strong sense of community. Our future is the network and the community.

TOMORROW'S LEADERSHIP

Learning from the military to develop leaders who can operate in a VUCA environment, there are three things we can consider:

1   *Leveraging strength*. Rather than identifying their weaknesses, leaders learn to leverage their personal strengths to deal with any new challenges they're facing. For example, a leader who wants to be calmer under pressure may take inspiration from a different strength that they already possess, such as win-win partnering. Thinking about the 'skills' they use successfully in win-win partnering (e.g. detaching themselves from the situation, being curious about new possibilities and asking clarifying questions) can provide practical insights that can help them to stay calm under pressure. Then they must learn to recognise the 'triggers' or warning signs that appear when the pressure is rising, so they can make a conscious decision to respond and behave differently.

2   *Understanding neuroscience*. Understanding more about how we learn, why we behave the way we do and how to make changes can help leaders to challenge their ingrained

habits and adopt new behaviours. As we understand
the neurochemistry of the brain more, we can challenge
ourselves to be driven by data and science as effective
sources to design our leadership.

3 *Simulations to retrain the brain.* Leaders can practise
moving out of the comfort zone of their default responses
if you give them opportunities to experience VUCA
situations in a safe and supportive environment. They
can be given a scenario – which can build to become a
full-on VUCA nightmare – and can review their own
performance and get feedback on how they collaborated
and responded to events.

In this chapter we have described the importance of defining and
developing leadership and culture in a shared context, particularly
from the perspective of cultivating a shared sense of mission and
attaining common goals.

The future of leadership and management is based not in the
factory models of the machine and in the context of a *foreman*
who controls. This core belief about the workplace of today is
still ingrained. In a digital context of networks and systems, of
relationships, of ethics and of purpose, the very word *manager* thus
seems archaic.

We need a new language to be able to imagine a new way. We
need facilitators who are free from administration and who coach.

There are consistent qualities among the best people managers.
They care about the people they lead. They know them as people.
They care about them. They connect with their purpose and are
purpose-driven themselves. They are rooted in themselves and
have confidence in their own alignment with their purpose. They
are values-driven and curious. This is no longer a controller or a
therapist but instead a *skilled continuous learner who emerges in the
right context, free of rank.* A coach, a friend and an advocate.

Leadership is beyond empowerment. It is not just getting your things done (productivity) or the company's things done (execution). It is now the real transfer of power. Power is energy.

NOTES

1   Northouse, P. *Leadership Theory and Practice* (7th ed.). London: SAGE Publications, 2015.

2   Schein, E. *Organizational Culture and Leadership* (4th ed.). San Francisco: Jossey-Bass, 2010.

3   Western, S. *Leadership: A Critical Text* (2nd ed.). London: SAGE Publications, 2013.

4   Schein, E. *Organizational Culture and Leadership* (4th ed.). San Francisco: Jossey-Bass, 2010, p. 156.

5   Spears, L.C. (ed.). *Insights on Leadership: Service, Stewardship, Spirit and Servant-Leadership.* New York: John Wiley & Sons, 1998.

6   Kets de Vries, M. INSEAD Leadership Institute, January 2015.

7   Fiedler, F.E. *Leadership Experience and Leadership Performance.* Alexandria, VA: US Army Research Institute for the Behavioral and Social Sciences, 1994.

8   Deloitte, 'Transitioning to the future of work and the workplace' survey, 2017. https://www2.deloitte.com/us/en/pages/human-capital/articles/transitioning-to-the-future-of-work-and-the-workplace.html. Accessed 3 December 2018.

9   Brafman, O., and Beckstrom, R. *The Starfish and the Spider: The Unstoppable Power of Leaderless Organizations* (reprint ed.). New York: Portfolio, 2008.

16

SPAGHETTI BOLOGNESE

'Of the five elements, none is always predominant; of the four seasons, none lasts forever; of the days, some are long and some short, and the moon waxes and wanes'

— Sun Tzu

In this chapter:
- why do we not understand change?
- why change is critical;
- using appreciative inquiry as a tool to facilitate the process of change;
- how to phase change to achieve optimal results.

Change is constant. We know this and yet we seem not to know it. It seems that change is another inconvenient truth that nips us when we are not expecting it.

> **Chris:** When I cook spaghetti Bolognese, I use my own particular method. Each of us does. No two home-cooked versions of this common dish are exactly the same. I am assuming that we all follow the same basic principles. I start with chopping herbs and onions and maybe peppers, then I move to frying them and boiling the pasta. Then I add a variety of things. I alter the temperature now and then and

adjust the speed of the cooking to suit and then add extra ingredients to taste.

But imagine instead that I had put all the ingredients together into a pot at the same time and just applied water and heat. I would make a strange-tasting mulch. It might serve the purpose of nourishment, but it would not be the same dish. There is a reason why we've learned how to cook. *Method* ensures that fewer people die of food poisoning – some foods are made more palatable, we have access to more food groups with proper preparation of food, etc. It is a learned aspect of a society. The older societies in the world have long-established ways of preparing food and the newer societies experiment with 'fusion'. Each has a method that is national or local; it is not random unless the randomness is designed (now a trend).

CULTURE CHANGE

As we look to culture change, our recipes seem so crude and inelegant. We consistently approach each change opportunity without realising or remembering that (a) people are at the centre of change, (b) change takes time, and (c) some aspects of change are predictable and can be mitigated with a plan.

We often throw in a bunch of change products all at once or ignore them completely; use minimal communication and try to rush through the change – in the end creating a dish that we would not want to eat.

This is not a new dialogue in the circle of business school or change and leadership summits. We seemed to know this all once. Or was that just from a halcyon era? Did we ever get change right? Did we ever have more time? Did we maybe lose knowledge of what to do in change management – even in the last 20 years of organisational practice? Did we get too obsessed with short-term expediency? Did change practice itself not evolve to our VUCA context?

APPRECIATIVE INQUIRY

What we will present in the following section of the book is an original change-based process to align around core themes and ideas and to enable an organisation to change. It is based broadly on experience, some theory and some science. We will guide you towards thinking about the change process to drive a sharing and empathic organisation.

The process that we propose combines multiple management theories, approaches and practices into a practical and tactical flow that we hope is of interest and use. We have based the process roughly on a body of work known as *appreciative inquiry*.

The concept of appreciative inquiry was pioneered in the 1980s by David Cooperrider and Suresh Srivastva, two professors at the Weatherhead School of Management at Case Western Reserve University. It is based on a belief that we accentuate the positive energy that arises from the release of the imagination. Imagination gives us energy. When we inspire our people, they will turn that will into the tactical processes, policies and practices that help govern and run our organisations. But it always starts with some direction – a change plan – what to do first and what to do after that – a recipe.

Linda: When Chris and I started the culture project for the largest bank in the world shortly after the financial crisis in 2008, there was a lot of negativity towards banking because of the way press portrayed banks at that time. Internally, employee morale was low due to cost cutting and staff reduction. We decided to teach appreciative inquiry methodology to a global network of learning and organisational development specialists and encouraged them to start local listening exercises with diverse bodies of leaders and employees.

Totally 1 per cent of the global workforce, about 3,000 people, answered one question and elaborated their experience on 'What was the proudest moment during your time here?' We collected thousands of stories that talked about the bank's values being rooted in its origin of facilitating independent trade, its deep concern for the communities and wider societies it operates in, its frugal outlook on money to ensure financial strength and sustainability in the past 156 years' history, so on and so forth. Before we knew it, people were re-telling those poignant stories to colleagues and customers without any nudging or instructions. They just did.

When we finally started to execute on the change plan, the whole organisation was ready. People were excited. We articulated the value statements first in English; local territories then took initiative to translate into their own languages through employee challenges that facilitated further debates and introduced even more narratives of personal experience.

What I learnt from that project as some powerful lessons are: 1) trust the process and follow through – there were times we were not sure where it was going and it required courage and humility to actively listen to what people were telling us; 2) start the change early – the storytelling, not only initially but also the re-telling of stories spontaneously became the most authentic, hence effective part of the culture change process early on and actually 'stuck'; 3) leverage the network of informal influencers – people trust those they know and respect, sometimes not necessarily those with titles or formal authority.

THE RECIPE: PHASES

The phases that we outline enable an understanding of who we are, as both an individual and an organisation. It can be where we find our purpose in the context of the wider world.

We realise the need first to ground ourselves in the history of the organisation. Edgar Schein tells us that the founders of any organisation have a significant impact on the practices and ideas of that organisation and thus we must take the time to rediscover what was true when it began, decide what is true today and think about what could and should be true in the future.[1]

Chris: Too often, management consultants and others who do such work in organisations use a gap-analysis approach to the problem. This method creates such a long list of work that it seems daunting; too many things are always unaligned. On my first attempt to influence culture, I remember starting here, with a long list that seemed to talk about everything. I had spoken to a cross-section of people, interviewed them about what we needed to change in the organisation and then collated the results. I was overwhelmed. It seemed that everything was wrong.

I recall that I was once working on a major project. Lots of analysis and focus groups of backwards-facing things that we needed to fix we captured and executives were presented with dozens of pages on every aspect of the organisation that needed to change. The problem with such an approach is that although data-driven and in-depth, it is too long and unfocused to bring about understanding. Attempts to implement such lists disrupt the rhythm of the business and the flow of the organisation. In my experience, the organisation is always put into a temporary period of chaos: I have seen many situations where the project infects the wider organisation and itself becomes the reason for failures. Drowning itself in multiple change initiatives, the organisation inevitably ends up with too much to do and so often the initiative fails. The project is put on hold and becomes the 'focus' work of the incoming new senior management team, who in turn pledge to stop the project and 'get us back to work'. The previous administration is removed because of its failure to drive change effectively. The new cultural effort becomes highly directive on a few emergency items. The long list of problems to fix is lost.

Good change process should allow all employees to build a shared understanding of who and what we are and what we want to be and do. This can and should generate energy and insight. We can invite the whole organisation to dream about possibilities. Possibilities rooted in the best practices and knowledge of the individual technical expertise and understanding of each of our customers, but also rooted in who we are and who we have been. We will introduce phases into this work, after dreaming together. How can we move to codify our collective dreams and then create congruence in the experience and make new habits?

THE INGREDIENTS: A NEW LANGUAGE

As we look forward towards a digital world, we have a big opportunity to change the language we use. To leverage in the change method a language suited to the new industrial age for which we are heading. Increasingly, we have new language in which to think – new words like *systems*, *networks* and *complexity*. In this new dialect, thinking about the organisations as process or machines is less relevant.

We know that taking the systems view is more appropriate to this time. We create change through activating random cells and networks in order to bring the whole system to life. We think that this is a more potent and appropriate approach. The fallacy of the organisation to be viewed as a machine requires an arrogance of control. Control issues have guided most traditional change-management models to date.

The dominant leadership mindset of change models and management approaches is one of *control and command*. Leaders are expected to control through carrot-and-stick measures. It implies an old concept that employees are serfs instead of colleagues, are children or slaves that need to be controlled. That they cannot be trusted to share in decisions that impact them. It is about *driving efficiency versus effectiveness*.

For the work we are describing and our new-networked age of knowledge workers and non-owned assets, of partnerships, we finally have to move on. This concept of higher- and lower-worth humans needs to be left behind. Instead, we need empathy. We need to eschew that Darwinian and Victorian thinking that echoes earlier, monarchical societies that assumes that some have better blood, have been naturally selected to lead others, and the rest need to be controlled and are not to be empowered.

> **Chris:** It is embedded in how we think about the world, and, for me, always goes back to the tribes of early Rome and Athens as an age-old struggle of *for* or *through* the people. Some seek an approach that is best for all, believing in the inherent worth of people; and some serve only themselves, their family, their tribe. To do the latter, with what we have learned from cognitive dissonance theory, we now know that we would have to believe that we are more human than someone else. That we are more deserving and better educated, have better values, better clothes, better families…Do we believe that many of us are less worthy and need to be culled from time to time?

That mindset reflects the societal view of the 1800s. For most of us, one of workhouses, mass poverty, servitude, deportations and debt bondage and versions of slavery around the world. The values and workplace of the time dictated the mindset of the approach to work and workers. Are those things that we value today? Our societies, and most of us as individuals, have moved on. We live in relative partnerships and with the advent of new technology we have such opportunity in front of us to invent new language. To dream into our legacy.

We can choose models and language of change that are based in beliefs of our inherent worth and regard for each other. Some new form of Magna Carta principles about the worth of a life. It's a basic thought but it shapes how we view the world and how we behave. If we believe in the value of each other then we have a duty to have a change process that empowers.

With the controller mindset we intend to manipulate the worker to serve our needs. In establishing such a process, we also seek to manipulate the visible and transparent enabling mechanisms. In our phased approach, we think about how we can become agile through better listening to the crowd. We think about principle-based decision-making, instead of rules, as a tool for discussing how individuals are released and empowered when they are trusted.

Individuals in every department, in every aspect of the organisation, are able to articulate and bring to life meaning for their work. When this work is done well, this includes the person who delivers the mail, the marketing department, the HR team, the strategy team, the sales team, each unique department figuring out how it should live the essence of the brand, its values and intent.

We become a sharing, empathic corporation and move towards truly becoming a share-based society through the articulation and redefinition for each of us personally and also at the company level. We use the intense intelligence to solve and share within the organisation, as opposed to having the view that humans are inherently flawed and an aspect of the organisation that needs to be controlled.

COOKING IN YOUR OWN KITCHEN
We believe that this work and this approach is truly unique to you, wherever you are. It has been tested; we give the guidelines in

the hope that they are followed carefully — much like following a recipe for the best results. Let's say we are a couple of chefs who have been cooking in a few kitchens and we want to share what we think is our best recipe with you, our readers.

We are intrigued to see how far such an approach to change could spread. Our context, of course, is the organisation. We think it would also be interesting to use our emergent technology solutions and technology assets to create trust and design work on a larger scale.

Of course, there is always local flavouring, many takes on the basic Bolognese sauce: some like it more or less spicy, salty, sweet, savoury — and no two kitchens are alike. So we know each chef will adapt. In the same way, we invite you to alter, adapt, amend and play with this process to suit your needs.

One thing we have found especially true is that the way the decisions are made in each organisation is unique. Like two families on the same street. Even within two organisations in the same industry sector, the way the decisions are made is totally based on the way the founders created the company.

Some organisations involve the use of formal papers and are almost academic in feel; others operate on PowerPoint presentations to convey sharpness of ideas; and then there are those that require a considerable amount of time lobbying syndicates, knowing the right people and building a coalition of the good. In some places, it's the decision of the single committee or one powerful individual.

For any would-be change artists who intend to work with our recipe, you have to understand the decision-making method and the nuances of your unique kitchen context. How decisions are made in your system and the role that you play in that system should guide your approach.

When thinking about the system and the decisions of that organisation, there are different points at which you, as the practitioner (cook), can sit; if we imagine a system represented by a circle, we can sit:

- inside the circle;
- on the boundary that defines the edges of the circle, or;
- outside the circle.

Chris: Each unique place in that system gives a particular vantage point from which to cook. To sit within the circle is to be part of the week-by-week struggle, to play the political games, to have the airtime attention and to feel the emotion of the protagonist in the work ahead. If I continue to use my analogy of cooking, this is about getting down and dirty in the kitchen, getting garlic on your fingers, buying your fish fresh rather than packaged, doing the frying and much or all of the prep work yourself. Let's consider this in the context of my children in preparing a meal of spag Bol.

When I invite my children to help me cook, the whole family is involved and we often break into units of work based on age, calmness and ability. We want everyone to be proud of the dish. Everyone attacks his or her role with enthusiasm. Maybe the spaghetti gets broken too small, maybe the garlic gets chopped too big, and maybe water boils over and spills all over the countertop. It is messy but everyone has felt involved and we have a meal to eat that we are all proud to have shared. After a highly involved cooking process, I will need to spend additional time washing my hands and cleaning the kitchen and anything else involved. This can be frustrating and annoying. I like things to be clean. This is how organisations get distracted and lose patience with change processes.

The disadvantage of being inside the circle is that we are so immersed in the process of cooking that we perhaps lose sight of the full eloquence of the meal and forget we have guests to serve. Or we are short on time, missing bedtime and the conciseness of the thing we are trying to cook. Sitting apart at a different place in the circle might offer me that perspective.

On the boundary I play a more formal role for the children and am less involved. I walk around the kitchen and coach and help where needed. I step in immediately any danger presents itself. On the boundary of the process, I'm doing some of the cooking and some of the prep work, but mostly, I am making observations and giving feedback. This is less messy. There is an element of supervision and advice with overseeing something. I have a better-tasting dish. It is produced at speed. I am able to give directions, to step in when needed; I am a situational leader.

In the third option, I sit outside the circle, delegating from afar and believing in my kids. If someone makes a mistake, it's a lesson; I have taught them how to use knives, how to stir carefully. Safety is a concern but I have taught them and I trust them. I watch and listen but allow them to make small mistakes and to learn to apply safety as they go. It can be messy. I am a consultant to the meal. I taste if asked, I'm able to give feedback but it's their choice to ask. I'm not involved, they are. And I have to have a high level of trust in the relationships. I have to eat whatever is served.

There are pros and cons to each of these approaches, and there are questions that determine how you set up your kitchen and approach cooking:
- what is the nature of the change you need to think about?
- what level of trust exists about what?
- how does the organisation make decisions?
- do you want or need to be in the change process and feel like you're *the* change agent?
- are you able to detach your ego from the involvement of the process?
- what are the drivers of what is important to you personally?

Knowledge of these things, knowledge of the organisation and clarity about your own purpose and intent (on things like status, recognition, personal purpose, control) are all essential in choosing where to cook your change (inside the circle, outside, or on the boundary).

Across all approaches and in every kitchen the importance of communication cannot be overstressed. So much is written about this, anything extra seems redundant. The opportunity lies in the new language with which we choose to communicate. We create new possibilities about how the work is to be done.

NOTES
1 Schein, E. *Process Consultation Revisited: Building the Helping Relationship*. Chicago: Addison Wesley Longman, 1998.

SECTION FOUR

A MODEL FOR CHANGE

THE 4-STEP APPROACH

'There are not more than five musical notes, yet the combinations of these five give rise to more melodies than can ever be heard.

There are not more than five primary colours...yet in combination, they produce more hues than can ever be seen.

There are not more than five cardinal tastes...yet combinations of them yield more flavours than can ever be tasted'
– Sun Tzu, The Art of War

In this chapter:
- the approach to change management;
- why the mindset of the 1870s can't enable change in current context;
- introduction of the 4-Step change approach.

We will now introduce our model of change: the 4-Step, or 4 Ds (Discover, Define, Develop and Deploy). In many ways this follows the process that we know as appreciative inquiry, but we present it here as a phased approach over time. The purpose of this chapter is to talk about the soul or the 'how' of the approach. If we just create another model, it joins the list of others on the shelf that come and go. All worthy and right in their own way, yet sometimes missing the point that the core aspect for success is about *coherence and congruence*: does everyone involved have clarity and make the necessary links?

CONGRUENCE

There is another old and oft-quoted principle: *Be the change that you want to see in the world*. This means to role-model what the future can feel like – to sprint, hack and play at being the culture in advance.

We know that if we want our corporates to take stronger ethical and empathic approaches to how they impact our societies, then we need those values to be inherent in *all of us* as corporate citizens. If we want to build an empathic, sharing-focused organisation, then the change approach has to be an example of those values. After years of working with culture and change efforts, one kernel of professional wisdom that we have acquired is that organisations must be congruent for people to have belief in the proposed changes. This means that we do what we say we will do. We deliver on a promise. If this is not possible, then all the work will be in vain and perhaps best not started at all.

Too often, we have seen an attempt at culture change work well until it meets a point of truth. Will the executive do the right thing and preserve the covenant made in the words of the culture articulations? A decision not to invite someone to a meeting, or the way someone is spoken to at the meeting; or a pay decision for someone who has made huge progress but at a cost. Executives and middle managers are visible. The organisation watches them for any deviation. Every deviation providing more evidence that the change, the work on culture, is not real. (The question is asked: why should *I* believe, if you cannot meet your promise?) This is sensible; we are trained, indeed genetically programmed, to avoid risk. Change implies risk. Risk is uncertainty. Sometimes we are more stimulated and fearful in uncertain situations than when under direct threat.

CHRIS ON THE RHYTHM OF CHANGE

In order to get on board with change, one must understand the *rhythm* of the change. I thought a lot about the importance of this as I reflected on the music that shaped my dancing years in my twenties and thirties – house music, drum and bass, and, yes, disco!

When I lived in south London I came to understand 4-Step, or four-to-the-floor rhythm, as it is sometimes called. The underpinning for garage music, which was once my genre of choice, it is a regular beat in 4/4 time, in which the bass drum is hit on every beat (1, 2, 3, 4). This deep bass beat, also used by some reggae drummers, makes it hard not to dance or at least tap your foot to.

We have seen that when change is done well it is possible to find a rhythm to how the work flows well into an organisation. As with dance, the movement is not jerky, but fluid – pleasurable to take part in.

When dance is good, it changes something inside you forever.

I rarely dance nowadays, only at weddings and the occasional party. There seem to be fewer and fewer work-related opportunities at which to dance. We seldom dance (or even cat festive meals) with the people that we work with.

Not so long ago, across workplaces, across cultures, we sang together when we worked. I attend the leadership development retreats at Silver Bay in Lake George, New York, probably the only such conference that I really find refreshing. At the start of each day, the whole group sits together and sings for around 20 minutes. This is a tradition for a conference started by Wall Street executives over 100 years ago. They would sing hymns together at the start of a meeting. They make it almost sacred in a way. Such habits and rhythms – based on the deep bonds of practice and trust – partly explain the longevity and success of some of the oldest institutions that have withstood war, depression and subprime.

THE 4 Ds

When we are in the flow, we dance. We want you to think about 4-Step approach like a dance, like a song, elegant, inviting and seductive – with a good bass beat. What we propose is a process called the 4 Ds: Discover, Define, Develop and Deploy. Something to tap your foot to. Each phase is loud. Each phase is distinct. And they are equally impactful and iterative.

D is for Discover

Ever since gurus started articulating their wisdom, we have been hearing something along the lines of self-knowledge being truth. Every major world religion espouses this idea. It seems that if we are aware, we have more control. This is the essence of sharing. With knowledge comes clarity – to create clarity, it is necessary to have information. To be empowered to have information and then to be able to reflect or dialogue on the relative truth of the information that we have. When it is possible to have information about ourselves, we are less triggered. We are less likely to be controlled by fear or old habits that have been built *for* us and not *with* us.

As it applies to individuals, so does it apply to entire organisations. We believe that it is possible and necessary to allow an organisation to build awareness and a joint participative process to talk about what the organisation looks and feels like. So we have to invite the organisation to discover itself. To seek self-wisdom and self-truth. To tell and hear the stories.

What is truth?

We are assailed today by the term 'fake news'. The expression comes from the German *Lügenpresse* (lying press), which used to be chanted at Nazi rallies to undermine critics of the regime. Before that, German intellectuals used it to denounce enemy propaganda during the Franco-Prussian War and the First World War.[1] Today, with so much data at our fingertips, it seems easy – and critical – to figure out what is true (and what is false). We look for peace and solace in this truth.

> **Chris:** In the context of culture, we *are* the experience, and we must remember that there are *several* truths, in a permanently revolving mosaic. In an average day in my office, I move from project to project, from room to room. I flow across these meetings with different aspects of my personal mosaic rising at different times. At times, I am leveraging the male camaraderie, at times I access my London roots, at times my humour. Sometimes I am placed in a box, because of my social, ethnic or organisational hierarchy or status. Across these scenarios, does (and should) the same experience of the culture play out in a congruent way as being true? How, then, to *discover* our current culture? For culture is shaped in an instant.

Who are we?

We need to know what we are dealing with, where we are, as the leaders of the organisation, but also for each member. We use the process of discovery to bring shared involvement of a discussion about who we are as an organisation and who we would like to be. It really is hard to imagine that we would start a journey towards being an empathic organisation without fully listening to the various realms within it; to conduct a 360-degree instrument review, to bask and wallow in the data, opinions, stories, then to allow the data to start to turn into 'facts', themes and stories that can root us in certainty.

We often discover that we already have empathy and share as part of our everyday lives, only in small ways. The question is: how can we make that occurrence of when we share – when it feels like we are doing the right thing – become habit? So that it is almost instinctual all of the time.

In order to discover what defines us, we must listen to the stories of others. We want to do so in an involving way. In one project, we asked every stakeholder in the organisation to tell us stories that showed us who we are at our best. And we took time to listen to all the stories – and there was great participation. People warmed up and jumped in. For many of us, it was like waiting for the right song to come along before committing to the embarrassment of dancing. These storytelling sessions allow us to start tapping our feet and think about entering the dance. We need to feel a pulse, a beat.

What are the themes of our story?
We have the opportunity to focus on how and when to leverage our strengths; through stories of when we performed that action of sharing, what it looked like, when it happened, who was there, what was so unique about it. As we listen to stories from across the organisation, we form our own versions of the truth. It is the opportunity to articulate the stories that best fit with the culture that we want. To create the *themes* of the stories that we want to hear.

Good stories people tell can delight us. Most have a point of principle, like a fable.

Here is one story that we heard from a financial services company, where the focus was on integrity:

> Sometime in the 1970s, a junior banking executive is sent to a new market opportunity in a developing country. The executive has been selected and schooled in the history and values of the organisation. The new market experience is part of a well-planned sequence of career moves for the executive – great things are in store for him. In the market, the executive is asked to employ the child of a local politician. He is told that this type of quid pro quo is part of the way business is done locally. He

is appalled; this goes against everything that he has been told about how the institution works. The executive refuses. When pushed by the local management team to comply, he resigns and writes a note to HQ, refusing to work under such ethics. The executive is promoted and the local management team is removed.

The story is interesting on many levels. Is it all right for a global organisation to put its own value system into a local market, or should it respect local customs and practices? Is the bank imperialistic in its approach? Is doing business globally not about accepting local customs? Should the executive not respect hierarchy? Is it safer to resign because the executive is 'known', is part of a programmed move and thus will be noticed? Is it safe for any of us to resign on a point of principle? The point is that the story not only provides a 'right answer' to ethics from the organisation's perspective – it also speaks to many wider issues in a way that no rulebook or policy does.

All of this can be intentional in the choice of stories that represent us, in the themes and context of the planned discovery.

If we are intentional, it is possible for us to flood the organisation with stories that we have discovered, and these stories ground us. They define who and what we are. We are, then, in some way, family. We have a shared history, a way of doing things. In the Discover phase, we create the themes from the stories that we tell. Truth emerges about *how* we share and what this means.

We must allow time for these stories to be discovered from deep within the organisation, up and down and across, again and again. Until, one day, it seems that it is everything that people are talking about.

Discovery is the phase of the work which is the least under control and which addresses issues of ethics and tone in the 4 Ds approach. Here are some of the unwelcome stories that are related to the theme.

Chris: One company I worked for invited discussion of projects and challenged a team to find opportunities to improve business. One proposal was to move away from using fossil fuels which had been a big part of the company's history. The team leveraged a video by a climate pressure group to help present their case about data and public opinion. More than half of the executives present walked out of the room as the video was running. It was too difficult for them to entertain the idea, or even to risk being seen watching the video.

We have become hardened in our views of our industries, for-profits, governments and NGOs. In many cases, organisations have become a machine that has lost its purpose, whose intent is not in sync with its actions, strategies or partnerships.

> **Here are the major questions an organisation must consider with regard to the tone of the Discover phase:**
> • is any topic off-limits?
> • are the employees allowed to share their grievances?
> • do we want to hear the stories of communities and stake-holders impacted by good and bad news?

D is for Define
In the Define stage, we take the themes from the dialogue in the Discover stage and craft them into simple and meaningful terms that will resonate with everyone. We keep them brief, and we illustrate the principles with stories, not with long definitions. As we ground ourselves, we need to pick some words, some artefacts to hold onto. We will speak of the beauty and power of these when they are done well.

Chris: One of the best projects that I have seen was at American Express. The mission was *To Become the World's Most Respected Service Brand*. Each word was defined and explained so as to make sense:

- *To Become* — accepting that we are on a journey and in an almost permanent time of change; always evolving;
- *the World's* — speaks to the consistent global enterprise and application of the vision;
- *Most Respected* — this was about the emotional connection that each of the organisation's stakeholders aspired to; it is aspirational and has meaning across cultures and personally for each individual from a quality perspective;
- *Service Brand* — it defines the industry that they wish to compete in.

The company took great pains and went to great expense to shape these few words, but they speak of the mental models within which the construct of an organisation operates. They *define* the way that the collection of people called the organisation actually think and behave.

Keep it clear and concise

Creating clarity through choosing the right words is important. We know from neuroscience that the prefrontal cortex can hold only a few things at a time.[2] So often, we talk about how to focus on no more than three things.

The theory around having this prefrontal cortex as part of our so-called executive functioning comes from work carried out in the 1960s that still holds true concerning the working memory. Baddeley's model of working memory contains three components: the *central executive*, the *phonological loop* and the *visuospatial sketchpad*.[3]

The central executive function directs us to what is relevant and actionable *now*. It brings clarity and dictates priority when more than one thing is happening at the same time. It co-ordinates across more dormant systems of the brain. One such system is the phonological loop, a storage system for sounds and phrases. It keeps it relevant in a rehearsal loop – of only a few things. The sharper and fewer the better for memory recall and thus for acting as a prime organising principle of processing. Another storage system is the visuospatial sketchpad, which creates mental maps, leading to less clutter, less confusion – and more meaning, more clarity. More of a chance of the thing that we are trying to define becoming possible.

There is a technique to make organisational attributes of *strategy*, *values*, *purpose*, *mission*, *brand*, *leadership behaviours* and *practices*. We have noticed that the attention to these varies widely across organisations. We heard recently that many organisations seem to need a point of pain really to understand that such things are critical. Without this, the organisation seems to flounder. It then competes or functions through a confederacy rather than a union. This may not always be the worst thing – for the right time and place, this may be the best operating model to work with. But without some core articulation of solid ideas, there is confusion. All too prevalent in organisations is a proliferation of all the ideas which have not been updated or refined and just add to the confusion.

> **Linda:** Sometimes a successfully defined external brand can resonate so strongly internally with its leaders and employees that they voluntarily use the succinct phrase to summarise the company's culture and values. State Farm's 'like a good neighbour' was a case in point.
>
> State Farm's long-time ad agency DDB created the iconic slogan in 1971, with a jingle written by pop star Barry Manilow that ended with the line '...State Farm is there'. It was pure marketing brilliance because of its simplicity, yet anyone could understand and probably describe what 'a good neighbour' was like. The slogan was also perfect for State Farm and suited its operating model well – with

19,000 agents and hundreds of claims operations offices across the US, most insurance contracts were signed in the agent's office, who also lived in the same small town, and claims were dealt with within 1,000 miles of the claimant. For almost 50 years, 'like a good neighbour' has endured and remains as part of the company's DNA.

I remember after I joined the company in its Bloomington head office and when I travelled around its field offices across the nation, employees and agents told me stories about 'helping others'; 'being there when others are in need'; 'being responsible and being good'. To them, these are not empty words. It meant being present at their customer's children's birthday parties, holding the hands of storm victims and making sure their claims were processed, chatting to a 75-year-old pensioner about his hip replacement surgery when he called in to enquire about his insurance coverage; the list goes on and on.

In 2015, State Farm employees volunteered 501,000 hours in education-related causes,[4] and the company won Corporate Social Responsibility Leadership Awards in 2016 and 2017, based in part on the number of volunteers and volunteer hours that employees put in.

Although State Farm decided to retire the slogan in 2016 and launch a new one, 'Here to help life go right' to reflect its shift from insurance to financial advice, the company deeply understood the influence of being a 'good neighbour' and strived to keep it alive. In 2017, State Farm launched its Neighbourhood of Good platform, which connects consumers looking to volunteer with charitable opportunities in their towns.

Chris: I recall one company where I demonstrated that the organisation had a number of strategies, vision statements, etc., all visible at the same time. The top team suggested that we extend the meeting to lunchtime and knock something out. While time-efficient, this was not the best way to get full involvement. The Define phase is the strategy stage. The work of strategy in culture should be seamless across the organisation.

Let's take Southwark Cathedral in south London as an example. The site has been excavated to reveal a history of worship at the same place for more than 2,000 years. Before the Roman invasion there had been ancient Britons, then worshippers of Roman gods and then the early Roman Christian churches, since built over. There is no doubt that the succession of religions in this space involved blood and pain, but we want to make the larger point about the transition of practices, the adoption of what worked best in one culture and belief system and that we built upon what was there before. All good principles for steering what we want to do when tasked with building culture anew.

In the Define stage, we take the themes from the dialogue and craft them into simple and meaningful terms that will resonate. We keep them brief and we illustrate the principles with stories, not with long definitions.

Too many cooks...
The main problem that comes at this phase of the work is the coherence among the groups accountable for it. In some of the best work, specialist agency assistance is utilised to help ensure that all the work serves the external brand and overall corporate strategy. In reality, it often flounders between the HR department, the internal communications team, the marketing department, the CEO's office and the legal department. The conflicting agendas of these groups and the power battles that always seem to ensue block the most effective articulation and definition of the work at hand.

It is best if final control sits above, from outside these groups – in so many cases, individual departments produce a suboptimal language which serves too many agendas; it does not serve its true purpose, especially given the power that it has to do so.

D is for Develop

Chris used to read a lot of Sun Tzu's *The Art of War*. It was an ancient Chinese strategy book adapted by business writers in the 1970s and 1980s who were interested in transferring the guiding principles to the industry, as the West sought to emulate and compete with Asian market growth. A central idea of the book is that you first look to avoid defeat by building a strong defence:

> The good fighters of old first put themselves beyond the possibility of defeat, and then waited for an opportunity of defeating the enemy. Thus it is that in war the victorious strategist only seeks battles after the victory has been won, whereas he who is destined to defeat first fights and afterwards looks for victory.[5]

At the Develop phase of the work, one is looking to establish policies, processes and procedures which are guided by the values and principles discovered and defined in the first two phases.

The cart before the horse

All too often what we see is that the organisations and our functional groups in particular rush to communicate intent or new policy without having done the work of the first two phases well. If the Discover and Define phases have been done well, then the language and thoughts are already embedded in the organisation and the transfer of these new ideas into the organisation will come easily and be recognised without incongruence. Too often this is not so.

This is the path of good politics: the people are made aware of a problem by the government, which wishes to draw their attention to the thing they want to fix; the media are used to stir up and confirm stories of how bad things are and opine on what should be done; and then the right government official or politician steps up with the solution that they have been wanting to implement. It is managed well. At times this is done well in organisations, too.

In some cases, the imposition of process and procedure needed to come first and then itself become the catalyst for change – the ending of slavery before the eradication of racism, for instance; women's suffrage; de-segregating schools; removing caste or religious privilege in the workplace. But when the Discover and Define phases are skipped, what follows is the inevitable struggle of and pain for society. We see society trying to catch up to make sense of the process, of the new laws, and their resulting reactions over decades of tension. There is a question of expediency – the judgement of when the passing of processes ahead of widespread buy-in rights a wrong, addresses the totem, or the egregious aspect of societal or corporate practice which needs to be amended.

Congruence
In the Develop phase, we seek congruence, aligning all the company to work to the same beat. In our experience, the development of values and principles, the development of a culture change, involves a new philosophy. This change has to be wide-ranging and includes the following:

- there is an organising principle for how non-executives manage;
- it is included in the terms and conditions of the company;
- HR policies and practices (pay, performance, hiring, promotions, and all other processes and procedures that impact the lives and experiences of our people) are governed by principles that are congruent;
- financial, real estate, marketing, brand, operations (and so on) practise what they as staff functions and executives preach. (Are their decisions guided by the defined values and principles?)

The ownership of such work cannot be by crowd or committee; it must be a reflection of the very real changes in all of those people as well as the people who draft and interpret the policies, who run the company and its functions, and create the day-to-day experience. It is important that functional staff groups are given special attention – to bring their members as a primary targeted audience to work in the first two phases.

D is for Deploy

> **Chris:** There are two schools of thought on the channels for deployment: the formal and the informal. When planning the Deploy phase, I have used the simplicity of the iceberg principle to review and describe the organisation. The iceberg ranges, of course, from what is visible to what lies deep within the organisation.

The formal channels

The formal channels of deployment are the speeches, the uniforms, the office environment, the public relationship speeches, the marketing and product communications and the campaigns. This includes what we measure and how we define concepts such as, among others, employee engagement and inclusion.

The informal channels

The informal channels are perhaps more important. If the Define stage has worked well, it will have catalysed the eager, who will look to be at the vanguard of the new changes. The passion is there – and the opportunity to harness it. With good work on the informal viral approaches, the opportunity is there to deploy the intent of the change far more deeply and in ways that cannot be envisaged by any change team. Like a wildflower that takes root everywhere, it will keep popping up, sustained by passion. This enables mass habit formation, new group norms, at scale and in a viral manner.

CONTEXT AND INTENT

We look at this work overall as a flow, to bring unity. If done well, this simple process creates the momentum to evolve culture. The challenge for the architect of the process in your locale is to plot the *nature* of the change.

In this context, we, of course, are proposing that the flow becomes empathic and more share-based. We have seen that the process can be used to create a new sense of history and shared purpose, and, to some degree, a revision of the organisation to be based on the ideals of the nature of the conversation that we want to provoke. The ethical issue is how comfortable we feel controlling each other's thoughts, actions and behaviours.

NOTES

1   Chandler, A. 'The "worst" German word of the year', *The Atlantic*, January 2015.

2   Preston, A.R., and Eichenbaum, H. 'Interplay of hippocampus and prefrontal cortex in memory', *Current Biology*, 23 (17), 2013, pp. 764–73.

3   Edward, D. 'Baddeley & Hitch (1974) – Working Memory', *Psychology Unlocked*, 2017. http://www.psychologyunlocked.com/baddeleyhitch1974. Accessed 26 April 2018.

4   https://neighborhoodofgood.statefarm.com/why/index.shtml

5   Sun Tzu. *The Art of War – Special Edition* (1st annotated English ed.). (L. Giles, trans.). El Paso: Digital Pulse Inc., 2007.

18

DISCOVER AND EXPLORE

'Tell me and I forget. Teach me and I remember. Involve me
and I learn'

— Benjamin Franklin

In this chapter:
- tactics of the Discover phase;
- how to drive high involvement;
- should we manipulate the crowd just because we can?

THE PROPOSAL

1. Conduct a 360-degree review of the organisation. This is an
   invitation for the keen and the early adopters to participate.
2. Consider the full breadth of the organisation in the discussion
   about the work:
   a. Employees — full-time, part-time, every-time. Care
      should be taken to ensure as fully representative a sample
      of employees as possible. Every nuance of segment,
      group, geography, tenure, gender, religion, etc., should
      be considered and carefully invited. It is not always
      possible to include every employee, so think about the
      right percentage of people to take part. If it is possible to
      get everyone to take part, then do so.

b Clients/customers – every segment of customer, all geographies and points of view across the business model, or any consumer groups – where there is no 'client' as such but where a service or government obligation is met by the organisation.

c Non-executive directors – the formally appointed groups which regulate the organisation and provide oversight.

d Partner organisations – the multiple partner organisations that impact the B2B, B2B2B or B2B2C versions of the networks of business models now in place.

e Public – where the organisation has a relationship with the public or the government, how does wider society view it?

3 Use the appreciative inquiry process. The organisation needs to be empathic. It is crucial to share more across our organisation and also in how we work with all of our constituents. It supports our strategy of involvement:

a What does it look like when we share as an organisation?

b Do your leaders or colleagues make decisions with great empathy?

c If you visit this organisation in 15 years' time and it is the epitome of empathy and sharing, what has changed? How is this possible? Tell me the story.

4 People are sampled in groups and in individual interviews. Some submit stories to an online hub, etc.

5 Evaluate the rituals and totems.

6 Theme the stories and data.

7 Link the emergent themes to strategy.

The very act of discovery will modify one's perspective. All the multiple journeys in our lives have changed us in some way.

Discovery literally has the power to transform each person as well as the collective, particularly if the journey is well designed and all involved are aware that it is a shared journey. The process breaks the machine free from the day-to-day routine and carries the promise of change through a carefully orchestrated process.

PROVOKING CURIOSITY

The more that is discovered about the organisation's strengths and weaknesses, the more the collective is empowered to forge change with *transparency*. Curiosity encourages and informs the start of the journey for the organisation. There had to be a reason to start the campaign for different methodologies for the work at hand. Curiosity is linked to discovery as an internal driver, like hunger or thirst. The drive theory sees curiosity as a naturally occurring urge that must be satisfied in a very similar manner to how we satisfy our hunger by eating. When curiosity becomes aroused, humans look to satisfy the desire for understanding. The specific dilemma, which precipitated the question, or necessity for change, drives the process. Wherever the incongruity enters the effectiveness of the workplace is the inception of the investigation, which will lead to the discovery process that will enable the most effective future structure, and culture, of the organisation. Our curiosity is piqued when we see something that doesn't fit into our universe as predictable and orderly and we are moved to explain it, which supports the incongruity theory.

Think about the early cave dweller or hunter-gatherer. At some point, in order to seek change, they had to (a) be curious, (b) be forced into it by a random and/or traumatic event, or (c) find an element of their cosmology which was incongruent for them. We are motivated by threat or fear. Perhaps we're naturally curious about incongruence.

In the absence of threat, how can we as an organisation provoke the curiosity to shift? In the Discover phase, we recommend inviting mass participation in a dialogue about the thing that you want to be. Children are naturally curious; some stay curious through positively reinforcing environments, and some don't. This curiosity links with the confidence to try something new and the motivation to practise until it becomes habit.

AN APPRECIATIVE APPROACH

An appreciative inquiry means focusing on the positive aspects of the thing that we want to see brought forth. We leverage this instead of the gap analysis done by many consulting firms, which usually entails creating a list of all that needs to be changed. Appreciative inquiry means asking the questions about what is best in the organisation right now and in the past – a discussion in the organisation about sharing and empathy: when do we currently do this, or when did we in the past? What does it look like when we do it? What are the stories of what this means and how it impacts?

These positive stories have the ability to heal wounds, to bridge. In one example, we had a situation where one organisation had acquired a number of other companies around the world. Each one had a rich history of practices, stories and habits, some shared and some not. By asking the stakeholders from all these various companies what the organisation looked like at its best, we began to see a picture of common practices, common ways of viewing the customer, common ways of talking about what was really important.

We also looked at areas where there was difference. In some cultures, sub-teams, departments or silos, one aspect of practice is so much more important than the other. Because of the shaping of the questions, one is able to shape the actual inquiry itself. This means that we shape the very conversations that are taking place in the organisation.

What we have found is that when people leave the interview or team discussion that was focused on such an inquiry, they tend to go and tell their neighbours, their friends, the family – they tell the story as an act of catharsis. We have disturbed something within them – to be curious about something.

So the very act of conducting the interviews is in itself provoking the very thing that we are talking about: sharing. It is, essentially, priming the organisation to be more conscious of a particular aspect by generating the conversation about the fixed aspect. Thus, asking someone about when they see sharing and what it means to them, asking them to explore empathy and to tell a story, taps into their imagination.

This approach is used to provide new schemata development in our brains. To learn a new thing. Imagination literally creates the potential for a new neural pathway. We enforce the imagination with stories and dialogue about the stories. We learn.

PRIMING

It is also possible in this stage to see particular stories again and again.

Chris: In some organisations I leveraged the opportunity to pick key phrases and keywords and watch them spread virally with intent within the organisation. In one particular case, I leveraged a phrase from a story that I had heard one executive tell in their interview in the Discover phase – it is an example about the attitude to the customer and links with how sales meetings should be held. The story had some distinctive characteristics and named another competitive brand. It was deliberately spread to show what excellence in the workplace looked like. About three months later, when attending a regional meeting, the sales head for that region told the same story back to me. Months had passed since I had deliberately spread the story. The story as part of the Discover process had done the rounds across the organisation. A mid-level sales manager shared it exactly as we had intended – as part of the Discover stage.

EARLY ADOPTERS

Some people are delighted when you ask them to participate in something big for the organisation – such as talking about what something means or inviting their involvement in focus groups. They are proud. And they talk about it to friends, work colleagues and family. They are fans, or *early adopters*. If we involve them early, they work tirelessly and invisibly on our behalf to drive the daily conversations that stimulate.

In *The Tipping Point* by Malcolm Gladwell, we see this opportunity for early adopters to become excited by the dialogue.¹ They can be called upon to help in any way possible. They will give a face to the change and will spread stories – they ask for opportunities to help administer the process of change, they will shift their focus and create energy and buzz in the organisation on the themes, which resonate for them. Everywhere we have worked, this group has been there.

The trick is how to know where to identify these people when starting such work. You need to create a beacon. They look like any one of us but in every organisation we've worked in we've found that this group of people is *loyal to ideals*. They show loyalty to the expressed values and to the organisation, they are impatient for change and they want to be involved in the opportunity to talk about meaning in their work. They want to be the first participants in a pilot.

This is part of what we're trying to do in the Discover phase – figure out who the champions are – and in many cases the champions of the idea that we seek to promote. The inquiry into the conversation will come from all levels of the organisation, which makes it powerful as a cross-functional slice if one cares to design the group interactions.

In our experience, these champions are found among non-executive directors, clients, government departments, partner organisations, and then more internally, a unique geographic group or business division, as well as employees from all levels. They always emerge. A warm and friendly greeting or a simple invitation to participate releases an energy that organisations otherwise would have attempted to buy with marketing, benefits statements, free toys and pizza lunches. But here it is not bought, it is revealed.

HARNESSING THE ENERGY

This positive energy release across the organisation can be supplemented by various forms of involvement: employee forums, stand-up meetings, blogs, crowdsourcing tools, video diaries.

There has to be a careful consideration of how much to genuinely leverage stories heard in these forums.

> **Chris:** In my experience, it is better to put the stories in the right places so that a great story can be used. With the use of video and the multiple storytelling techniques that we have available in this digital age, there are few boundaries to the spread of information. Sometimes something anomalous to the normal host culture of communications, but done in a sharing way and with empathy, can be used right away to impact and signal change. In one organisation, we moved to a quarterly and then a monthly dialogue where the CEO reacted live to crowdsourced themes from an inquiry. The power of the CEO to paint a story and show vulnerability and empathy to a story live signalled a shift.

TOTEMS

A totem is something we hold sacred within the organisation. To use another metaphor, it is the 'sacred cow', the thing we do not touch.

> **Chris:** I once visited Hong Kong for a long work trip. After a busy, hardworking day, I invited my team for a drink in the bar that was housed in the headquarters building. I had

previously been taken there by expatriate colleagues. My team were almost exclusively HK Chinese. Even though the gathering was held well before the time most people left the office, many of them declined the invitation, making polite excuses about family or other commitments. Eventually, as trust was established, I was told that the local Chinese employees traditionally were not invited to the bar – it was used exclusively for the whites and Indians who formed most of the expat community. This was an aspect of colonialism in this particular organisation which dated back over 100 years and which was still an ingrained habit in the twenty-first century.

While the organisation spoke to diversity, the equality and openness of who is allowed to be where in the building still existed even though no one today thought these norms were a good idea. They were historical habits which no one had thought to discontinue. They benefited some, but often because they simply had not been articulated as incongruent. When such totems are examined, it is hard to justify their continued existence. Some fall fast and symbolically in the Discover phase. It requires mental toughness and readiness from the executives to acknowledge and amend.

In one acquisition, we found different doors to the organisation's HQ being used by different ranks; some elevators, some toilets, some parts of the building are often segregated based on the salary rank or some other quirk of the enterprise. In another organisation, a graduating management development class presented the CEO with an engraved gold-plated revolver in appreciation of the educational opportunity the organisation had given them. The gift reflected the rural, relatively conservative, gun-owning history of the organisation, yet was contrary to all the HR policies and espoused ethics on safety.

Another organisation had a history of being direct in its questioning of the quality of work – similar to a PhD viva examination.

This quality test originates from a history of deep intellect and precision – yet is intimidating and counter to the culture espoused. In the context of the history of the organisation all these things *seem* normal. Be careful not to overlook the worth of seemingly innocuous habits or patterns for sometimes their impact is invisible. Sometimes they are a symbol of organisational strength. The bars and the exclusive restrooms drive a sense of a personal club – they also drive deep, trusted connections. Those deep relationships with the executives help steer and bring agility over time and in crisis. They are exclusionary to some but the totems once had a purpose. Asking the hard questions, however scary, ensures that you know what you are doing.

When invited to have a dialogue about when we are at our best, stories of when we are not at our best also crop up. Often these totems also appear in the stories. They emerge as incongruent to what we know and believe on an individual basis to be true in the context of sharing. When asked about how we are empathic, I tell you when I am also *not understood*. It is important to capture and highlight these examples and show them to executives through local employees and to engage in the conversation bluntly. In one organisation, we hired a film crew and interviewed people all over the world about what they thought about the emergent themes and about totems. They captured live, candid interviews in canteens, car parks and corridors. We showed the footage to the executives and asked them to have a dialogue about incongruence.

This is part of the Discover stage: an opportunity to talk about who we are, to challenge some of the rituals and the ways that we have always been, to think about what needs to be true moving forward to express ourselves as congruent.

STRATEGY
It is important, of course, that we are able to tie any themes that we wish to discuss in the Discover phase back to major strategic

competitive themes as a business. If we are to examine aspects such as empathy, there must be a compelling logical tie to how these things will also make us competitive, make us stronger and enable us to win.

For what we are trying to evolve, we need to cherish the best of what we have, moving from doing it only a small percentage of the time to it becoming the default way.

FEEDBACK AND DIALOGUE

Chris: I often smile when asked to think about how we can encourage a feedback culture – for us to be more open and to reveal more of our real selves at work. In life, we have the skills we need. I'm able to take a T-shirt back to the shop if it doesn't fit, and give feedback; I'm able to complain to the restaurant that the food is too salty. I am sometimes skilled at difficult conversations with members of my family – sometimes highly emotional – but competent. Outside the organisational world, the skills of empathy, criticism, giving feedback, being positive and being accountable are well seasoned in our homes, and we practise them daily. Some of us find it easier to return things to the shops than others, some of us will accept cold soup, not wanting to make a fuss, but even in the most timid there is the ability and need for us to use these skills in order to function in daily society.

In the organisation, there is this element of psychological safety that is critical to address as a prerequisite to embracing this work. The tone and attitude of senior management in allowing dissonance and noise, in being vulnerable to the employee and other stakeholders, and thinking about how this expression is linked to the strategy of the organisation and how it is expressed, is absolutely critical.

This phase of the work must be embraced, talked about, known and understood by all levels of the organisation. It must be believed that ultimately this will make us better. It is relatively easy to change things that need to be changed when faced with a crisis. The challenge for most organisations, of course, is to change *before* the crisis occurs. So the belief and links to strategy must come from multiple places and also be expressed as part of the inquiry process in the set-up.

NOTES

1   Gladwell, M. *The Tipping Point: How Little Things Can Make a Big Difference*. Boston: Little, Brown, 2000.

DEFINE AND ELEVATE

'Always aim at complete harmony of thought and word and deed. Always aim at purifying your thoughts and everything will be well'

— Mahatma Gandhi

In this chapter:
- how to discuss what is most important and make it clear;
- leveraging collaboration and partnerships to achieve clarity in strategy;
- get alignment on congruence.

THE PROPOSAL

1 Codify the intent of the organisation to be more empathic and share-based in its core language.
2 Do all of the above in a collegiate and unifying way — avoiding ego, tribalism and silos to impact, while leveraging specialist direction and help.

In the previous chapter we shared discoveries from our education and work in the first phase (Discover phase). In this chapter we will identify key themes based on those experiences and insights (Define phase). Sometimes the themes have been self-evident; in some other cases, Chris has needed to hire an external marketing data department to classify the data into core stories and themes.

It is important to link the themes of how we can share better and be empathic, from different audiences, to the existent brand, strategy, values, mission, history and relevance. The senior team, which owns the existing brand, strategy, values, mission, etc., will need to be fully engaged to consider the legacy of this moment, review the totems to build and destroy, and then figure out where to put up signs of change.

ASSUMING GOOD INTENT

Chris: When I was about 10 years old, I moved to north-west London from Guyana. I went to middle school and high school in a Jewish neighbourhood. People invited me into their houses and treated me as one of their house members. From there, I went to college and made more friends who also took me into their lives and introduced me to their parents and siblings. Like many college students, I was poor. I lived on tinned sardines, chilli and instant Ramen noodles. Near where we lived was a Sikh gurdwara. Some evenings, I went there to get the hot vegetarian food they had cooked to share with visitors at the Sikh community's customary communal meals.

After college, I spent two years travelling all over the world. In my early twenties, I travelled across Europe on something called Interrail, a cheap way for youth and students to travel. One day, on a trip in Turin, Italy, we paused in front of a two-star Michelin restaurant, in smelly clothes and with no money. To our astonishment, the owner came out and invited us in. We said we had no money and were obviously not dressed for the venue, and yet we received a table and a free meal.

On another trip, I was robbed in Brussels. I was left without money, my passport or spare clothes. I needed to get back to the UK. We have all seen people lost at places such as railway stations, begging for money to get home. I was one of those people and everyone ignored me. I spent a day and a night begging. I got nothing. Late one night, an old Hasidic Jew gave me money for food, for transport to the harbour and to call home. I have never forgotten him. For me it's the tale of the Good Samaritan that pops up across many religions throughout history and inspires the Golden Rule (see Chapter 2). Why did he give his money to a stranger? This was a very religious man. He had been praying loudly in a corner of the station. Many people bypassed him and made fun of how loud he was. At the end of the prayer, he helped me. I could go on and share many more stories…So, what's the point I am making?

The point is that I have consistently experienced more sharing and love in the world when I have needed it than hate. I find that in almost everyone there is a need to be kind. In the examples above, people shared food or money – the most important of resources – *because they believed in something*. There was a *reason* for doing it. We know that as human beings we are wired neurologically to share, and we see that when we collectively have a sense of purpose – a collective belief system. Then we are not afraid to share, for it defines us as humans. The difference between us and other species is our ability to imagine. To believe in something called purpose – it allows us to band together and help each other as strangers and is an advantage over other species in how we compete.

The words that we choose to believe in are so important, for words shape the communication and the mental models of thought. It can be very difficult to choose the right words to express our feelings but it is also critical that we get it right.

DIPLOMACY

With such work, Chris has often leveraged help from a specialist agency. It is a skill to be able to craft language that resonates globally (i.e. works in every part of the world that is tied to the brand) and respects the past and inspires a vision for the future. Not all of us are good with this stuff. Our experience tells us that it is hard to articulate something which meets the need of the committee. This work requires such sign-off that in almost every organisation the scripts and phrases they use require a certain political deftness. So many departments are involved (communication, corporate and public affairs, legal, risk, brand, marketing, etc.) that good internal navigation and conviction are paramount.

INVOLVING THE CORE GROUP

Art Kleiner describes a core group at the heart of every organisation. This is the senior team but also extends to others in the organisation who have relationships with them. This small group directs major decisions for the organisation. Normally a visible power elite, they have the power to make things happen, or to stall things. It sometimes challenges our egalitarian values even to think about such a group existing in human societies. But leveraging this group consciously can also positively influence the decisions an organisation makes for the good.[1]

The Define phase is focused on getting this group to buy in and help define this work. Failure to take the time to do this well causes the work to fail. The solutions look like the cursory team-building work – a management offsite consisting of a speech by the sponsor, and at worst, a presentation from the change team on the side, communications and HR people who go away and do the work while the core group are engaged in the 'real work' of the organisation. Rather than this, they need to be involved. They need time to dedicate to their own rite of passage to induce the cognitive-dissonance adoption of the new practices.

The process that we have seen work best seeks to create a rapid learning environment where all data can be processed and assimilated by business leaders themselves and not the proxy departments. For example, we once used a large, ballroom-sized space and filled it with centrepieces to show the work of the different segments that we had talked to: employees, customers, analysts, NGOs, market perceptions, non-executive directors, etc. Each segment had its stories to tell, on video, with real people. Then we showed the history of the company and where it was going in terms of competitive landscapes, new products, etc. Competitor analysis was shown as well as a review of global trends.

The whole experience was presented as if in a special exhibition in a museum. There were guides and data curators who accompanied the senior team and representatives from the various other departments and regions. We took them around from one exhibit to another in groups of four or five. At the end, we asked them to think about how best to summarise all they had seen or heard in pictures. We then asked them to turn the pictures into themes (yes, again) and form their own 'language' and phrases that should guide the work moving forward. The right words emerged naturally – without the need for subcommittees – and were refined by a specialist. And owned by the executives. With executives, it is often beyond personal power – if possible, make it about *legacy*.

Many of us suffer from imposter syndrome. For many, making it to the so-called C Suite, or being invited into the core group, is a dream – and they have sacrificed a lot to get there. We are trying to create a sacred space – one that stops in time and makes it a moment of legacy for these leaders to feel special. It is hard for executives to sponsor rapid change – especially for something like culture. They have been programmed all their lives to behave in a certain way.

Often brought up in the host organisation, it is difficult for them to adjust. It is very hard for them to be anything else – they have achieved their position by enabling and running, in some cases, the culture they are now considering changing. Why is this so important? We need them to adopt something new. There is an important and critical element of emotional attachment. People copy the passion, language and words of their leaders. It is a crucible moment for the top team to dream and believe new things. To want to embrace what sharing means to each other, how it impacts business.

In the first phase, the work discovered must be translated. The organisation continues to be in some cases like a family – the children copy the things their parents do because that is the path to new success. In every organisation there is a core group.

BEING THE HELPER

In a medieval court, there would be clans, issues of power, fear of retribution and constant politics. Fear of saying the wrong thing might literally mean death, not just for you but also for your family and clan. In an organisation, death can come in the form of removal from the organisation, career 'suicide', loss of pay, etc. How to navigate this phase of the work and stay alive?

In the court, the jester was the only one who could speak truth to power. Jesters, also known as fools, in the medieval European royal courts were dressed in a brightly coloured coat, with donkey ears, bells or other decorations. They served not simply to amuse but to criticise their master or mistress and their guests. Elizabeth I is said to have rebuked one of her fools for being insufficiently severe with her.

Excessive behaviour, however, could lead to a fool being whipped, as King Lear threatens to punish his fool in the eponymous play. So in the organisation, if you are working within the culture, regardless of the position, if you are the one concerned with designing the process in some way then you need to be able

to tell stories, make observations, speak the truth to powers that
be and ensure that people can trust you as a safe source. Not a
threat to the organisation but someone who is there to help. This
means suspending your ego in the process while understanding
professionally the power politics involved and being sensible.
A 'jester' for the organisation cannot of course wear bells and
donkey's ears. However, you distinguish yourself as helper, find
some personal aspect that allows you to recall that you are in the
organisational system and yet on the edge seeking to help.

TURNING WORDS INTO CONGRUENCE
In the film *Inequality for All* Robert Reich talks about the huge
increase in the pay gap between the minority (1 per cent) and the
rest of the population in the West.[2] Some of the decisions about
how to compete, what to be transparent about, how to share
differently, how to steer the work of the company differently have
to be taken after very careful thought. Almost every company has
elements of integrity in terms of how they have competed. Almost
every industry has a history of current success based on decisions
that might not be seen as ethical. In a period when the power of
the unions has been considerably weakened and executives earn
a multiple and are often taxed significantly less than the rest of
society, why should I as an individual give that up? To do so puts my
family and social status at risk. I have to be altruistic about the future
of the organisation I have been groomed to lead. This issue of pay is
important. Changes in how we share pay have, according to Reich,
the ultimate trickle down in creating the new values/mission of the
organisation to share and be more empathic. We catalyse this group
to impact social change.

In the service industry there is the service-profit chain on how
leadership and culture impact growth: happy workers deliver
customer service with excellence. Happy customers spend more
money, give the organisation more share of wallet and talk up the

brand (\$). This reduces the cost on acquisitive growth and boosts organic growth and thus requires less investment – more can be spent on training, leadership development, intrinsic and extrinsic motivation elements. The employee is better trained and happy. The cycle repeats. The top service brands all reflect something like this.

Reich suggests something similar.[3] Executives decide to cut their pay and/or agree to higher taxation. Government gets more tax revenue and spends more money on education, workers are better equipped to compete and get better jobs and provide a more skilled workforce, the economy grows and real wages grow. The middle class spends more – consumer spending is the biggest driver of most economies – and the economy as a whole grows. Executives ensure growth and wealth distribution. This allows for elements of fear to be reduced in society – we hate our neighbours less and feel more confident about the future. Maybe...

The work of changing the culture makes this a significant phase of this work. It sounds super-liberal and 'fluffy' to say we aim for a share-based, empathic culture internally. The people who drive the decisions must ground it in the competitive landscape. Unless more urgent and drastic change is required. If it is serious, then drastic policy change is sometimes required. The work of the Define phase continues to be critical. What are you prepared to sacrifice in your own life or change for a wider purpose?

NOTES

1   Kleiner, A. *Who Really Matters: The Core Group Theory of Power, Privilege, and Success*. New York: Doubleday, 2003.

2   *Inequality for All* (2013), [film] Dir. Jacob Kornbluth, USA: Radius-TWC Pictures.

3   Ibid.

20

DEVELOP AND ENABLE

'The overall name of these interrelated structures is system. The motorcycle is a system. A real system... There's so much talk about the system. And so little understanding. That's all a motorcycle is, a system of concepts worked out in steel. There's no part in it, no shape in it that is not in someone's mind. I've noticed that people who have never worked with steel have trouble seeing this – that the motorcycle is primarily a mental phenomenon'
– Robert M. Pirsig, *Zen and the Art of Motorcycle Maintenance*[1]

In this chapter:
- the issues of congruence in the formal aspects of the organisation;
- the importance of having a structure to implement the change strategy;
- the articulation of core areas which guide the change work.

THE PROPOSAL

1 Articulate the direction of the organisation.
2 Pinpoint the decision makers and attract new talent.
3 Determine which processes to keep or cancel or create.

4 Influence with external and intrinsic motivation.
5 Create an environment where the freedom of speech is assured.

The formal aspects of the organisation are the visible things – artefacts that can be seen and read, that impact our lives through rules, regulations and policies. The STAR Model from Galbraith (2002) is a simple way to think about areas to be addressed.[2] Those areas together form the structure to allow the intent of the strategy to take shape.

There are several core areas to consider which guide the work in the Develop phase. First and foremost is the direction of the organisation. It is critical to have clarity. Can the average employee understand it and articulate it? Can it be simply articulated? Can it be used in a mission brief?

COMMUNICATIONS

Chris: Success of the strategy is all about communications. In the past few years I have used some of the techniques created and used at West Point and other military schools. Giving a command brief (the mission, objective, reason and tactics) is seen as critical to create clarity. It allows the individual to understand why they are doing what has been asked of them and to connect their work to the strategy and mission. In the command briefs, the leader is also able to make it relatable by linking it to his personal values and mission.

In the case of building a share-based culture, define it in the context of your organisation and make sure it is clear. What does empathy or empowerment of the workforce mean? Is this understood in the commercial context of this work, and is it translatable to the employees?

DECISION MAKERS

Second, consider where the decision-making is done in the organisation. This work articulates where the power lies in the organisation and how power, decisions and relationships are managed in the context of the strategy. How does this best align to new opportunities? What competitive capabilities or other aspects of the company need to be made stronger to deliver on the promise of a share-based culture?

PROCESSES AND PEOPLE

Third are processes. This refers to the flow of information within the organisation, including how data are managed in the system. What are the most important processes to align? Which are critical new processes that may need to be implemented or cancelled because of the change in strategy? What is urgent?

Next, influence the motivation of people to perform and to focus on organisational performance by using cash, bonuses and pay. From a Maslow perspective, the basic human needs are about food, shelter and physical safety.[3] These are still the biggest drivers for compliance, or fear. Since the first industrial revolution, so much of the HR function's time, attention and energy has been focused on the calculation of the money. This thinking hasn't really evolved. There is a lack of creativity or desire to have a dialogue about other intrinsic motivations, such as personal ambitions and life goals.

Some progressive organisations start to look at 'wellbeing' as a bigger concept, attempting to understand employee needs and then provide payment for things that bring joy and align with what is most important for the individual. Others step into the gig economy and allow freedoms of choice by paying the bare minimum, blanket piecemeal work. We spoke to an Uber driver recently about his choices moving from customer service to retail sales to other sales across a career. He had taken a pay cut along the way to pursue more freedom to choose where and how he worked. How could a payment for services enable more freedom?

Let's talk a little more about people. This concerns the policies, which influence the skills, knowledge, ability and aptitude of the workforce to work in a way that enables the strategy.

In the Develop phase, we identify the most critical people and other organisational processes. Those include the attraction and induction of new talent, providing learning and development opportunities, managing their performance and rewarding them for their work. Other core processes such as risk, compliance, finance, security, etc. will also require reviewing to ensure congruence to drive the new behaviours and culture. For example, the processes around managing various forms of risk (operational, financial, reputational, systemic risk). The concept of business is about the management of risk and the weighing of factors to form a value proposition. How will these work with the new strategy?

LABEL AND LINK
A phrase we learned for ensuring alignment is 'label and link'. This means linking each piece of the work to a plan and in turn explaining that plan in the same language in a consistent way. If a process change is made, explain the process change in the context of the new strategy and how this change reinforces or creates it. It sounds simple, but this is very rarely done. Each change in people appointment or in their responsibilities should link back in the communications to the wider story that is being told with every action. Linking everything to everything else is critical to help people make sense of changes happening around them and use their own pattern recognition to understand the messages.

HEROES AND VILLAINS

As new practices are defined, and established totems challenged, a new understanding of culture will emerge. Some things may or may not be on the wrong side of what the organisation defines as a minimal level of accepted behaviour. We have seen this in many organisations:

- the group who thinks this work is all too 'soft' for them. They ignore it and continue to behave in the 'old way' and take care of the 'real' business;
- individuals whose behaviours genuinely are unaligned with new culture but were not confronted or corrected;
- the 'rainmakers' or technical specialists who command a premium for their expertise or relationships with clients/customers. They have a history of delivering huge value for the organisation, so senior leaders shut their eyes to their behaviours or comments;
- those in their late careers, who see the change but feel too close to retirement or their next job to adopt new practices. This is often referred to as 'coasting'.

A call has to be made about how to work with each of these groups, what is tolerable and what is not, given the speed of change, the messages, the congruence of the messages and the organisation's tolerance of risk. There is no one formula or hard rule. A good question to ask is whether your decisions are guided and explained by the values and principles already defined. Is it worth sending a message of zero tolerance loud and clear, and, if so, how?

FREEDOM OF SPEECH

How is the average employee expected to act in the new organisation? A focus on a culture of seeking perspectives and listening to feedback is a critical step alongside the introduction of new policy. How can you create an environment in which people feel psychologically safe to be able to speak up? This is done by role-modelling and creating one safe environment at a time. Think about creating shared space for dialogues without hierarchy. Those are places like the water cooler, cafeteria or a lift, where people can speak freely without fear of retribution and leaders' egos are not threatened by difficult questions. We need to establish more spaces like those so that the workplace feels more like a community where each employee plays a part and his or her voice is important.

OMBUDSPERSON

It is hard to write policy and train leaders to coach, so one of the most critical structures to put in place that encourages a speak-up culture is that of an ombudsperson. An ombudsperson enables the speaking of truth to power. It provides a safety net for the workforce to call out incongruence for the collective good. Outside such a function, it is very difficult for any individual to speak up freely and be brave without fear of potential consequence. In many organisations, there is fear. In the absence of safe channels of communication, the risk the organisation runs is that it is blind to how the employee base may really feel on the most important things. The hardest conversations to have are those about how we are not putting money where our mouths are and where there is an elephant in the room. In every conversation there is a problem with how people can open themselves up and speak truth to power. *Consistently, when incongruence happens with new policy and process or existing practice jars with the new intent, one needs to hear the unfiltered voice of the organisation.*

PEOPLE STRATEGY

Often the whole people plan is one of the first places to look for alignment. If the working towards a more empathic and share-focused organisation emerges along with other new capabilities required for success, then the range of people strategies seems sensible to align. Too often this is started but not completed. Elements to consider are:

- how the talent and succession process are aligned to find and place people who demonstrate the required mindset;
- how to bring the strategy into the performance-management process;
- how processes such as performance, recognition and reward enable (and do not block or are contrary to) evolving practice;
- which learning strategies and organisational development practices can be deployed to ensure new capabilities are developed to support new strategy.

CONSIDER THE AMBIENCE

Chris: One more thing to think about in the Develop phase is how to tweak all the other aspects of the surrounding system to bring further alignment and congruence. Aspects that I have tackled include:

- the look and feel of the reception area of the HQ. When going into a new organisation, I often get there early and sit down and absorb the look and feel of their reception area. Consistently, it tells me something about the culture;
- the design of all offices and working spaces;
- the need (or otherwise) for dress codes or uniforms and the design of both; what decisions employees can be trusted to make;
- security, real estate, technology, finance, etc. The key here is that all these functional groups combined bring

an element of creating the culture. The best method I have seen is to focus these teams on time to discuss and align their work to the refined purpose or intent of the organisation. These experts can adapt to strategy change if involved early, and if time is taken to bring their leadership and participation forward.

ONE LAST POINT ABOUT CONGRUENCE

It is important that you come across the same, consistent messages wherever you go. This fits all the elements of consistency and congruence and builds adoption of learning. This really helps with the knowledge around such questions as: what is my job and how do you expect me to perform it? People are clear about the expectations. They see, feel and accept and then enable the congruence. As we will discuss in the next chapter, congruence will enable a sense of pride and that feeling that 'I'm part of something bigger than myself'. When we start to feel part of something, we start to own it. We take decisions and actions in the style of the thing that we start to believe in. The organisation helps us to arrive at our destination by removing the element of doubt created by dissonance.

NOTES

1 Pirsig, Robert M. *Zen and the Art of Motorcycle Maintenance: An Inquiry Into Values*. New York: Bantam, 1976.
2 Galbraith, J.R. *Designing Organizations: Strategy, Structure and Process at the Business Unit and Enterprise Levels* (3rd ed.). San Francisco: Jossey-Bass, 2002.
3 Maslow, A.H. *Maslow on Management*. New York: Wiley, 1998.

DEPLOY AND EMPOWER

'The most courageous act is still to think for yourself. Aloud'
— Coco Chanel

'People don't complete us. We complete ourselves. If we
haven't the power to complete ourselves, the search for love
becomes a search for self-annihilation; and then we try to
convince ourselves that self-annihilation is love'
— Erica Jong, *Fear of Flying*[1]

In this chapter:
- formal and informal elements of communication;
- viral change;
- how to let go of control and trust the crowd;
- how habits build to congruence; any change is a change
  in habits.

THE PROPOSAL:

1 Involve everyone.
2 Plan channels of communication that are formal, informal
  and viral to activate and then sustain the work.
3 Set up communities, areas of interest or practice,
  opportunities to talk, create solutions and then to own the
  work locally.

4 Build incremental micro behaviours into a congruent culture.

In the previous few phases, we have talked about people who are mostly invisible to the organisation. These are people in the CEO's office, strategy teams, HR teams, finance, legal, brand, communications and a host of other functions. It also includes in-between internal CRM roles and divisional representatives that are common in a matrix organisational structure. We have deliberately focused on the functions as they wield the power to create the environment.

COMMUNICATION

Outside functional areas there are other groups that will be unique to your organisation that you need to plan for. It is worth doing the stakeholder analysis of sponsors, advocates, power players, early adopters, holdout areas, etc. From this, plan your sequence of who to approach first, where to build allies, and so on. This is covered heavily in so many leadership and change management texts that it would seem redundant to add more here. Our advice is to plan well for this phase in advance and to build the political alliances that are necessary to get traction and enable change. In building sponsorship, it is important to realise that each person may have his or her own agenda in terms of relationship to the work; personal, political ambitions to lead or be actively engaged with the work; or for reasons totally unknown. Having a plan, understanding individual motivations and involving those willing at the earliest possible stage is the key.

In the Deploy phase of the work, one will need to think about all the formal communication channels and anticipate how each can be used to tell stories that describe, elucidate, inspire and motivate others to follow and adopt new practices. Again, this word *congruence* and the concept of *label and link* are paramount (see Chapter 20). Equally important is the idea of having multiple mass approaches. What is the tolerance of the organisation to deal with more chaotic communication approaches? Outside the formal communication channels today, we are faced with multiple viral channels that represent opportunities. Many organisations remain intolerant of internal social media, which allows employees to speak openly. Instead, we see conversations taken outside the corporate firewalls and more honest information exchanged on independent platforms such as Glassdoor, which features popularity rankings of CEOs as voted by current and ex-employees. There seems to be this strange phenomenon of 'official truth' in most corporate environments under the disguise of 'engagement' or 'loyalty' – only good news, telling the story that is palatable to the senior executives and causes the least risk to the current state of things. It is the most comfortable way and ensures a sense of control. 'Don't rock the boat' – does this sound familiar to you?

One problem is that the very departments that are tasked with change have traditionally occupied the role of protecting the organisation from risk. The communications team sees a message that differs from the brand book and immediately raises a red flag of brand risk exposure. Similarly, the HR team looks at comments which might seem heretical or challenging the status quo. The benefit of the new work needs to be weighed against the potential risks of open dialogues and the sentiment that 'things could be different'. These departments are often more traditional than the rest of the organisation in terms of protecting hierarchy and existing powers. This is like expecting someone to play the dual roles of police and social change leader. The two roles are incompatible. That is why ensuring the sponsorship of the core group is essential.

Drums of change

Chris: At some point, the wider organisation has to be involved. I recall one story, which talked about a change team being assembled, and they played a drum in their meetings. I think only really to be trendy and 'change guru'-ish. We had moved beyond bean bags. To motivate and break the cycle of normal organisational patterns, change teams often take unusual measures to shock and awe – for example, using talking sticks to grant permission to speak up, wearing funny hats that stand out as change agents, and so on. They visibly demonstrate a new way of speaking and behaving, becoming an alien clique to the rest of the organisation. Oftentimes they are seen as weird, irrelevant and too clown-like by others. Very little is changed.

MASS PARTICIPATION

Let's talk more about early adopters – those who want to be involved first (see also Chapter 18). They are different – some are inspired by the change and love the organisation and want to take part; some embrace the idea of a share-based workplace and yearn for an environment where we are more empathic. It will appeal either intellectually or emotionally to them. For others, they just like to be the first to try new things. One should plan on how to use their energy.

Chris: An executive once gave me advice on allowing the crowd to spread the work that we were trying to do. He told a story of wanting to promote all things British in Manhattan for one weekend. They communicated their intention across all the Brit communities in New York and had a few rented spaces booked. They were inundated with suggestions, ideas and volunteers, more than they could handle. Their solution was to set up a committee that listened to ideas and said 'yes' to everything except the outrageous. (One idea that didn't make the cut: put people in the stocks and throw vegetables at them – an injury and lawsuit waiting to happen.) In forming this committee, they released the natural energy of the crowd to participate. The whole enterprise was a success — it was broader and more diverse, creative and energetic than they could possibly have anticipated. *Their approach was not to control, but just to give permission, and to empower.*

Linda: In one culture project I consulted, we asked the top 100 executives to identify 'influencers' that were two levels down in their hierarchy, from about 200 mid-level managers. Initially, people were sceptical. On the first call, most wanted to know why they were selected before anything else — were they on some kind of 'secret' list held by HR? After we clarified what we wanted them to do — which was nothing other than having dialogues within their immediate circle, asking questions about how the others were feeling, understanding concerns and a lot of listening, there was this hesitation, almost disbelief, that there was no 'official script' and they could speak the 'truth' in their minds. Then they took off, we heard and learned so much from the real pulse of the organisation and had a head start with changing the would-be 'frozen middle'.

If we were talking about a more share-based community, what would this look like in terms of getting mass participation?

HABITS, NOT REVOLUTIONS

In the 1950s, plastic surgeon Maxwell Maltz said it took his patients about 21 days to form new habits. He wrote about these experiences then founded a whole craze based on self-help and motivational speeches, which sold books and videos on this popular belief.[2] More recent research says that it takes more than two months before a new behaviour becomes automatic, 66 days to be exact, depending on the behaviour, the individual and the context. In a University

College London study, it took up to 254 days for people to form a new habit.[3]

> **Linda:** I always have a chuckle when I see those 60-day or 90-day workout programmes being marketed as 'transformative' within that short period of time. Having tried a lot of them, I know they don't work. Or you may be able to see some fast results if you are super disciplined about diet, but the results don't last. One of my trainers, who is 5' 1" tall with an amazing body of steel, says that everyone wants to know how she gets those incredible muscles – 'What they don't realise is that those are the result of 10 years of pumping iron, day in and day out.'

Hence, we need to set expectations appropriately. *Habits are a process and not an event.* Understanding this from the outset makes it more sensible to commit to small, incremental micro behaviours, i.e. small, regular improvements versus thinking that we have to do it all at once. We also need to forget about the number of days that it will take and focus on doing the work.

We suggest the use of leveraging habit formation as the principal focus to increase the capability of the organisation and to adopt the new practices of empathy and sharing. If we were asked to create a solution for long-term behaviour change, we would not jump straight to training or a communication plan. We have other tools in our bag. Imagine if we were talking about giving up smoking or changing diet or exercise routines? We know that we would need to focus first on the cognitive elements of why and then to practise in small ways in adopting the new. We should focus on micro behaviours that are standard and that can almost become routine.

The military does this very well. The team works on small, repeatable behaviours that are simple and standard. They are easily applied into the flow of work and can be practised one at a time. A good example is briefback. This is simply having each member of the team repeat the orders or information after receiving them. It is a standard procedure in the military prior to critical or potentially dangerous missions. Other than the obvious need to make sure orders are clearly understood and will be carried out precisely, additional benefits are first that the receiver, knowing he is expected to repeat the information back, is most likely going to pay close attention, and secondly, that the officer who gives the orders, along with other team members, may spot things that were previously neglected and that could improve the plan.

For your organisation, take the time to break down what habits look like. Imagine, if we measured habit adoption and not satisfaction, what great progress might be made. Bad engagement scores might be evidence of the struggle for new habit adoption.

Habit controls our daily lives. It reduces our brain activity when we can make it a habit. We do things, make decisions in an instinctual way. A series of habits that we can do together gives us the opportunity to create new norms for a new society, regardless of its size, scale and breadth. It is critical to understand how important this is. 'Changing mindsets and risk management…any company that embraces the status quo is on a collision course with time,' said Howard Schultz, when he was CEO of Starbucks.[4] We need to re-examine our habits and steer the ones we want for the life that we want and not be complacent.

It is through this that, over time, we will get local interpretations of what it means to have the culture and society that we want. Habits allow for congruence, it becomes sustained and means that we can move to continuous improvement towards the culture, the values that we want. One small habit at a time in a process of continuous, involved choice.

NOTES
1   Jong, E. *Fear of Flying* (reprint ed.). New York: Berkley, 2003.

2 Manz, C. *Emotional Discipline: The Power to Choose How You Feel*. San Francisco: Berrett-Koehler Publishers, 2003. https://books.google.com. Retrieved 2008.

3 Lally, P. 'How are habits formed: modelling habit formation in the real world', *European Journal of Social Psychology*, July 2009.

4 Berman, J. 'Starbucks' Schultz stresses the need for supply chain to have a seat at the table', *Logistics Management*, October 2015. https://www.logisticsmgmt.com/article/starbucks_schultz_stresses_the_need_for_supply_chain_to_have_a_seat_at_the. Accessed 1 December 2018.

2 2

OUR SUPERPOWERS ARE OUR WEAKNESSES

'Not all who hesitate are lost. The psyche has many secrets in reserve. And these are not disclosed unless required'
— Joseph Campbell, *The Hero With a Thousand Faces*

In this chapter:
- a challenge to be conscious and take responsibility;
- a call to challenge conformity;
- exploring the question: why now?

If you have made it this far in this book, then maybe you feel committed to doing something about our current situation. We can all act. We can all take responsibility. One of our own small steps was to write these words. In order to be able to share, one must be self-aware, to be 'in choice'. Research tells us that it is much easier to initiate feedback by asking for it. To ask for feedback, we must be brave. We may or may not always *feel* brave.

COMING TOGETHER FOR THE GREATER GOOD
All too often, corporations seek to boost and motivate by chasing the latest shiny object, including a recent trend where employees were encouraged to strike a superhero pose. This focus is linked to the

adoption of *positive psychology*, which makes connections between positive thoughts and attitude and confidence and wellbeing. We are in an endless search for the new. Too many HR teams and organisations drift from what is in vogue to what is interesting, losing patience in developing and implementing the deeper work.

Our argument is that at some point in human history there is a need to avoid competition and the superhero myth and come together. To have shared mutual conversations for the greater good, or the greater purpose. There were moments when great treaties were written and alliances were formed. Those moments could have been ordinary; instead, they became steeped in history and legend.

Chris: When I wrote the first book, *Rewire*, one of the things that I did unconsciously in preparation was to visit the Polish town of Kraków and the Nazi death camps of Auschwitz and Birkenau. The most stunning discovery I made concerned the history of building the camps and the logic behind choosing their locations. Kraków presented the best location because all the railways across Europe were connected to it. This ensured the most efficient way of transporting Jews and others across the continent. The people who made the plans, ran the trains and performed many other tasks were people like us. They had been trained in corporate institutions to work effectively. But the purpose was so wrong. Choosing the right purpose will save us from a lingering death and create an opportunity to leap forward with hope.

I also visited Cambodia and again reflected on why others didn't decide to act or speak out in the face of great evil. I reflected on the possibilities of standing up. We believe each of us is called to act. We each have the opportunity to spend our lives working towards a purpose and meaning, by speaking up and asking the difficult questions. Because, if we don't, the greater fears would become true: chaos and radical shifts.

When the transcontinental railroad came to connect the east and west of America, it did many things. It allowed the country to heal wounds after the Civil War. It allowed the poor from the east and Europe to have land. It changed prairie grassland into wheat and grain fields. It created new towns and cities. It created America as a true continental nation and the world power. However, it also led to the decimation of the Native Americans, who had existed for thousands of years. Whole peoples were gone forever. All of this happened not that long ago.

We have much more recent examples of the damage rapid technological advancement can do if ruled only by the law of the jungle and pure profit. People suffer. Are we content to sit by? Who do you serve?

If the changes to date were to be done all over again, should they be done in the same way? Should the nature of technology and societal advances be driven purely by profit, with the associated loss of human life and the impact to entire civilisations? Or should we try to make these changes with care and with a plan or, at a minimum, and given the speed of change, some principles.

We know that the way in which an organisation works with the rest of the world is based on the way that the organisation itself works internally and what it believes in. We need you, in whatever role you play, to step in and step up.

Enterprise was created, funded and executed by corporates and by corporate-funded support from governments. This changed the nature of America. It created cities where there had been dust. It created wealth. Wheat and other cereals were introduced to where there had once been prairie grass. Buffalo went from millions to extinction.

CONFORMITY AND COMPASSION

We have studied conformity theory time and again. We see this play out at the times when humans are asked to conform so that we can be moulded to what government or corporation needs. We have a history of leadership and organisational development solutions that goes back over 150 years.

We know that organisations are most effective when people are engaged. Jeff Weiner, the CEO of LinkedIn, cites the Dalai Lama as the inspiration for his management style, which he calls 'compassionate management'. Managing compassionately is about putting yourself in another person's shoes and seeing the world through his lens or perspective, Weiner says.[1] It is also knowing that you're not going to get the best out of your people if you're constantly holding them up against your own lens or requesting them to do things in precisely the way you do.

> **Linda:** I spent a year and a half taking improvisation classes at Second City, a well-known comedy theatre based in Chicago and associated with popular TV programmes such as *Saturday Night Live*. The most valuable skills I learned were not making things up and being 'funny'; instead, they were active listening and teamwork.
>
> When you are part of an ensemble standing on the stage, facing an audience that could throw any request at you, that could be really daunting *on your own*. The moment one of your teammates says or does something, you do three things: 1. look each other in the eye, so that you not only hear and see, you also *feel* what he or she is conveying; 2. totally suspend any judgement, commit to whatever idea is put forward and build upon it, *even if* this is completely not what you expected; 3. do your best in the moment, then stand back and let others take turns to lead. These might sound like simple steps, but it is surprising to me how often I see talented actors become so focused on

what *they* want; or trying so hard to control the flow of the story that they sabotage the scene. The audience intuitively senses the friction and disconnect among the ensemble and it stops being *fun*.

It's the same in a work context. How often do we really listen, hear and *feel* what others are telling us? When others express emotions, do we acknowledge it and empathise, or pretend we didn't hear because it's inconvenient, awkward or unusual? When a different idea is put forward, do we always give full consideration or simply brush it aside? Lastly, do we feel our colleagues have 'got our back' and do we make them feel the same way?

At an airport lounge, a bus stop or any other place we encounter a fellow traveller in trouble, crying or distressed, many of us will reach out. With empathy naturally wired in us and reinforced by most cultures, we know what to do in order to help. As human beings, we are capable in the moment and intuitively to say and do the right things. If we have these innate skills, why would we need the organisation to show us what to do?

For this book, I spent some days in a commune and then at a communal retreat. A small taste for me of what a share-based culture might be like. People were people, they worried and gossiped and fretted the small things. I went expecting wisdom from these communities that might bring nuance and insight to the book. The only 'aha' that I had came from the role of elders in the community. That on some issues, people put their trust in others who are often not elected but placed in a position of authority because of their expertise. This trust in the integrity of others and respect for their values struck me as most different from life in the big 'bad' world outside. It seems we have lost the innocence, in our disconnected world, to trust – and if we can't trust then why should we listen to other views? We can wait for the superheroes to arrive or we can look around and see that they are all around us; 'elders' not in age but in wisdom and ethics. Maybe they are even in the mirror.

OPPORTUNITY

In some businesses today slavery still exists. Conflict materials are used in numerous electronics products that many of us use every day. Is this okay? Nation states cannot match the scale of the corporates. Can the potential horrors of globalisation and the fourth industrial revolution be fixed by the people who created this? You can choose to be conscious. To act. To be your own hero in your lifetime (with or without a superhero pose). We don't choose to be born or when to be born; rather, we are prepared for whatever time we are born into as much as anyone in history.

NOTES

1   Feloni, R. 'A top LinkedIn exec says the Dalai Lama parable CEO Jeff Weiner told him at their first meeting changed his management style', *Business Insider*, April 2017. https://www.businessinsider. com/management-advice-linkedin-jeff-weiner-2017-3. Accessed 11 February 2018.

FINAL THOUGHTS

'Thousands have lived without love, not one without water'
— W.H. Auden

Chris: I once saw a play at the National Theatre on London's South Bank that concerned the history of the UK. It showed that every 50 to 100 years there has been another group of immigrants. The story followed a cycle. Wave after wave of immigrants came in over the centuries. Each wave was met with racism, suspicion, occasionally murder. Over time, their descendants intermarried among those already established, these new families became locals themselves, and the prejudices and fears were eroded. And then, in turn, their children became suspicious of the *next* wave of immigrants and so it continued.

The cycle continuously redefined who 'we' were. It showed that, over time, we could get over our differences, but that it was always a painful process.

There has always been difference. It is only when history becomes personal to us, to our lives, that it can truly consume us. Being in a building next to the Twin Towers on 9/11 brought violent history to my nostrils and eyes. It seems sad that maybe only when we have such a personal connection can we have context and meaning to enable caring. Or else it is perhaps only a story that we read and can distance ourselves from.

We think the whole world is here and now. We are surprised when older biases still have power over the present and emerge as monsters from our past, or like a plague, or cannot imagine that those who are now in the majority were themselves once victims. Each is a story of change.

When I was at high school in the UK I was dating a white British Protestant girl from the same school. The dinner-with-the-parents invitation came and, at one point, I found myself alone with her father, who started telling me that he was not happy with me dating his daughter. 'The children won't belong to one or the other,' he explained, referring to the possibility of biracial offspring. As I was just a teenager, I assured him that it was in no way part of my plan to have children and that he was getting way ahead of himself. He replied, 'Well, at least you're not Catholic. I could never have let one of them in the house.' For him, better black than Catholic. The story has stayed with me because of the layers that it revealed about who we are and how little we have progressed.

I recall from a history class that entire villages of Viking settlers were massacred in England by Saxons in the Middle Ages. That Catholics were killed *en masse* for long periods of English history and the Welsh, Scots and Irish were also brutalised by the English. But time seems to heal – if love and cross-breeding does not always prevail there is at least some unity and dialogue. The old tribal differences in Britain today are played out through football rather than burnings and massacres.

We are so obsessed by the immediate that we forget what history has to teach us about where we came from. We learn little about our potential for hatred of each other and why we are driven to fear through short-term thinking. We operate from fear, sparked by uncertainty of the different. It makes concepts of sharing hard to understand.

Linda: To some extent, being born Chinese has its advantages –
one of which is that I immediately 'fit in' with another
1.3 billion people in the world. Before I left China in my
twenties, I had no idea what 'diversity' was. In the 1970s
and 1980s, everyone dressed in the same way, had the same
home appliances and listened to the same music. The only
differences within China are dialects/accents and regional
food. To this day, whenever I see Chinese people travelling
abroad they inevitably do the following: they spot another
Chinese-looking person at the airport, or at a sightseeing
spot, they strike up a conversation, quickly ask which city
the other person is from and then conclude they know
everything about the stranger. Why not? It is comforting to
believe that, within seconds, they can fit the stranger into
a known profile, including personality, values and likely
thinking patterns.

Except it is not true. We are all different, with individual
experiences and backgrounds. We were just taught to
believe all Chinese are the same. This 'we' identity is really
what made China unique and formidable. It also made
encountering different cultures and values exceptionally
uncomfortable, at least in the beginning.

Many times, I hear Chinese colleagues complain about
foreign bosses – the rants usually end with: '*Lao Wai* [the
term Chinese use for all foreigners] are just like that!' Such
generalisation often makes me feel uneasy. I sense the 'us
versus them' mentality probably creates half of the problem
and exacerbates the situation. But it is almost impossible
to convince the person to change his viewpoint because
we are all shaped by our individual experiences and often
those experiences are deeply emotional. So I keep quiet.

A lot of Chinese students and employees with overseas
education and experience are increasingly attracted by the
booming economy and decide to return to China. I am

happy for them. An overwhelming proportion still decide to stay where they are because of better opportunities and I'm happy for them, too. Today, those Chinese immigrants think and behave very differently from those who had fewer choices one or two generations ago. Most of them belong to a completely different socio-economic class and are much better integrated into foreign societies. However, I still see many of them living in a 'Chinese bubble' characterised by an over-emphasis on financial stability and a desire to be insulated from political uncertainty and chaos.

Time to rethink that. There's a strong sense right now in societies across the developed and developing worlds that economic opportunities are not evenly shared by everyone. Most of us are fortunate enough to be on the right side of the divide and therefore are well positioned to take advantage of technology, artificial intelligence and digitalisation; however, to those who feel they are on the other side, it is a time of extreme anxiety. We see politics becoming polarised in many countries and governments in gridlock, attempting in vain to make progress. A prevailing number of young people who were born after 2000 (the so-called 'centennials') don't trust governments and instead turn to social media in the hope of change.

I think that we, as CEOs, executives and human resources practitioners, should be concerned about this. Because if people lose faith in democracy and the value of work, we could be killing the goose while it lays the golden egg. To start with, we could encourage honest and transparent conversations within our own organisations about societal and technological changes and how those are impacting jobs and skills. We could focus on plans to bring people with us in our work for change and build confidence for the future. I hope this book gives you some ideas to start with and to inspire further dialogues.

Chris: In the most industrialised areas of the world, we are running out of water. Our factories' use of carbon-based fuels has altered our biosphere and poisoned our air and water. We have filled the seas with plastic and junk. I learned that in Seattle, where I now live, opioids are present in the most basic creatures in the food chain and antidepressants are found in marine life near the coast of the UK.

I hear that orca will probably die out, as they are 'top predators' and what they eat is the sum of all of the other poisoned creatures in the ocean – they are often now unable to breed successfully. We have lost a large percentage of the animal species in our planet in the last 50 years. These seem like big things. We know that some islands and cities are falling back into the sea and that greater storms and increased heat will change how and where we humans live.

This was all, to some degree, caused by the creation of corporations. In this link between corporation, society and the individual, we have seen the average global mortality rate fall; fewer of us die of disease, and we are less hungry and better fed as a race of humans. The rise of corporations has facilitated this, but has also caused huge population growth.

The corporations have created the concept of 'global', which has aggravated aspects of diversity, difference thrown together in trade but not culture and causing fear, leading to slavery, war, refugees, rape and horror on a scale not seen before this age that we live in. Wars are now fought in cities and in our streets and not in fields or forests.

The fear that our children will not experience the good times we once had drives us to seek strong leaders with simple solutions. They blame immigrants, other religions, other races, the rich…and we listen to (or ignore) this, because it is easier to do this and follow than to do something different.

Most of us have taken things for granted for most of our lives. We take it for granted that things will only get better (or at least stay the same). We take water for granted. We take peace for granted. When it seems that uncertainty is coming, we operate from fear. I fear for the planet that I will leave for my children.

We can imagine a better life. Our corporations can be steered towards good intent beyond profit alone. So can our governments. It does not have to be a move towards a utopian agrarian commune, post-apocalyptic or otherwise. We can try to share better with each other today. We can try to make our corporations more accountable and driven by a noble purpose beyond mere profit. We can influence our governments to be more collaborative instead of competitive. To serve.

Our future will be dominated by the use of artificial intelligence (AI). We have the opportunity for AI to grow from the best of human values. We can build from the human gifts. We can imagine a world where society, industry and science work more closely together in shared partnerships to co-create our future, as opposed to always playing catch-up. We need regulatory environments that are confident and that are written for our future and not driven purely on fear-based reasoning from our past.

We have to release the need for power and step into the unknown just a little in order to be able to share.

This requires a change from within. It requires you, the reader, to do something other than just vote.

It means new habits, new accountability and hard conversations.

It's a difficult path, but what other choice do we have?

BIBLIOGRAPHY

Adkins, A. (2016), 'Employee engagement in U.S. stagnant in 2015',
  Gallup News. https://news.gallup.com/poll/1F88144/employee-
  engagement-stagnant-2015.aspx. Accessed on 20 August 2017.

Angelou, M. (1978), 'And still I rise', *And Still I Rise: A Book of Poems*.
  New York: Random House.

Autor, D. and Price, B. (2013), 'The changing task composition of the
  US labor market'. Massachusetts Institute of Technology.

Avatar: The Last Airbender (2005), [TV programme], Nickelodeon Studios,
  18 March.

Bennett, N. and Lemoine, G.J. (2014), 'What VUCA really means for
  you', *Harvard Business Review*, Jan–Feb. 2014: pp. 16–17.

Bennis, W. and Slater, P. (1964), 'Democracy is inevitable', *Harvard
  Business Review*, Sept–Oct, 1990, pp. 167–183.

Berman, J. (2015), 'Starbucks' Schultz stresses the need for supply chain
  to have a seat at the table', *Logistics Management*, October. https://
  www.logisticsmgmt.com/article/starbucks_schultz_stresses_
  the_need_for_supply_chain_to_have_a_seat_at_the. Accessed on
  19 October 2017.

Birkinshaw, J. and Ridderstråle, J. (2015), 'Adhocracy for an agile age',
  McKinsey Quarterly, https://www.mckinsey.com/business-functions/
  organization/our-insights/adhocracy-for-an-agile-age. Accessed on
  30 July 2017.

Bowman, A.K., Garnsey, P., Rathbone D. (eds) (2000), *The Cambridge
  Ancient History*, Vol. 11, pp. 326–27. Cambridge University Press.

Brafman, O. and Beckstrom, R. (2008), *The Starfish and the Spider: The
  Unstoppable Power of Leaderless Organizations* (reprint edn). Portfolio.

Burkus, D. (2016), *Under New Management: How Leading Organizations are
  Upending Business as Usual* (1st edn). Boston and New York: Houghton
  Mifflin Harcourt.

The Butterfly Effect (2004), [film] Dir. Eric Bress and J. Mackye Gruber. USA/Canada: FilmEngine/BenderSpink/Katalyst.

Chandler, A. (2015), 'The "worst" German word of the year', The Atlantic, January.

Deloitte (2017), 'Transitioning to the future of work and the workplace' survey. https://www2.deloitte.com/us/en/pages/human-capital/articles/transitioning-to-the-future-of-work-and-the-workplace.html. Accessed 3 December 2018.

Durkheim, E. (1974) [1953]. *Sociology and Philosophy.* Translated by D.F. Pocock, with an introduction by J. G. Peristiany. Toronto: The Free Press.

Dweck, C. (2007), *Mindset: The New Psychology of Success.* New York: Ballantine Books .

Economic Policy Institute (2018), 'The productivity–pay gap'. https://www.epi.org/productivity-pay-gap. Accessed on February 3 2019.

Edward, D. (2017), 'Baddeley & Hitch (1974) – Working Memory', *Psychology Unlocked.* http://www.psychologyunlocked.com/baddeleyhitch1974. Accessed on March 10 2019.

Feloni R. (2017), 'A top LinkedIn exec says the Dalai Lama parable CEO Jeff Weiner told him at their first meeting changed his management style', *Business Insider*, April. https://www.businessinsider.com/management-advice-linkedin-jeff-weiner-2017-3. Accessed on December 1 2018.

Fiedler, F. E. (1994), *Leadership Experience and Leadership Performance.* Alexandria, VA: US Army Research Institute for the Behavioral and Social Sciences.

Frischmann, B. (2013), *Infrastructure: The Social Value of Shared Resources.* Oxford: Oxford University Press.

Galbraith J. (2014), *Designing Organizations: Strategy, Structure and Process at the Business Unit and Enterprise Levels* (3rd edn). San Francisco: Jossey-Bass.

Gallup (2017), 'The state of the American workplace'. https://www.gallup.com/workplace/238085/state-american-workplace-report-2017.aspx. Accessed on May 19 2019.

Gastroenterology Journal ADD MISSING INFO: article title, date, author, issue

Gladwell, M. (2000), *The Tipping Point: How Little Things Can Make a Big Difference.* New York: Back Bay Books.

Gleick, J. (1987), *Chaos: Making a New Science*. London: Penguin Books; Anniversary, Reprint edition (26 August 2008).

Grobman, G. (2005), 'Complexity theory: A new way to look at organizational change', *Public Administration Quarterly*, 29 (3/4), pp. 350–382.

Hamel, G. (1996), 'Strategy as Revolution', *Harvard Business Review*, July–August 1996 issue, pp. 69–83.

Hammonds, K.H. (2002), 'The strategy of the fighter pilot', *Fast Company*, June.

Hofstadter, R. (1966), *Anti-intellectualism in American Life*. New York: Vintage Books.

Inequality for All (2013), [Film] Dir. Jacob Kornbluth, USA: Radius-TWC Pictures.

Jacoby, S. (2009), *The Age of American Unreason*. New York: Vintage Books.

Jong, E. (2003), *Fear of Flying* (reprint edn). New York: Berkeley.

Judge, T. A., Piccolo, R.F., Podsakoff, N.P., Shaw, J.C. and Rich, B.L. (2010), 'The relationship between pay and job satisfaction: A meta-analysis of the literature', *Journal of Vocational Behavior*, 77 (2), pp. 157–167.

Katz, L.F. and Krueger, A.B. (2016), *The Rise and Nature of Alternative Work Arrangements in the United States, 1995–2015*. Princeton University and NBER.

Kets de Vries, M. (2015), INSEAD Leadership Institute, January.

Kleiner, A. (2003), *Who Really Matters: The Core Group Theory of Power, Privilege and Success* (1st edn). New York: Doubleday Press.

Kohn, D. (2015), 'When gut bacteria change brain function', *The Atlantic*. https://www.theatlantic.com/health/archive/2015/06/gut-bacteria-on-the-brain/395918. Accessed on 20 July 2017.

KPMG (2017), 'Future of work'. https://assets.kpmg/content/dam/kpmg/fr/pdf/2017/05/fr-Future-Of-Work-report.pdf. Accessed on 5 August 2018.

Kruger, J. and Dunning, D. (1999), 'Unskilled and unaware of it: How difficulties in recognizing one's own incompetence lead to inflated self-assessments'. *American Psychological Association Journal of Personality and Social Psychology*, 77 (6): 1121–1134.

Kuo, I. (2018), 'The "whitening" of Asian-Americans', *The Atlantic*, 31 August. https://www.theatlantic.com/education/archive/2018/08/the-whitening-of-asian-americans/563336. Accessed 17 December 2018.

Lally P. (2009), 'How are habits formed: modelling habit formation in the real world'. *European Journal of Social Psychology*, July.

Le Bon, G. (2009), *Psychology of Crowds*. Southampton: Sparkling Books.

Lorenz, E. (1963), 'Deterministic nonperiodic flow'. *Journal of Atmospheric Sciences*, vol. 20, Issue 2, pp. 130–148.

Manz, C. (2003), *Emotional Discipline: The Power to Choose How You Feel*. San Francisco: Berrett-Koehler Publishers. https://books.google.com. Retrieved 2008.

Marx, K. (1844), *Introduction to Critique of Hegel's Philosophy of Right*.

Maslow A.H. (1998), *Maslow on Management* (1st edn). New York: Wiley.

The Matrix Reloaded (2003), Dir. Lana Wachowski and Lilly Wachowski. USA: Warner Bros. et al.

Mayer, M. (1955), *They Thought They Were Free* (1st edn). University of Chicago Press.

McCracken, H. (2016), 'Satya Nadella on Microsoft's new age of intelligence', *Fast Company*. https://www.fastcompany. com/3064030/satya-nadella-on-microsofts-new-age-of-intelligence. Accessed on 15 October 2017.

Michaels, E., et al. (2001), *The War for Talent* Harvard Business Press.

McKinsey Global Institute (2016). 'Independent work: Choice, necessity and the gig economy', October. https://www.mckinsey. com/~/media/McKinsey/Featured%20Insights/Employment%20 and%20Growth/Independent%20work%20Choice%20 necessity%20and%20the%20gig%20economy/Independent-Work-Choice-necessity-and-the-gig-economy-Executive-Summary.ashx. Accessed June 2018.

Michaels, E., Handfield-Jones, H. and Axelrod, B. (2001), *The War for Talent* (1st edn). Boston: *Harvard Business Review Press*.

Mills, C.W. (1956), *The Power Elite*. New York: Oxford University Press; New Edition edition (17 February 2000).

Mishel, L. and Davis, A. (2015), 'CEO pay has grown 90 times faster than typical worker pay since 1978', Economic Policy Institute. https:// www.epi.org/publication/ceo-pay-has-grown-90-times-faster-than-typical-worker-pay-since-1978. Accessed on 3 October 2017.

Mishel, L. and Schieder, J. (2018), 'CEO compensation surged in 2017', Economic Policy Institute, 16 August. https://www.epi. org/publication/ceo-compensation-surged-in-2017. Accessed 17 December 2018.

Nichols, T. (2017), *The Death of Expertise: The Campaign Against Established Knowledge and Why It Matters*. Oxford University Press.

Northouse, P. (2015), *Leadership Theory and Practice* (7th edn). SAGE Publications.

Nuwer, R. (2017), 'How western civilisation could collapse'. BBC. http://www.bbc.com/future/story/20170418-how-western-civilisation-could-collapse. Accessed 10 April 2018.

Oshry, B. (2015), 'Power and Love: A System Perspective', https://newstories.org/wp-content/uploads/2015/01/Power-and-Love.pdf. Accessed on 11 August 2017

Pirsig, R. (1976), *Zen and the Art of Motorcycle Maintenance: An Inquiry Into Values*. New York: William Morrow Paperbacks; 1R edition (2 August 2005).

Preston, A.R. and Eichenbaum, H. (2013), 'Interplay of hippocampus and prefrontal cortex in memory', *Current Biology*, 23 (17), pp. 764–773.

Pulp Fiction (1994), [Film] Dir. Quentin Tarantino, USA: Miramax Pictures.

Raymond, R. (1990), *The Cathedral & the Bazaar*. Sebastopol: O'Reilly Media; 1 edition (15 January 2001).

Saramago, J. (2005), *The Double*. New York: Mariner Books.

Schein, E. (2010), *Organizational Culture and Leadership* (4th edn). Jossey-Bass.

Schwab, K. (2016), 'The fourth industrial revolution', World Economic Forum, 11 January. https://www.weforum.org/about/the-fourth-industrial-revolution-by-klaus-schwab.

Senge, P. (1990), *The Fifth Discipline*. New York: Doubleday Business; 1st edition (1 August 1990).

Spears, L.C. (ed) (1998), *Insights on Leadership: Service, Stewardship, Spirit and Servant-Leadership*. New York: John Wiley & Sons.

Stanley, M.D. and Lawrence, P.R. (1978), 'Problems of matrix organizations', *Harvard Business Review*, May.

Sternberg, R.J. and Zhang, L.F. (eds) (2000), *Perspectives on Cognitive, Learning and Thinking Styles*. NJ: Lawrence Erlbaum.

Sun Tzu, *The Art of War*, East India Publishing Company (4 December 2018)

Sundararajan, A. (2016), *The Sharing Economy: The End of Employment and the Rise of Crowd-based Capitalism*. Cambridge: The MIT Press.

Taylor, F.W. (1997), *The Principle of Scientific Management*. United States: Dover Publications.

Taylor, F. W. (2003), *Scientific Management* (includes 'Shop management', 1903, 'The principles of scientific management', 1911, and 'Testimony before the Special House Committee', 1912). New York: Routledge.

Tomasello, M. (2014), *A Natural History of Human Thinking*. Cambridge: Harvard University Press.

Waldrop, M.M. (1992), *Complexity: The Emerging Science at the Edge of Order and Chaos*. New York: Simon & Schuster.

Wallace-Wells, D. (2017), 'The Uninhabitable Earth', New York, 10 July: 1–2.

Waterman, R.H. (1993), *Adhocracy: The Power to Change* (book summary). New York: W.W. Norton.

Western, S. (2013), *Leadership: A Critical Text* (2nd edn). London: SAGE Publications.

Wongsrikeao, P., Saenz, D., Rinkoski, T., Otoi, T. and Poeschla, E. (2011), 'Antiviral restriction factor transgenesis in the domestic cat', *Nature Methods*, 8, pp. 853–859.

ACKNOWLEDGEMENTS

This book has taken us four years to complete from the original idea to publishing. During this time, much has changed in both of our personal lives: our jobs, our hometowns and, as a result, our perspectives. What didn't change was a sense of responsibility that we feel to generate a broader dialogue within industry. At times, we argued about whether we were being too forward or critical, but in the end we decided that speaking the truth as we saw it and progressing new thoughts may eventually drive change and make the status quo better.

We are immensely grateful for all the encouragement, input and help we've received along this journey, from families, colleagues, friends and even strangers. The strangers we can never really thank enough – the taxi drivers, random plane companions and restaurant staff who all had opinions and encouragements.

We are not the same now that this book is born. What made us stronger is knowing we are not alone and others will pick up from here, carry on the cause. One of those people could be you.

It is impossible to list all who have contributed to this book but there are a few we specifically want to thank.

For generously giving time and feedback on early drafts: Mary Mikel, Pooja Sachdev, Sophie Cammish, Elizabeth Yates, Megan Carpenter, Meghan Staley and Linda Chavis – thank you! We would also thank our work colleagues and professional partners who inspired with their perspective and practice in innumerable ways. LaShana Jackson – you are an amazing source of inspiration, thank you for your encouragement and support! A special thanks to all of the Seattle people who contributed: Joy & Anne, Ilene, the Simons, the TLI crew and the other various sages that came out of the Salish Sea to offer wisdom and support at the end of this journey.

Krissy Roleke – you were simply fantastic! Thank you so much for all the help. You took us to the finish line and made the book possible.

And, finally, and most importantly, the many work colleagues and our families:

Kyle: for your love, trust and partnership. For being the rock of the family when we went through international moves and job changes, for never giving up on me even when I was frustrated and for being a debate partner to help articulate concepts and ideas.

My parents, Cai Yufa (蔡育发) and Zhu Xianzhen (朱娴桢): for raising me with a curious mind, always encouraging me to travel and learn from different perspectives. You taught me to be confident and humble, to be self-reliant and empathetic at the same time. I hope I have made you proud.

Eden, Anais, Solomon and Rea, you all inspire me and teach me every day. To open the door on a bad day and be greeted with your energy and love fill me with strength. My recent move to the Pacific Northwest has inspired me with a love of our planet. Thinking about the legacy that I leave to my children has moved me. They are my tutors and in many, many ways, the reason for writing the book.

INDEX